I0812713

IMAGES
of America

NORTH KINGSTOWN
1880–1920

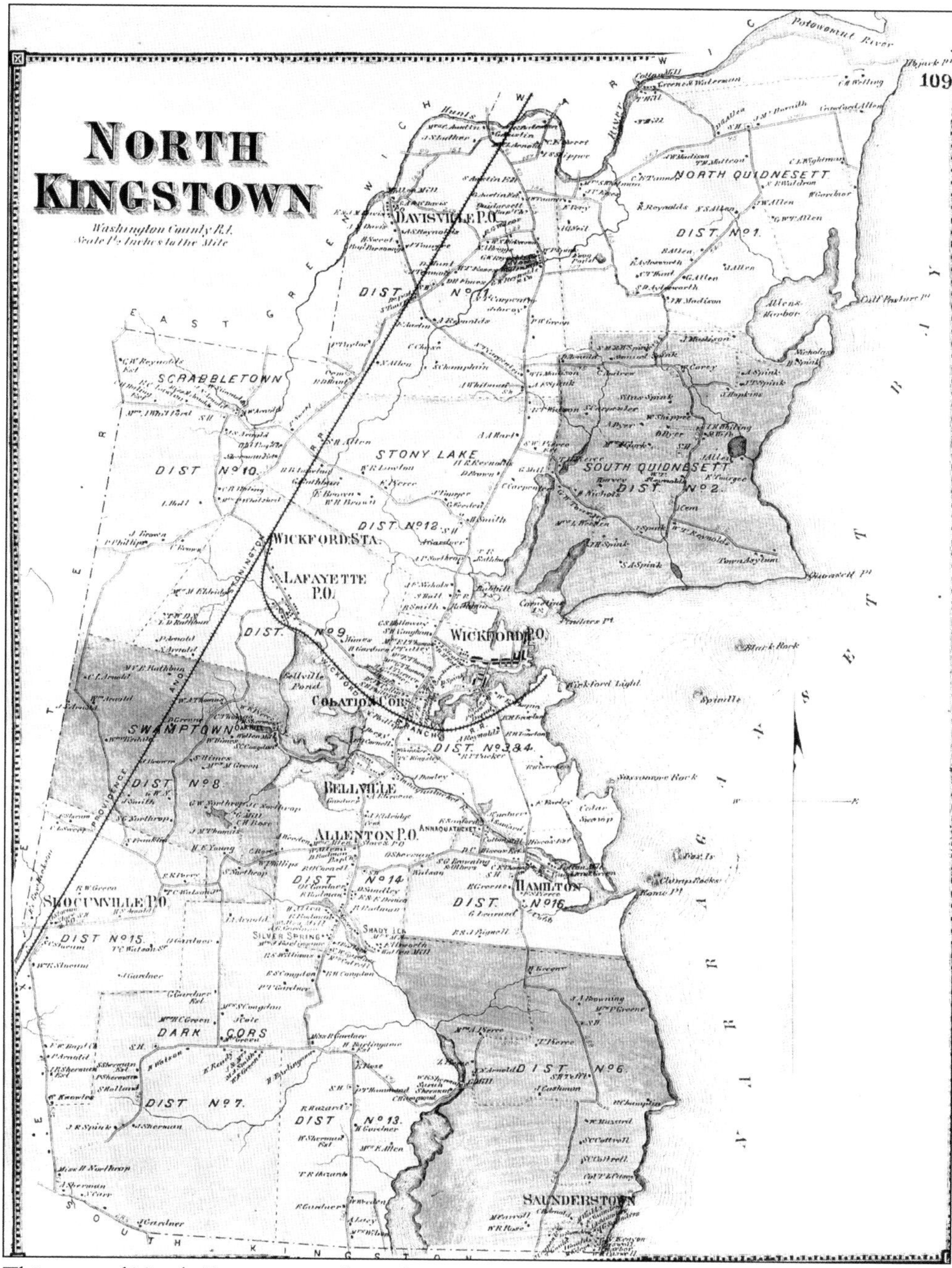

This map of North Kingstown is from the 1870s and shows the many small farming and mill villages that make up the community.

IMAGES
of America

NORTH KINGSTOWN
1880–1920

G. Timothy Cranston

ARCADIA
PUBLISHING

ISBN 978-0-7385-3908-9

Published by Arcadia Publishing
Charleston, South Carolina

Printed in the United States of America

Library of Congress Control Number: 2005928932

For all general information, please contact Arcadia Publishing:
Telephone 843-853-2070
Fax 843-853-0044
E-mail sales@arcadiapublishing.com
For customer service and orders:
Toll-Free 1-888-313-2665

Visit us on the Internet at www.arcadiapublishing.com

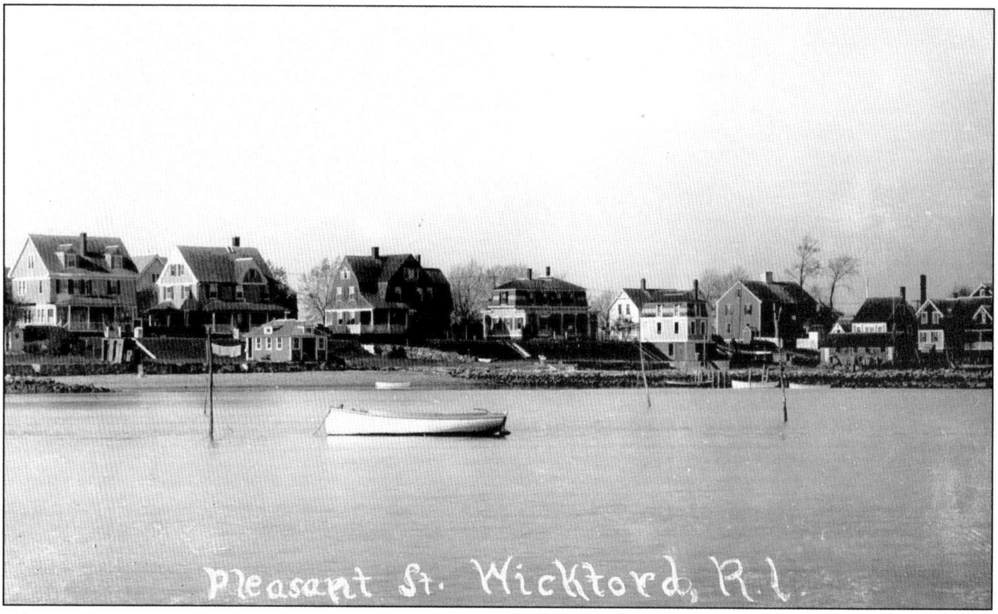

This view shows the Pleasant Street shoreline. Elwin "Doc" Young's magnificent home can be seen in the center of the photograph.

Contents

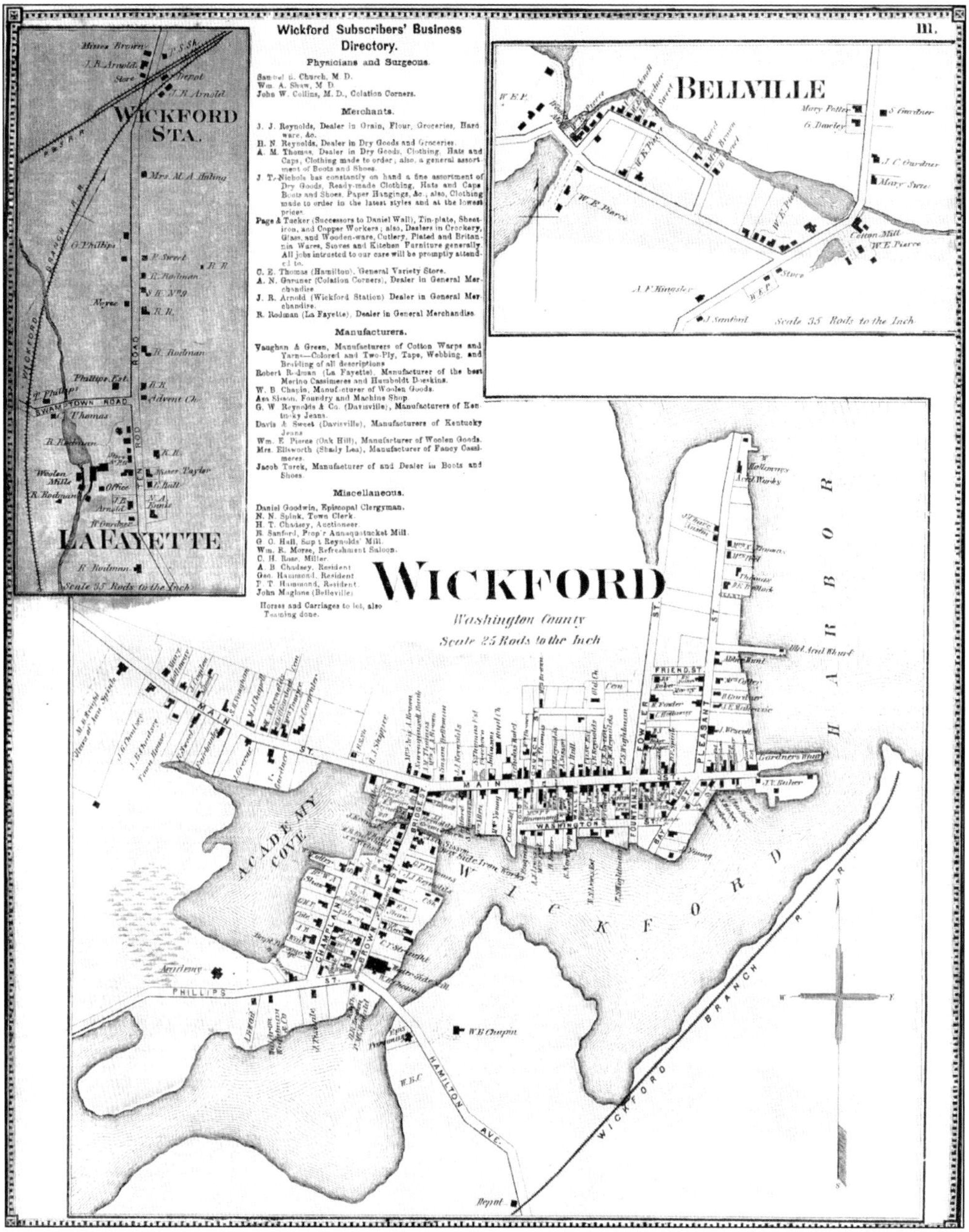

This 1870 map shows Wickford, North Kingstown's central village, and the two largest textile mill villages, Lafayette and Belleville. Also featured are the tracks of the Newport and Wickford Rail and Steamship Line.

INTRODUCTION

Elwin Edgar "Doc" Young arrived in North Kingstown at what was coincidentally a turning point for both him and his newly adopted home. Young had just finished his training as a pharmacist and was eager to begin a new life in the then sleepy village of Wickford. The town of North Kingstown was at a crossroads of its own. Once primarily a farming region with one substantial commercial port in Wickford and a smaller one at Saunderstown, North Kingstown was about to undergo a massive change. The grand homes of Wickford, at one time owned by prominent merchants, bankers, sea captains, and ship owners, had fallen on hard times as the shipping trade that had made the village one of the prominent ports on the Narragansett Bay had slowly either gone north to Providence or had been displaced by the arrival of permanent rail service between New York, Providence, and Boston. North Kingstown was no longer a seaport town; it was a textile town, and little mill villages were springing up wherever a rushing stream could be dammed to provide power to run a loom. A number of the larger mills were already switching over to the newfangled Providence-built coal-fired Corliss Steam Engines that would soon revolutionize manufacturing across the nation. Folks who had worked the land for generations were now working in the mills. A boom time had begun, and nothing would ever be the same in this or countless other small communities across New England. Sadly—or maybe not—Wickford was unaffected by this prosperity. The grand colonial homes continued to decay, as no one could afford to maintain them. As Lafayette, Davisville, and Belleville prospered at the onset of the age of the textile mill, Wickford, once the crown jewel of the western side of the bay, continued to decline. That all changed when the Newport and Wickford Rail and Steamship Line constructed its rail spur from the main line station at Wickford Junction, just west of Lafayette Village, down to its steamship dock at Poplar Point. Now Wickford became a port of importance again. This time, it was not freight that was going in and out of the village, it was the nation's elite going back and forth between their homes in New York, Boston, Chicago, and points beyond to their cottages in Newport. The age of *The Great Gatsby* and F. Scott Fitzgerald had arrived, and it arrived through Wickford. So, at the same time that the economic prosperity of greater North Kingstown was forever being altered by the onset of the textile manufacturing revolution, its central village was being revitalized by the "train that saved Wickford" and the affluent citizens who utilized it. As time passed, a number of the wealthy folks who often passed through the village on their way to Newport were captivated by Wickford's charm and peaceful ambiance and purchased or constructed their summer retreats here on her colonial-era streets and byways.

Throughout this time of change, Doc Young was there to record it with his tripod and camera. His original plan was to take some photographs and have them made into postcards to sell in his pharmacy in the village. The folks who came and went on the Newport train were later joined by another group of tourists and sightseers who came here via the Sea View electric trolley that brought people from Providence, Warwick, and other points north through North Kingstown on their way to the beaches and casinos of Narragansett. So, he had a ready clientele for these picture postcards. Young, though, was not satisfied with just photographing the typical tourist sights and scenes of the day. Along the way, he also chronicled the people and places that made up the real North Kingstown. Through his camera lens, we are able to travel back 100 years and see the fair town during its golden age.

With this book, I hope to be able to afford all of those who care about North Kingstown a glimpse of how it must have been back during that wonderful time between 1880 and 1920. Through the foresight of another Wickford Village pharmacist, Howard Ericson, the original glass-plate negatives of Young's photographs were preserved exactly as they were in the 1930s, when an elderly Elwin Young handed them off, along with the keys to his store, and retired. Ericson, in turn, entrusted them to me. As a way of honoring the memory of old Doc Young and all of his contemporaries, the photographs appear here, along with a number of additional images. I can only hope I have done them justice.

Acknowledgments

At this time, I would like to thank the following people who, along the way, have made this effort possible. Many thanks to Thomas and Erma Peirce and Henry Beckwith for assisting me in identifying what was happening in each and every photograph. Without the continued effort of Mr. Peirce, much of what we now know about the village of Wickford would have been lost to the ages. I would also like to acknowledge the contributions of Karen-Lu LaPolice and the Murray family for allowing me access to their wonderful postcard collections. Thanks as well to the North Kingstown Free Library and the North Kingstown Arts Council for their continued support, and thanks also to Kristen Cyr, Betty Cotter, and everyone at the Independent Newspapers for taking a chance on an unknown entity. Without the "bully pulpit" they offered up to me, this would not have happened. And, again, thank you to Howard Ericson for saving these photographs and entrusting them to me. Last but not least, I would like to thank my family—my wife Linda and my sons Ryan and Eric. This book is dedicated to them.

One

Elwin "Doc" Young

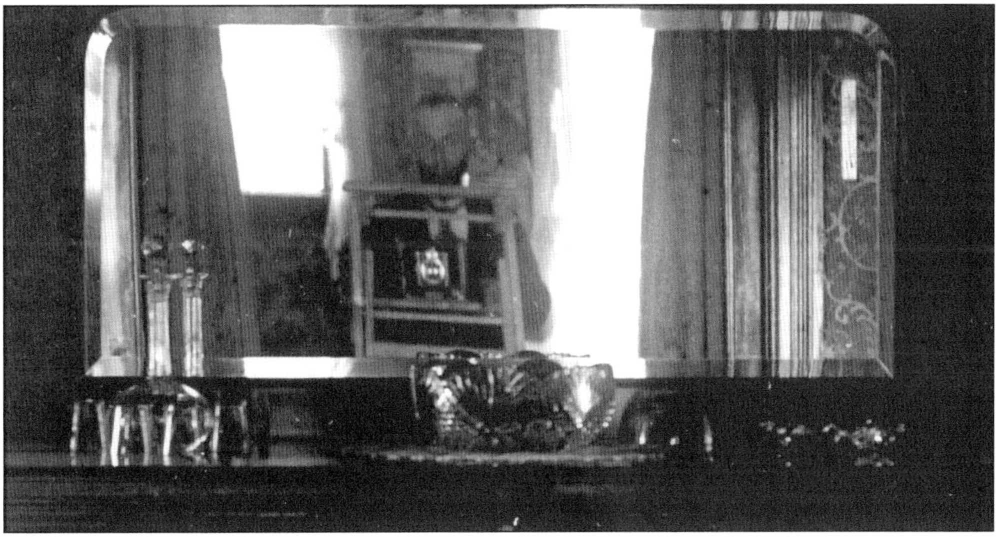

In this image, an enlargement of a portion of the photograph on the following page, Elwin "Doc" Young and his camera reach out to us across more than a century of time.

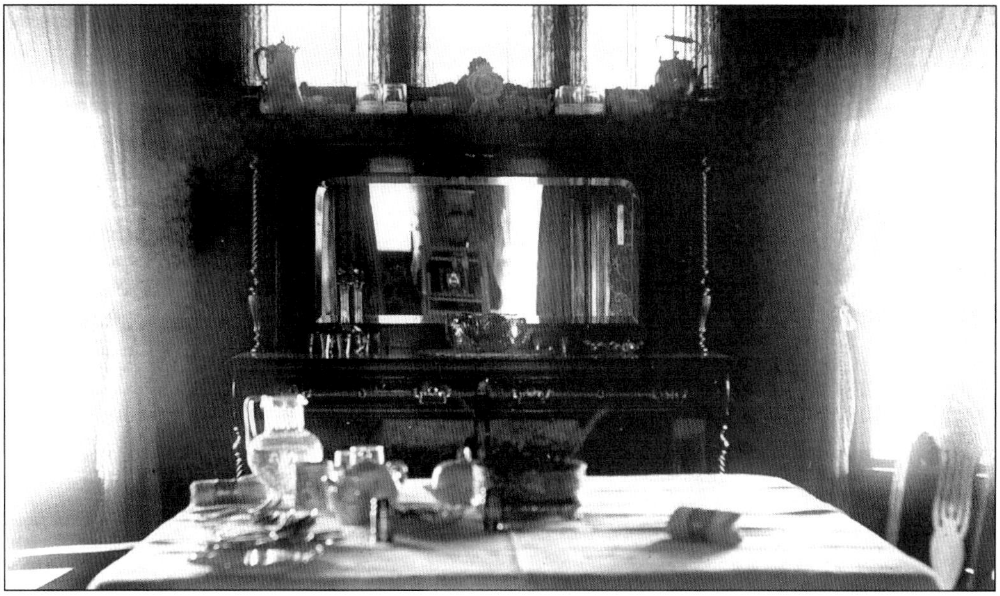

Doc Young records his own image in the mirror of his Pleasant Street home dining room. Elwin Young earned his nickname by providing much-needed medical advice to the less affluent members of the community who could not afford the services of a real doctor. He was much loved by the community.

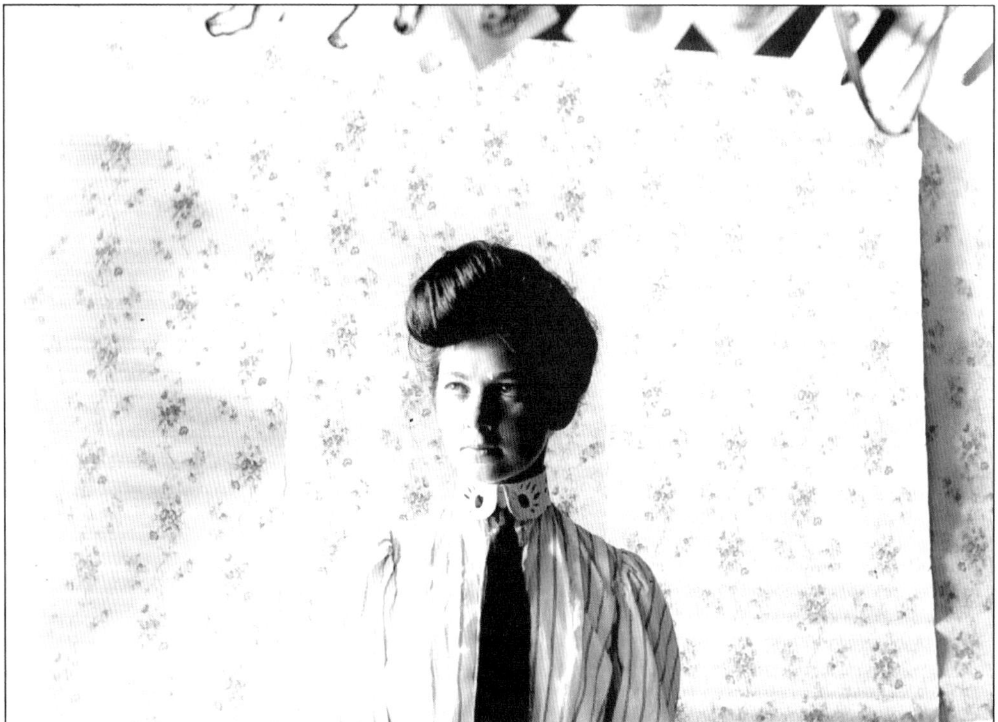

Toward the end of 1896, Doc Young married a young schoolteacher named Mamie Urell. A number of handmade holiday cards, most likely made by her students, can be seen in this photograph hanging above the doorway.

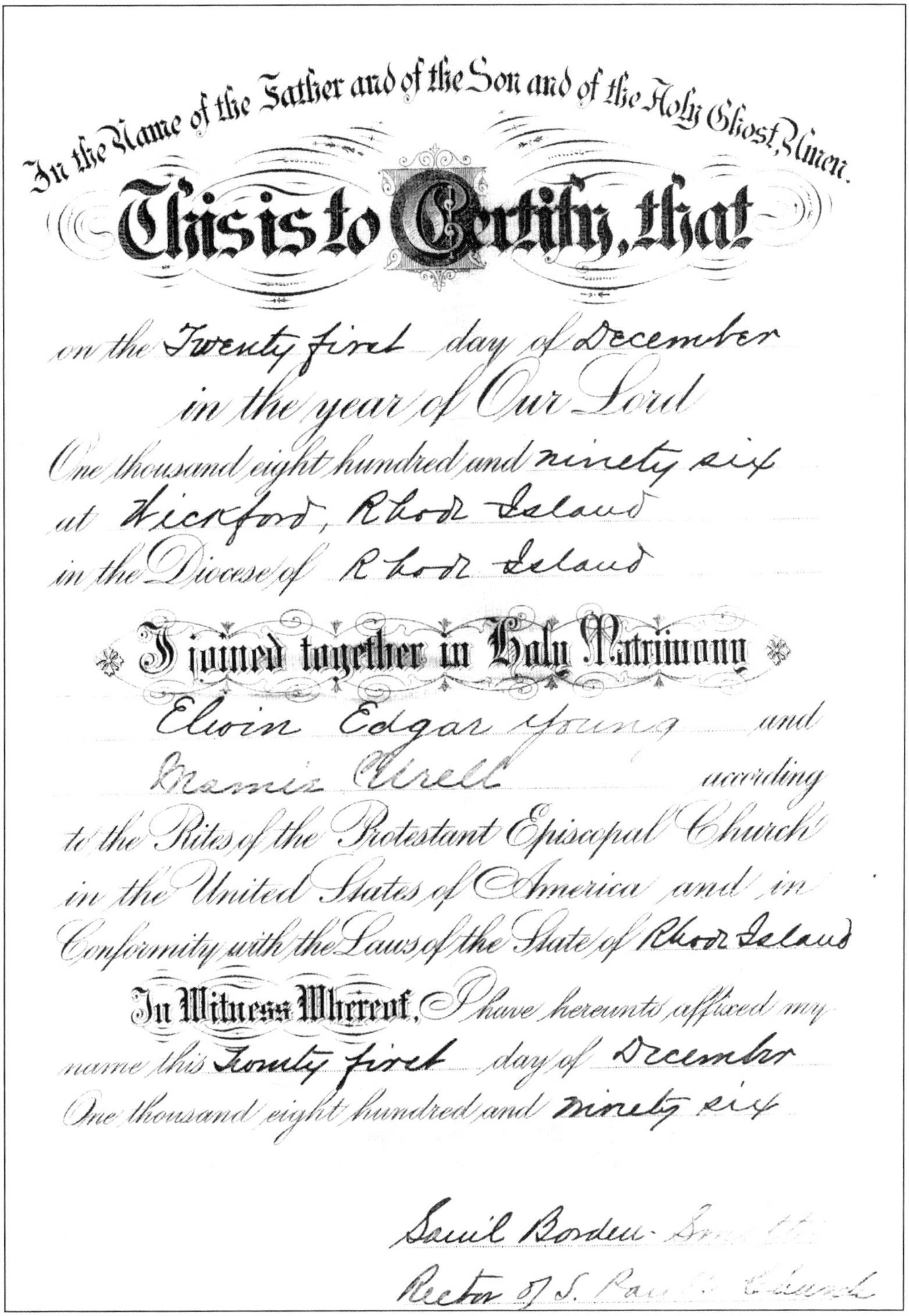

In the Name of the Father and of the Son and of the Holy Ghost, Amen.

This is to Certify, that

on the Twenty first day of December
in the year of Our Lord
One thousand eight hundred and ninety six
at Wickford, Rhode Island
in the Diocese of Rhode Island

I joined together in Holy Matrimony

Elwin Edgar Young and
Mamie Urell according
to the Rites of the Protestant Episcopal Church
in the United States of America and in
Conformity with the Laws of the State of Rhode Island

In Witness Whereof, I have hereunto affixed my
name this Twenty first day of December
One thousand eight hundred and ninety six

Daniel Borden-Smith
Rector of S. Paul's Church

Shown here is the marriage certificate of Elwin Young and Mamie Urell. They were married in the village at St. Paul's Episcopal Church by Rector Daniel Borden-Smith.

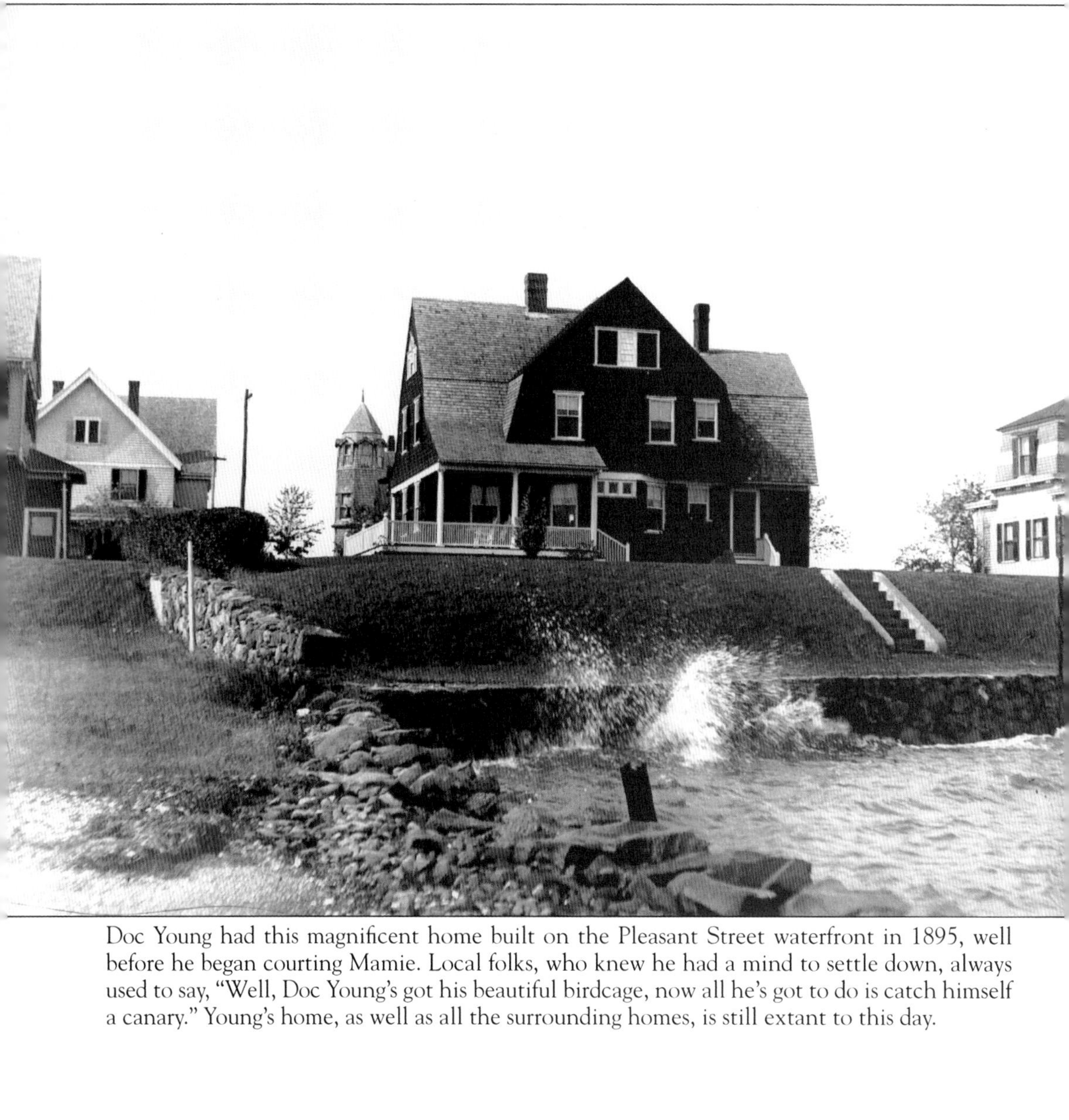

Doc Young had this magnificent home built on the Pleasant Street waterfront in 1895, well before he began courting Mamie. Local folks, who knew he had a mind to settle down, always used to say, "Well, Doc Young's got his beautiful birdcage, now all he's got to do is catch himself a canary." Young's home, as well as all the surrounding homes, is still extant to this day.

Mamie Young sits on the back porch of the Young home, sharing a moment with local character Capt. Ezra Thomas. Thomas was purported to be the last of the great clipper ship sailors who raced across the oceans carrying precious cargo from port to port. Although he was known to be only a first mate on the ships, he was called captain by all out of an endearing respect.

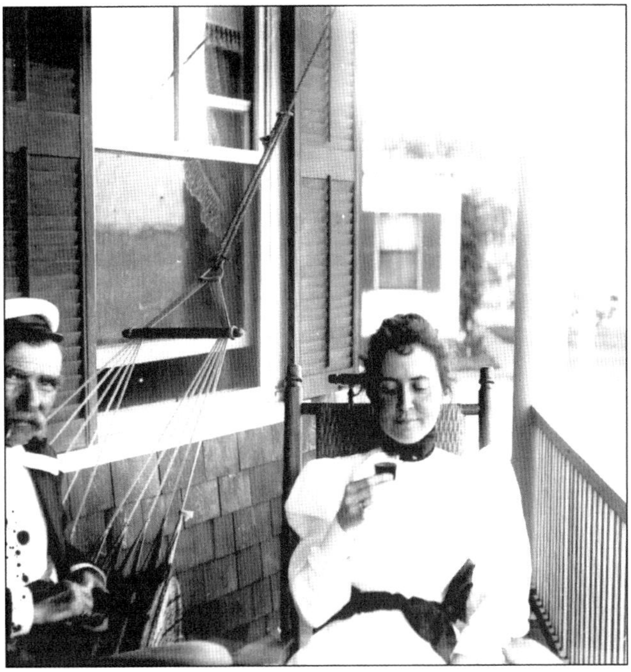

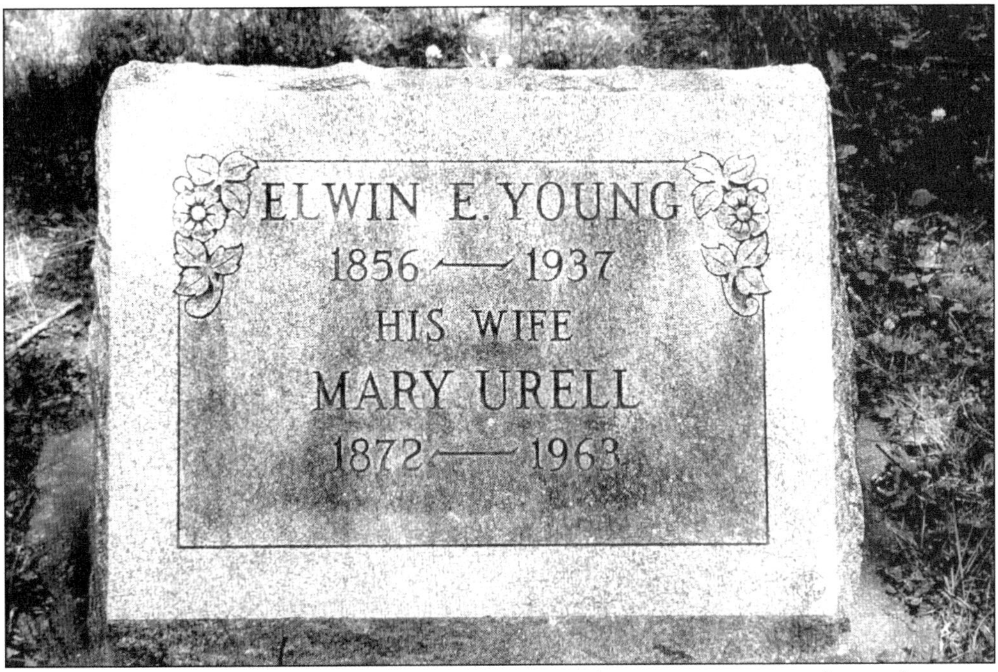

Doc and Mamie Young are buried side by side at the Quidnessett Cemetery in the northern part of town. Mamie outlived Doc by many years and, until her death, remained in the "beautiful birdcage" on Pleasant Street, which he had constructed to help win her heart.

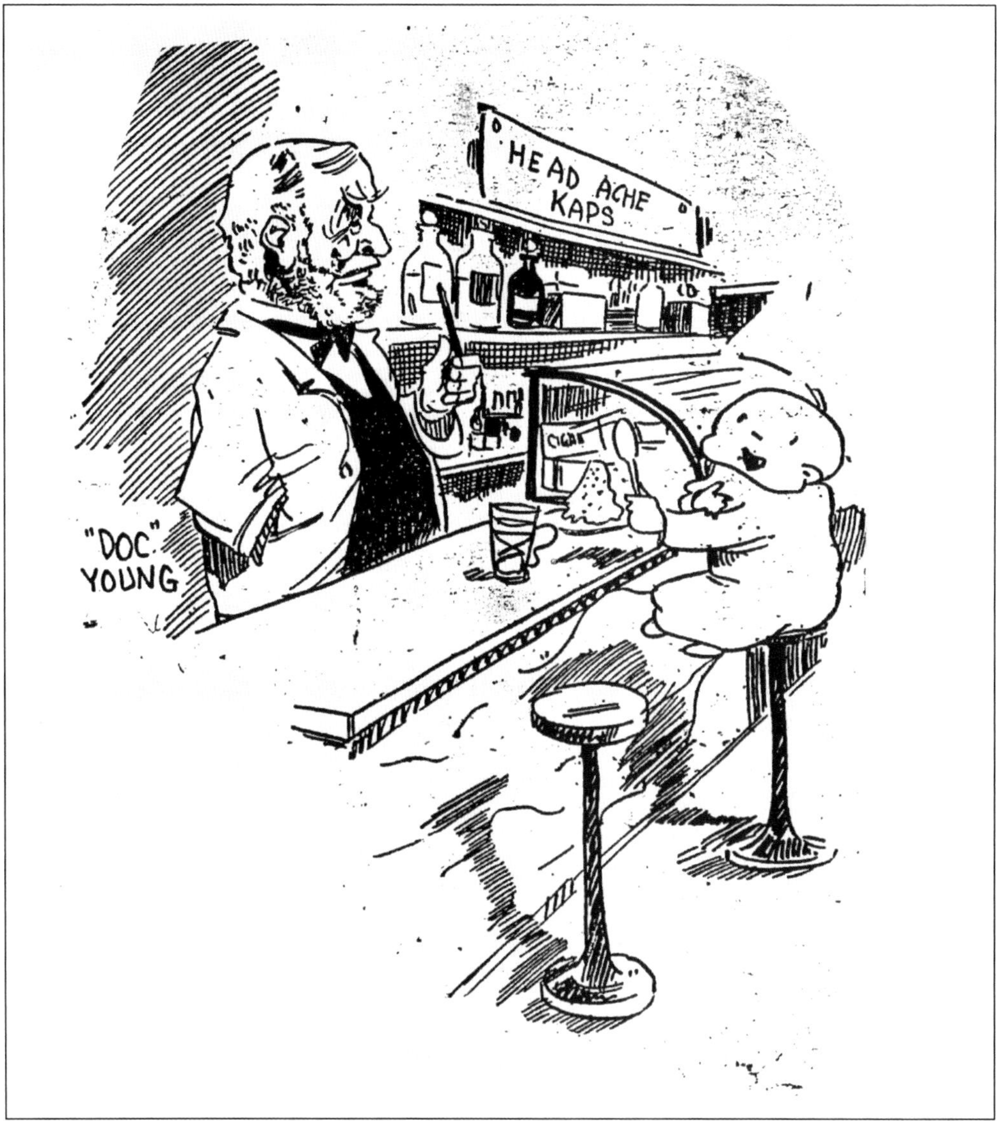

Years after his death, Doc Young was remembered by all. Local artist and editorial cartoonist Paule Loring created this cartoon version of the good pharmacist in his shop. (Used with the permission of the Loring family.)

Two

TRAINS, TROLLEYS, AND STEAMSHIPS

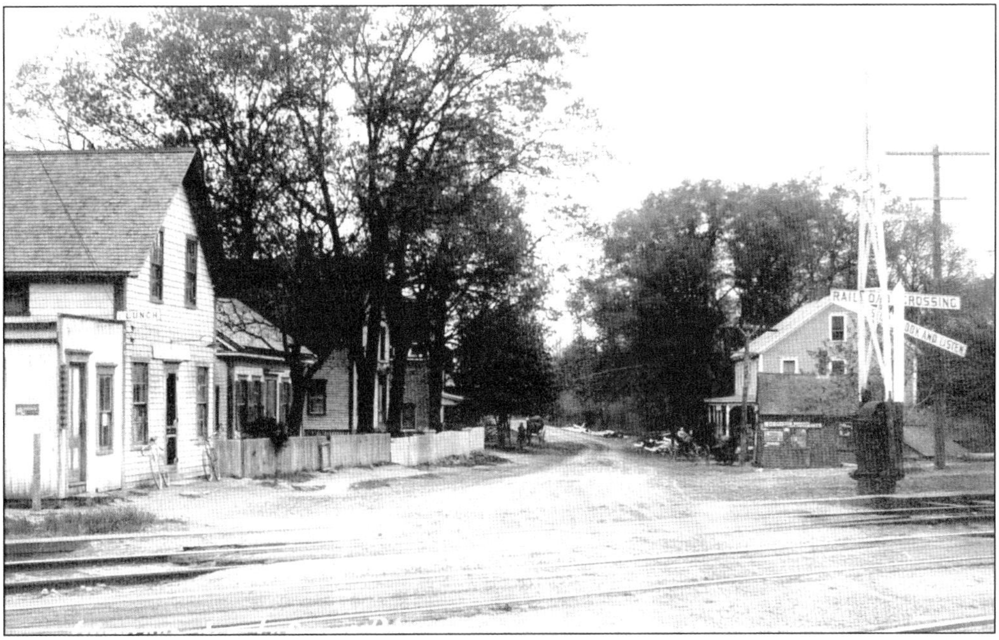

This is the view afforded to the wealthy passengers as they waited at the Wickford Junction Rail Station for the train down into Wickford Village proper and, eventually, a connection on the steamship that would take them to their ultimate destination—Newport, the city by the sea. The road shown in the photograph, Ten Rod Road, dates back to colonial times, when it was utilized to drive livestock on the hoof into Wickford to be shipped out to points up and down the eastern seaboard and beyond. The road's name refers to the width of the road's right of way, which was composed of grazing areas to help feed the livestock as the herds made their way to the village.

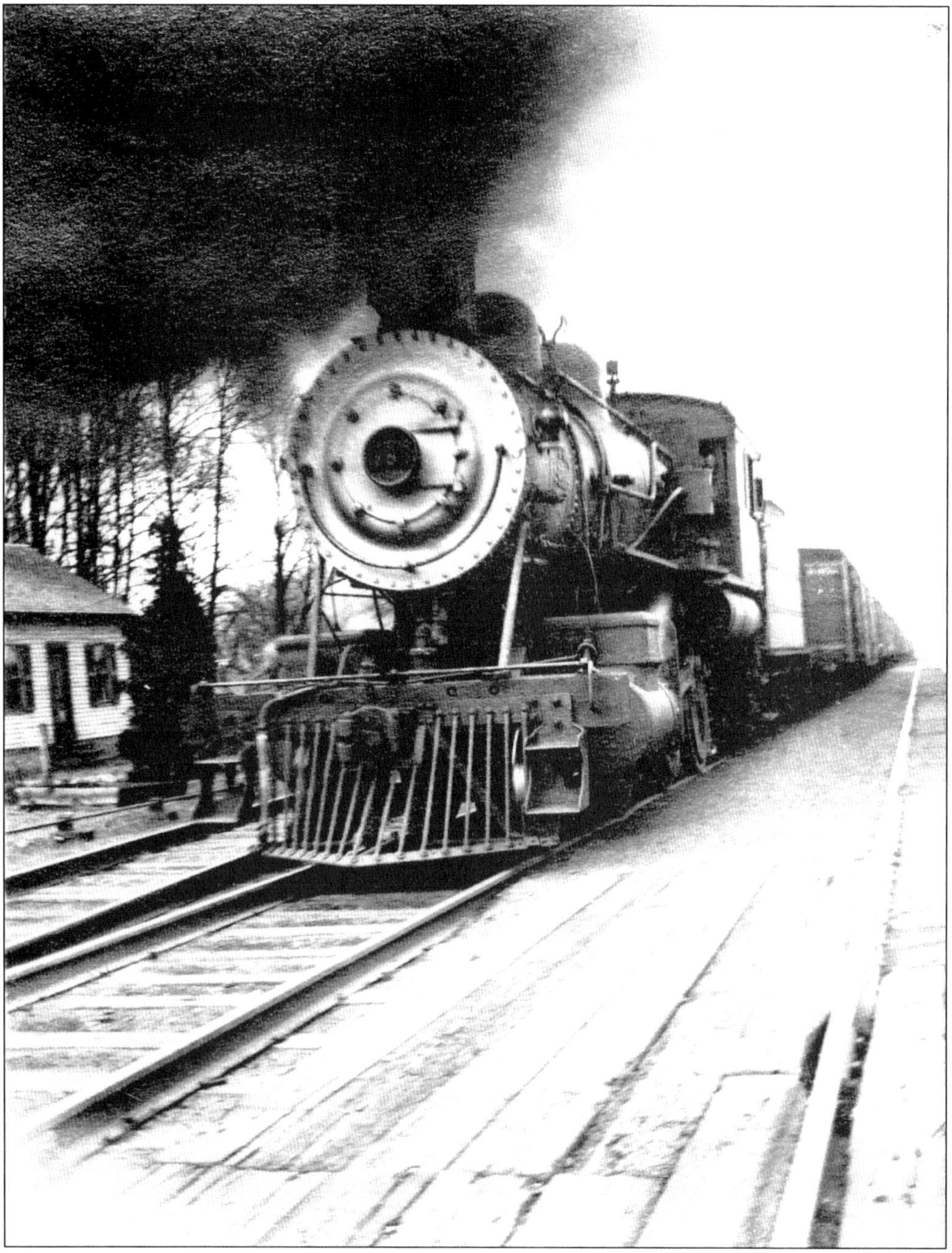

With a billowing puff of sooty black smoke, a freight train pulls into the Wickford Junction Rail Station. The largest single-freight delivery to be off-loaded at Wickford Junction consisted of just about every component necessary to build Robert Rodman's new textile mill, constructed in the mid-1870s in nearby Lafayette.

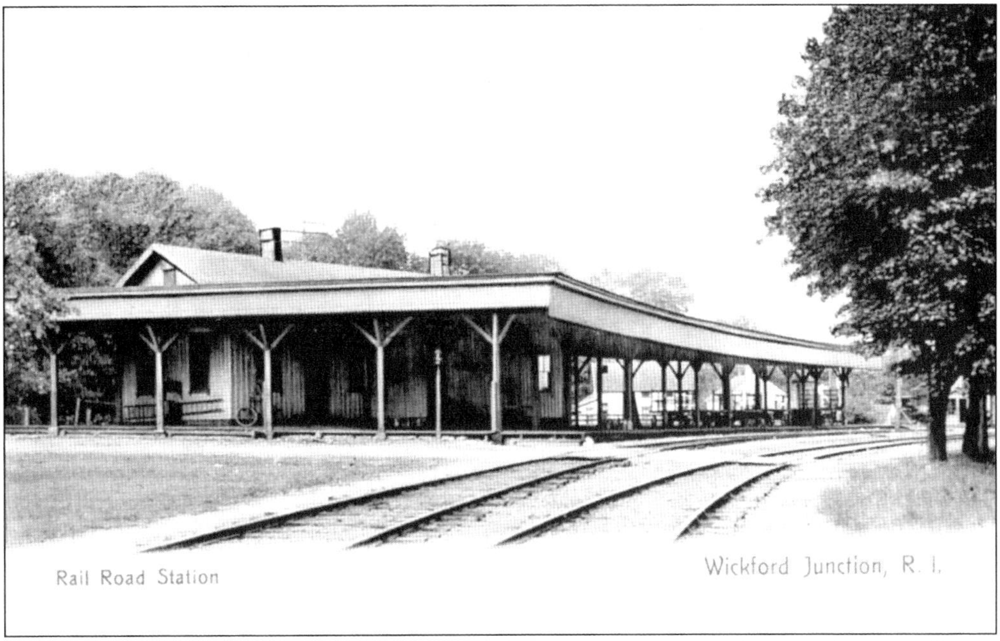

This postcard shows the Wickford Junction Rail Station as it appeared in its glory days. These postcards were sold at the Rodman Manufacturing Company store in Lafayette.

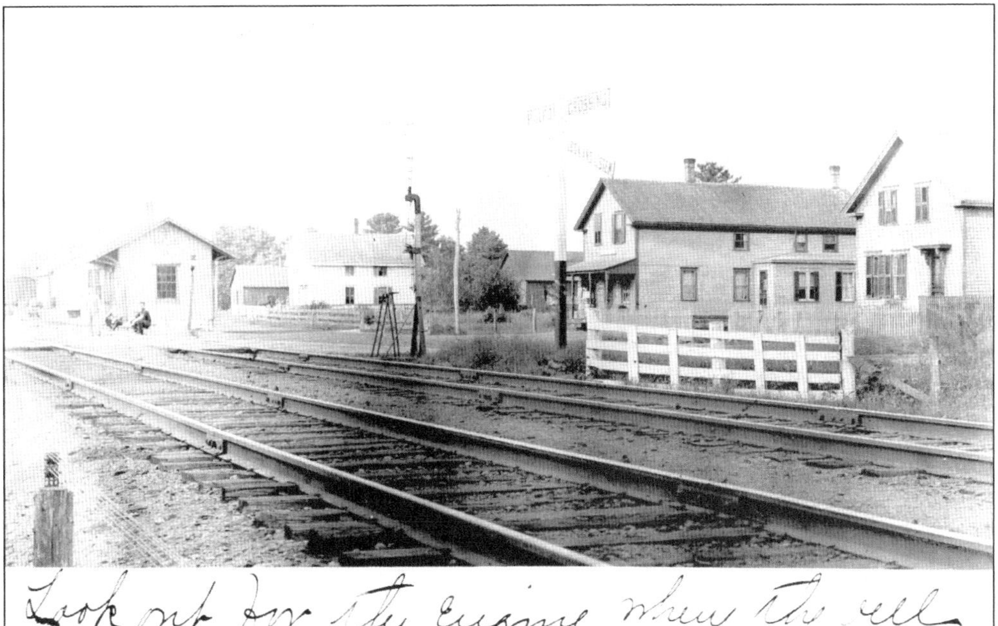

The next station north of Wickford Junction on the main line was the Davisville Station, shown here. This village was centered around a textile mill founded by the Davis family many years prior.

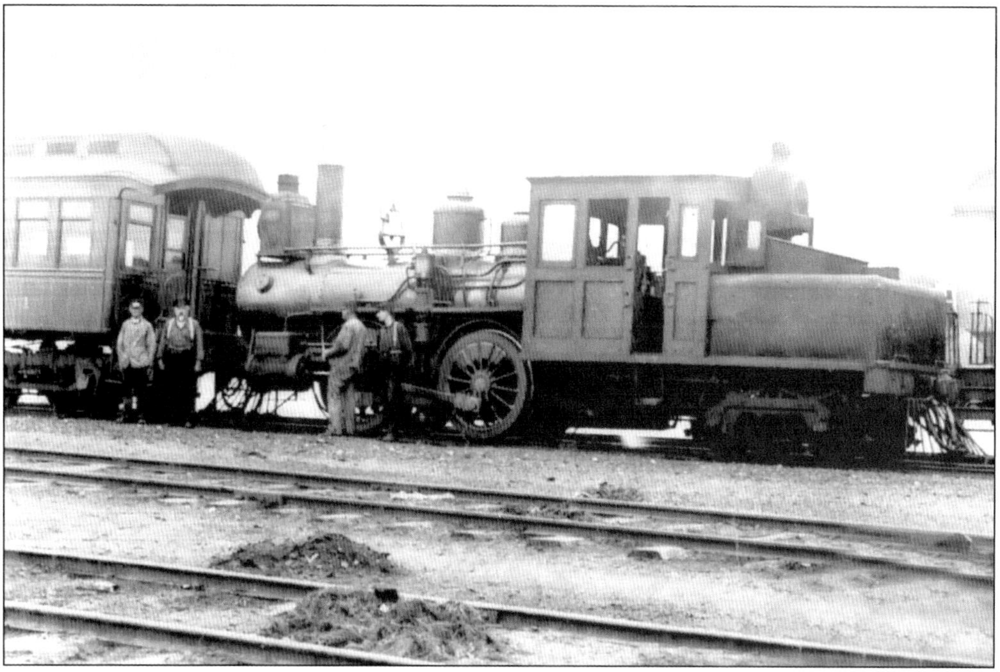

These two photographs are the only known images of the original "train that saved Wickford," the Newport and Wickford Rail and Steamship branch line. Also shown in one of the photographs is a portion of a passenger car. At the line's peak, the true elite did not even leave their opulent private railcars. Families like the Astors and Vanderbilts stayed in their own cars while they were switched onto the branch line. While in Newport, their private cars were stored on spur lines at the Steamboat Landing until summer's end when it was time to leave.

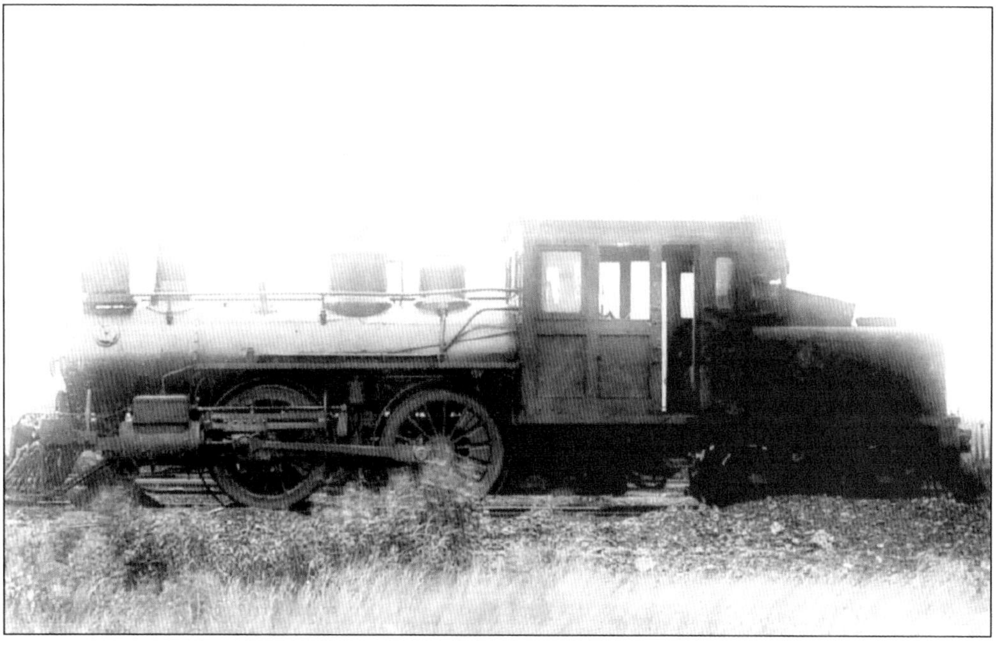

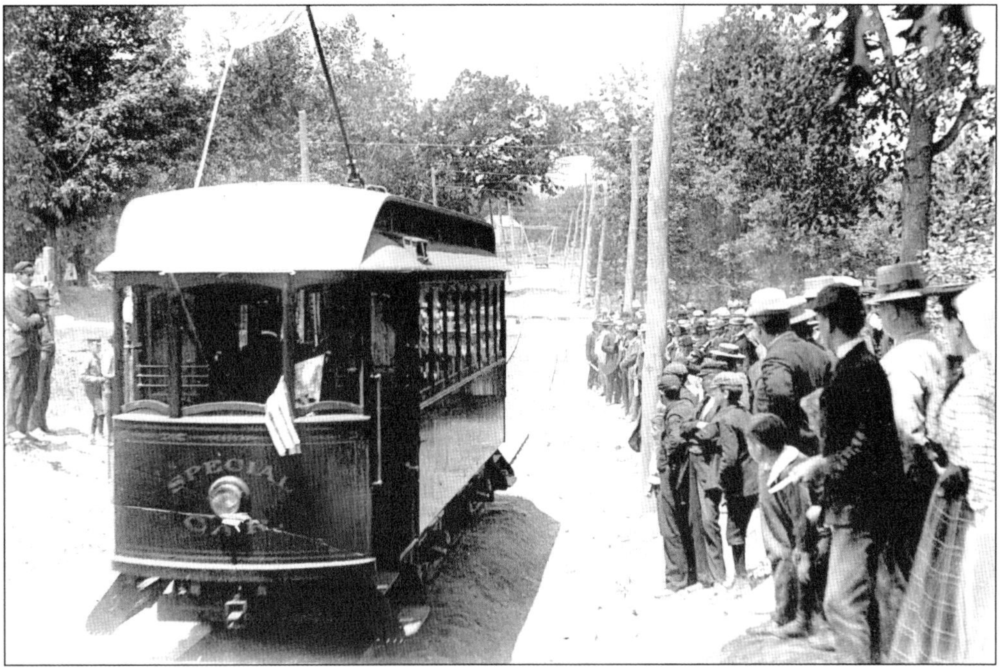

Another way to get to North Kingstown was to utilize Rhode Island's extensive network of electric trolleys. Switching to the Sea View line in nearby East Greenwich allowed virtually any southern New Englander the opportunity to take a day trip to North Kingstown or to Narragansett Pier. The line was also a boon to the local folks along its path, because in the days before cars, a person could inexpensively seek work outside of his hometown or attend a college in Providence. A daily freight run afforded an opportunity for local farmers to get their wares into the city on a daily basis. These photographs were taken on the line's opening day (note the uniforms and band members).

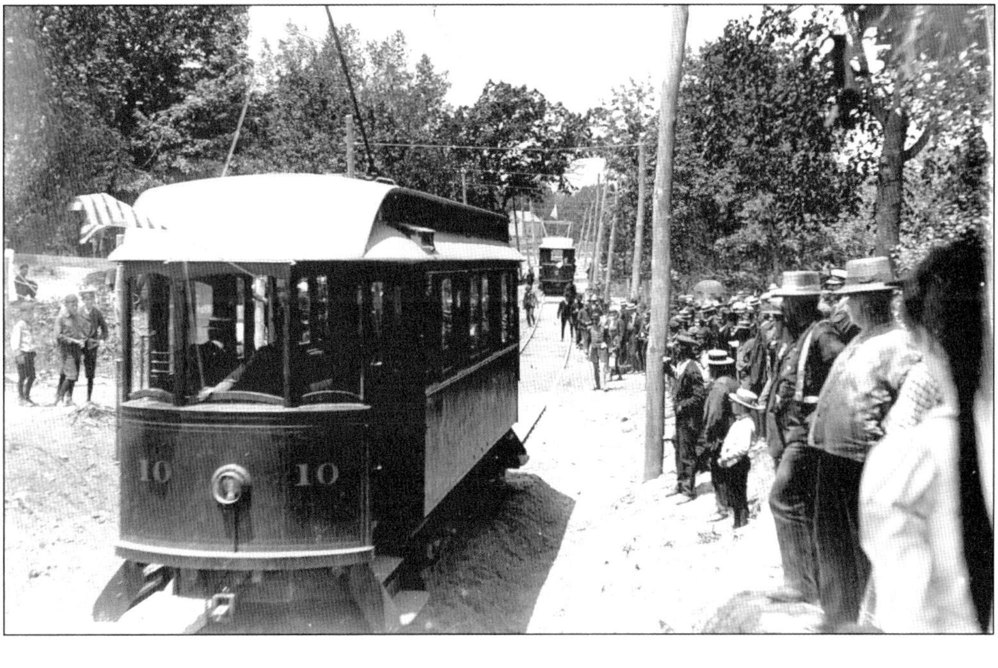

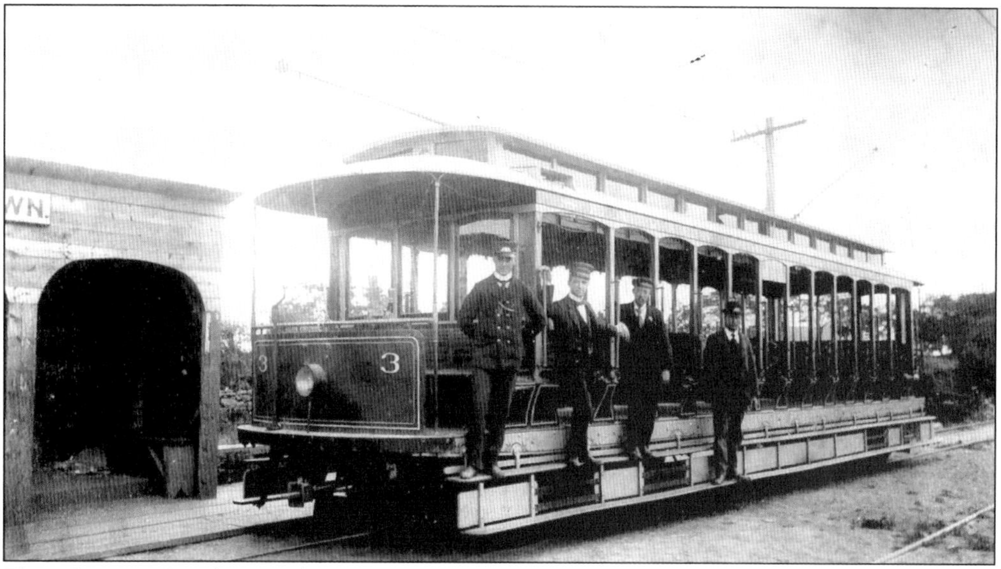

This photograph, taken at the Saunderstown Station, is of a Sea View open-air summer car. Folks would get off here to spend time in the nearby village of Saunderstown, a summer writers' colony of sorts centered around the La Farge and Wharton families. Teddy Roosevelt was a frequent guest at Saunderstown.

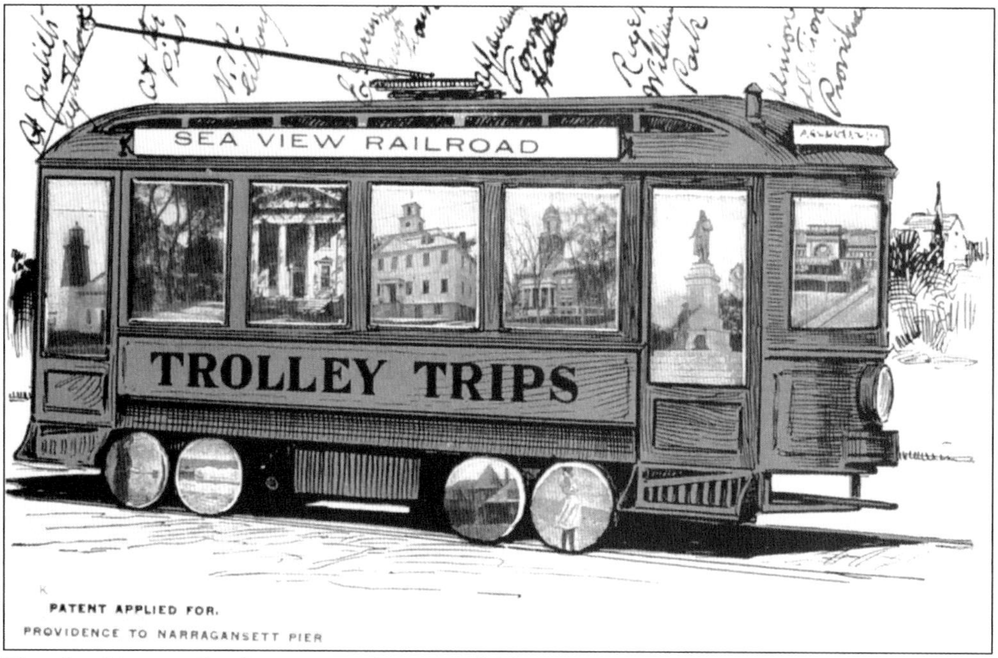

This Sea View trolley line postcard was available at many of the major trolley stations from Providence to Narragansett Pier. Shown are vignettes from Providence, Warwick, East Greenwich, North Kingstown, Narragansett, and Point Judith.

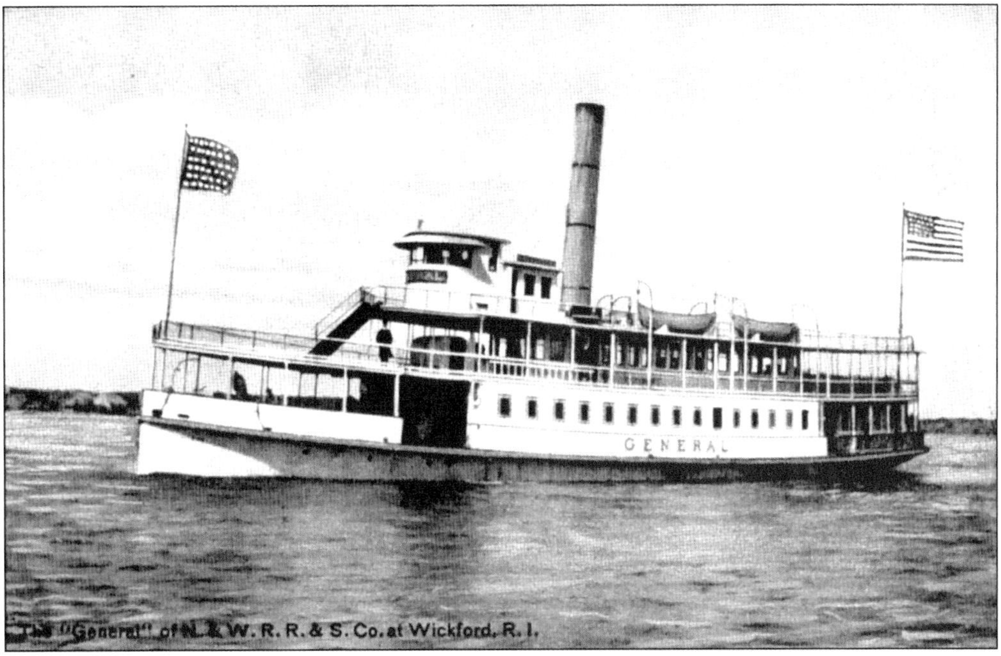

This is a postcard view of the steamer *General*, which would make numerous runs from Wickford to Newport on a daily basis. The *General* was the third ship to serve this line and was preceded by the *Eolus* and the *Tockwogh*. This was a Doc Young–produced, colorized card that sold exclusively in his shop.

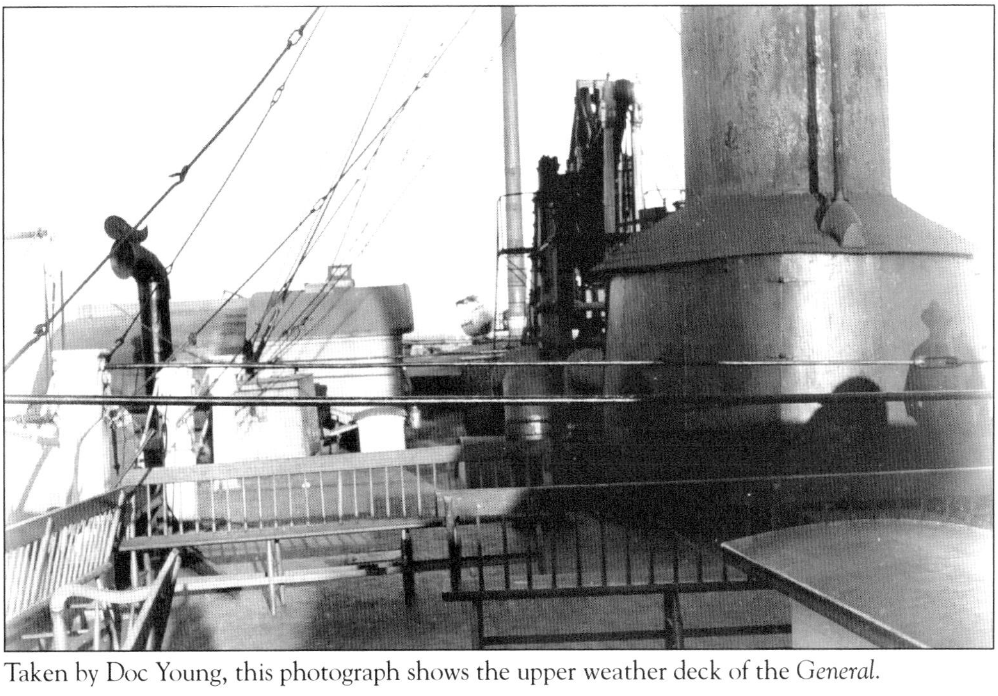

Taken by Doc Young, this photograph shows the upper weather deck of the *General*.

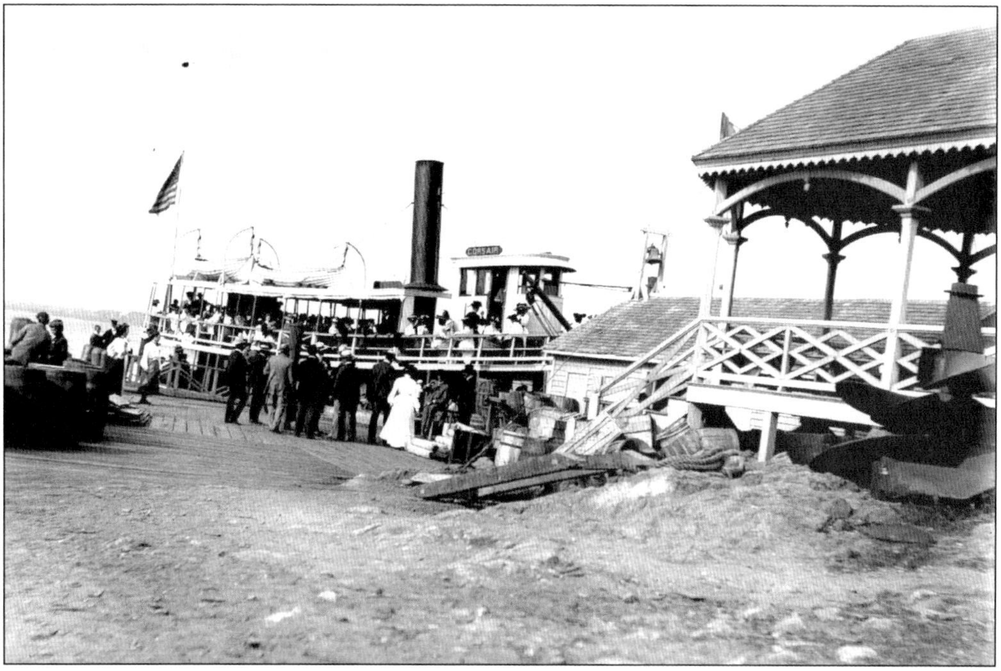

Another feature offered at the Poplar Point Steamboat Landing was an opportunity to board an excursion boat for a day trip in and around Narragansett Bay. Folks are boarding the *Corsair* for just such a trip.

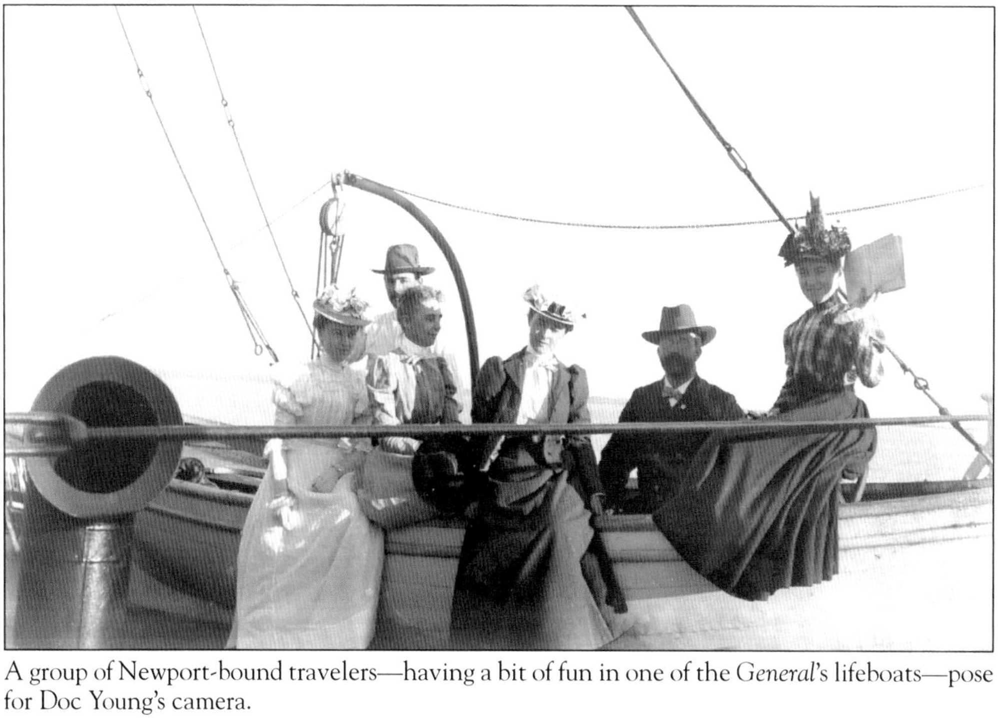

A group of Newport-bound travelers—having a bit of fun in one of the *General*'s lifeboats—pose for Doc Young's camera.

Three

HOTELS AND INNS

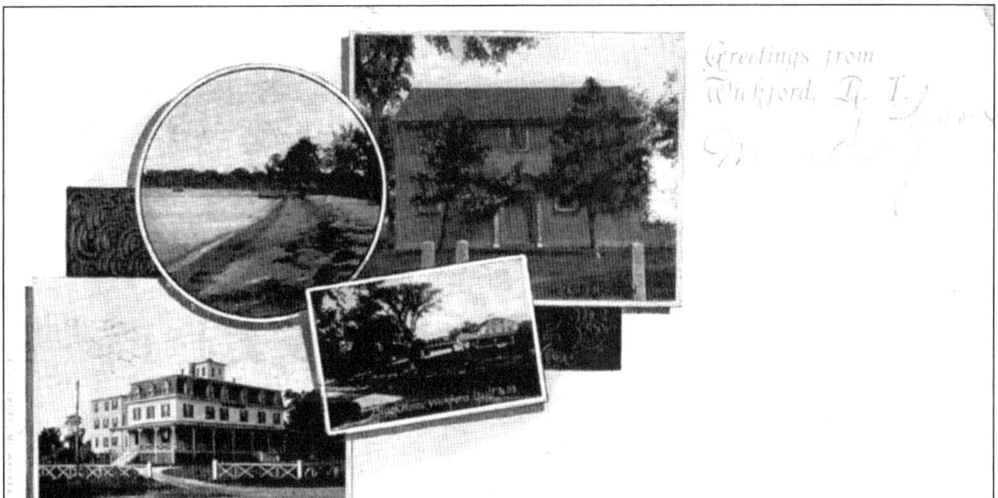

This is a typical Wickford postcard that would have been sold at the Cold Spring House, the village's premier summer hotel. Inset photographs on the card include the Cold Spring House itself, along with its beach, Richard Smith's Blockhouse, and the Old Narragansett Church.

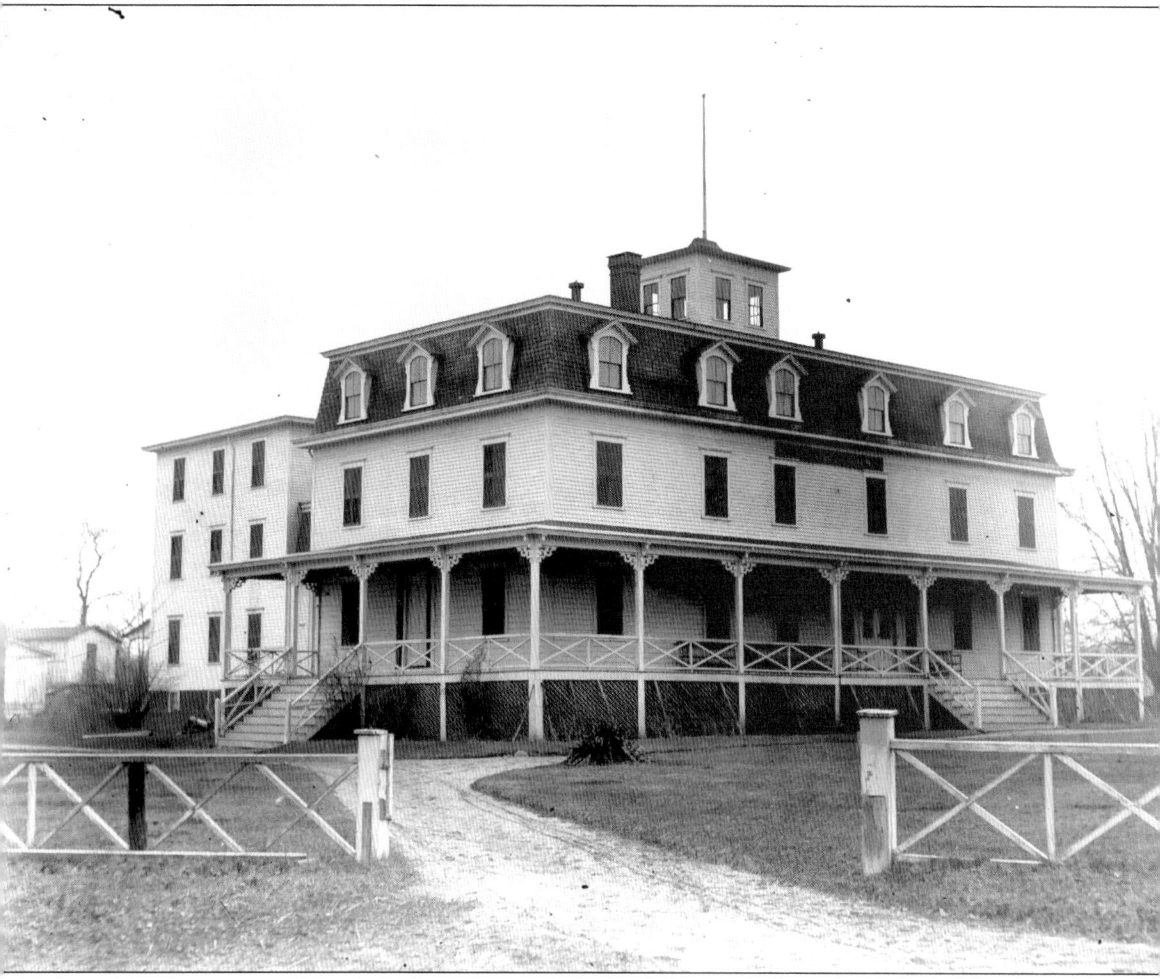

Here is a view of the Cold Spring House photographed by Doc Young. Opened in 1881 by Thomas Peirce, the 75-room hotel was constructed specifically to take advantage of the influx of visitors brought to North Kingstown by the Newport and Wickford line. In 1909, the then 80-year-old Peirce leased the hotel to schoolteacher Henry Carpenter. Carpenter eventually purchased the place from Peirce and ran it for 43 years.

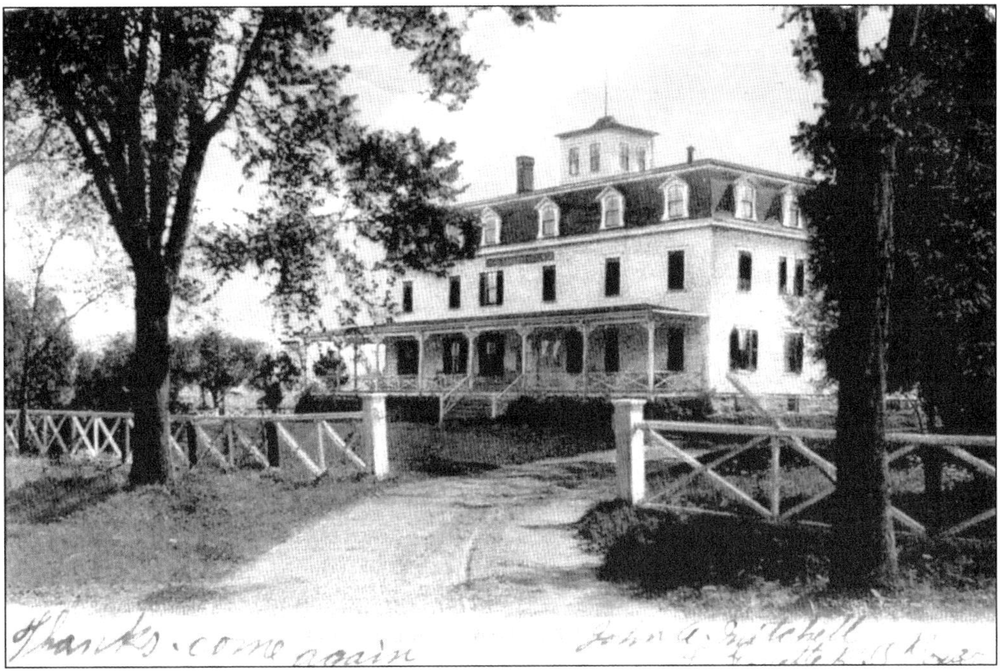

This is a postcard view of the Cold Spring House published by Doc Young's competitor, Sealey's drugstore, which was located just down the street from him. Both pharmacies continued in business beyond their original owners. Young's shop became Earnshaw's Drugstore and Sealey's continued on as Seavey's Drugstore.

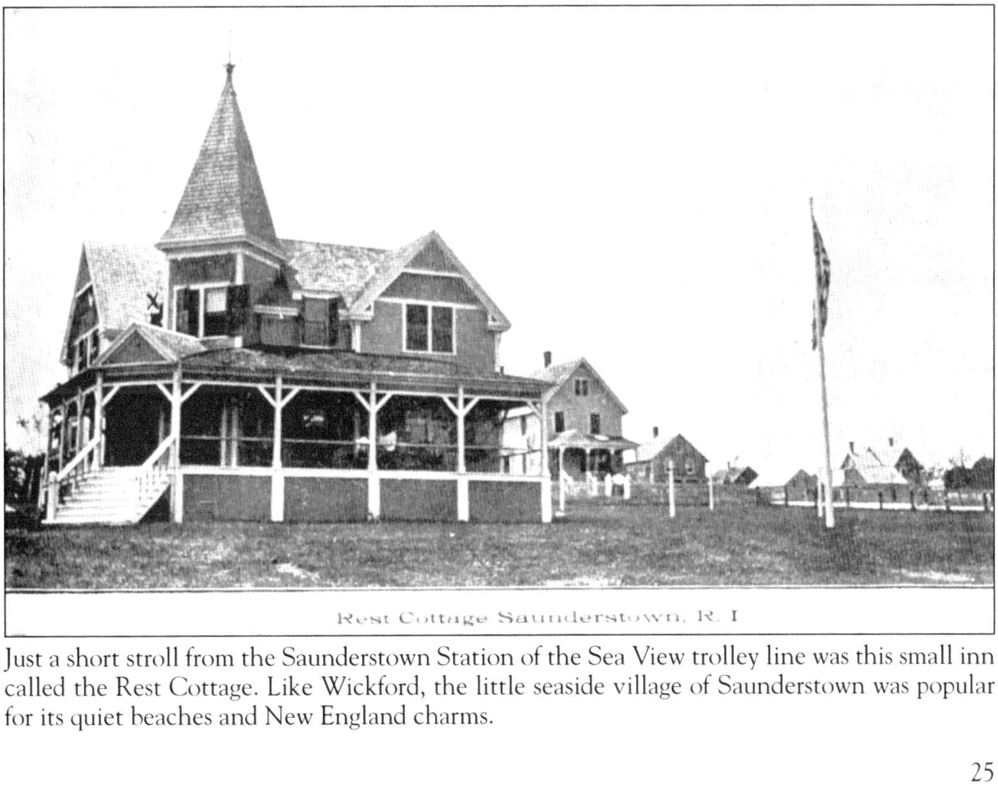

Just a short stroll from the Saunderstown Station of the Sea View trolley line was this small inn called the Rest Cottage. Like Wickford, the little seaside village of Saunderstown was popular for its quiet beaches and New England charms.

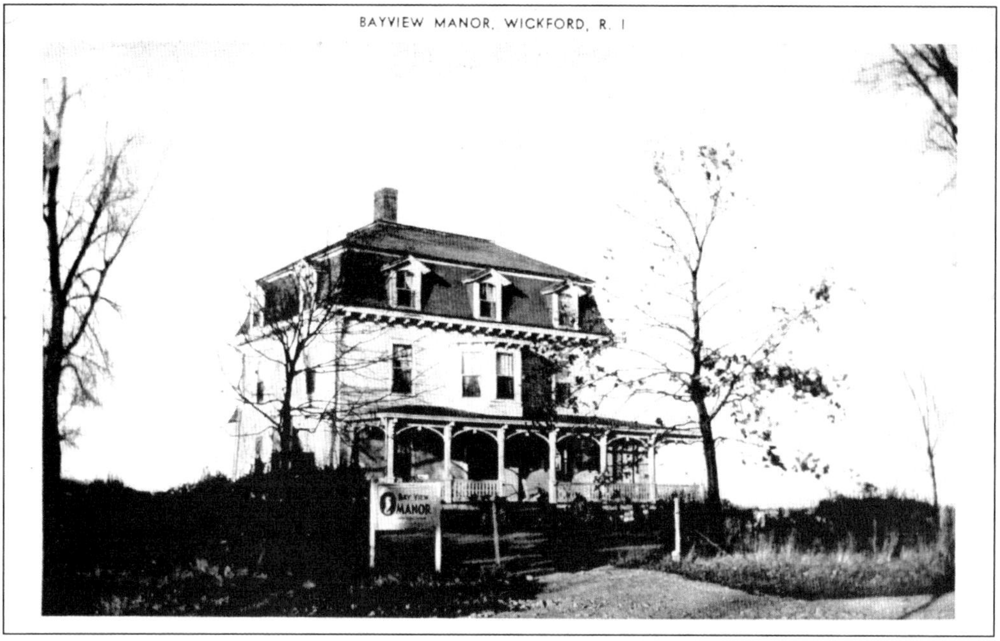

Just north of the much-larger Cold Spring House in Wickford was the Bayview Manor. Like the Cold Spring House, it was located within walking distance of the Wickford train station shared by the Newport and Wickford line and the Sea View trolley. Demolished long ago, it was located on the site of the present-day North Kingstown Town Beach.

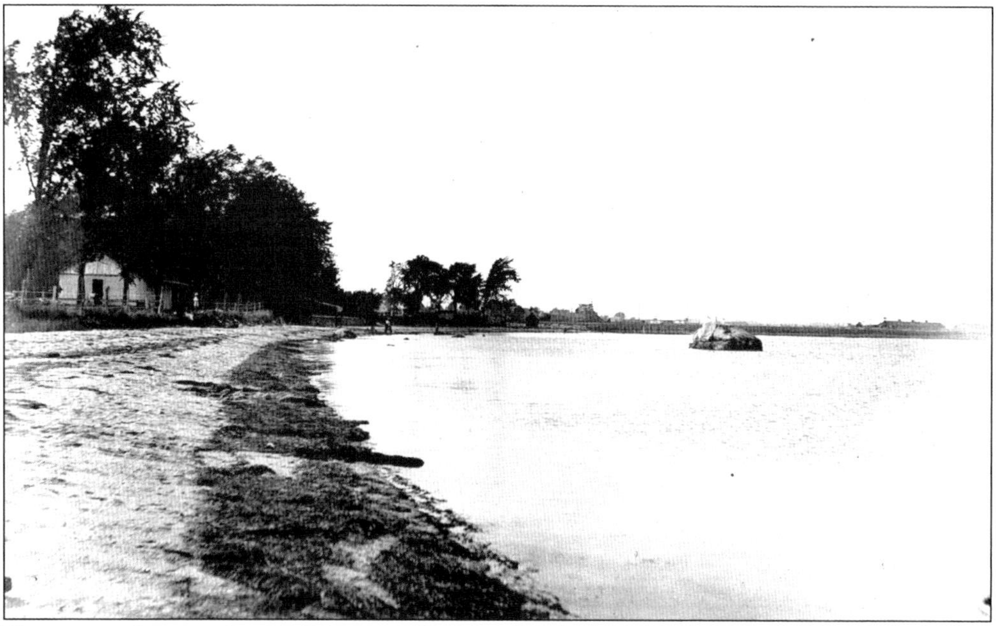

These two photographs show the quiet bathing beach shared by the Cold Spring House, the Bayview Manor, and the Beachwood. Nestled in a sheltered cove, it was, as it is today, prized

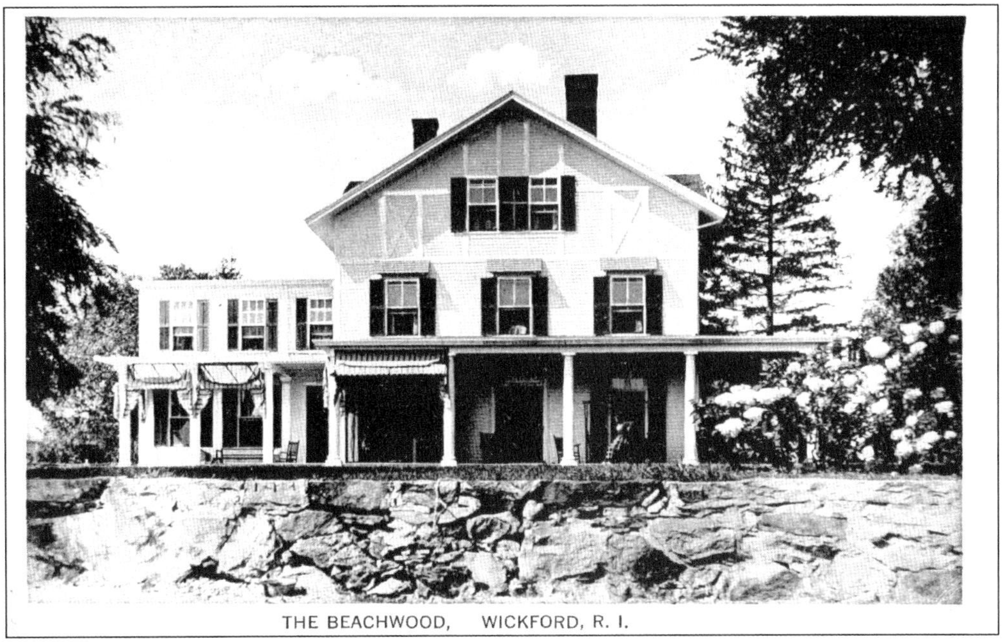

The Beachwood was another small inn located within walking distance of the train station, which was shared by the Newport and Wickford line and the Sea View trolley. It had formerly been the summer residence of Gov. Elisha Dyer and was to one day become the North Kingstown Senior Center.

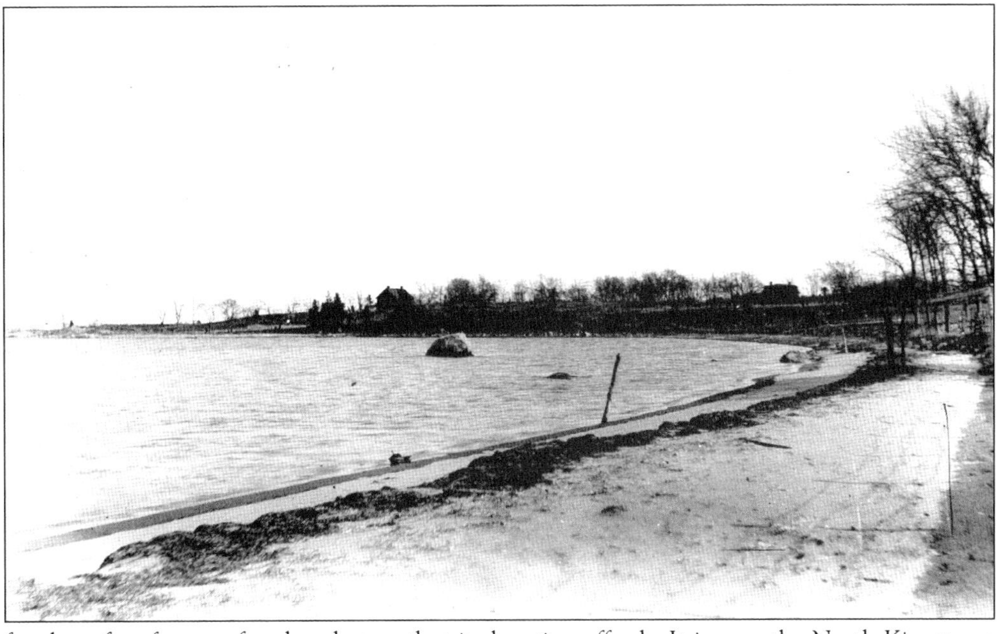

for the safety from surf and undertow that its location affords. It is now the North Kingstown town beach.

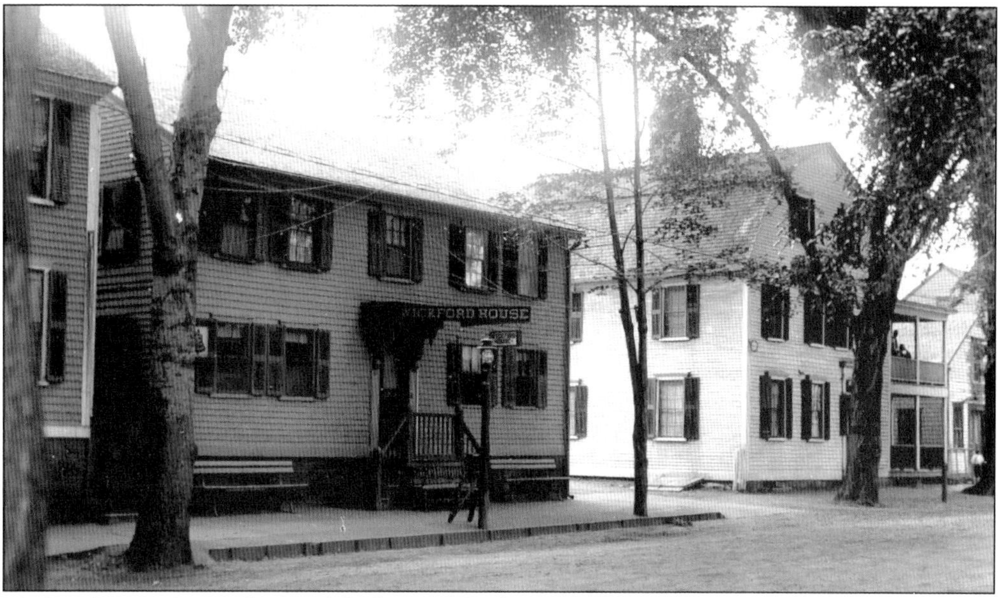

Mother Prentice's popular Wickford House had a wide-ranging reputation for hospitality and wonderful food. It was always booked to capacity during the busy season. Eventually, the Prentices, George and Ellen, purchased the large gambrel-roofed house next door from the family of Rev. Lemuel Burge and converted it into rooms to absorb the overflow. The building known as the Wickford House Annex was, sadly, demolished in the 1950s to make room for St. Paul's Parish House. Ironically, Reverend Burge had spent the majority of his life in service to that very parish.

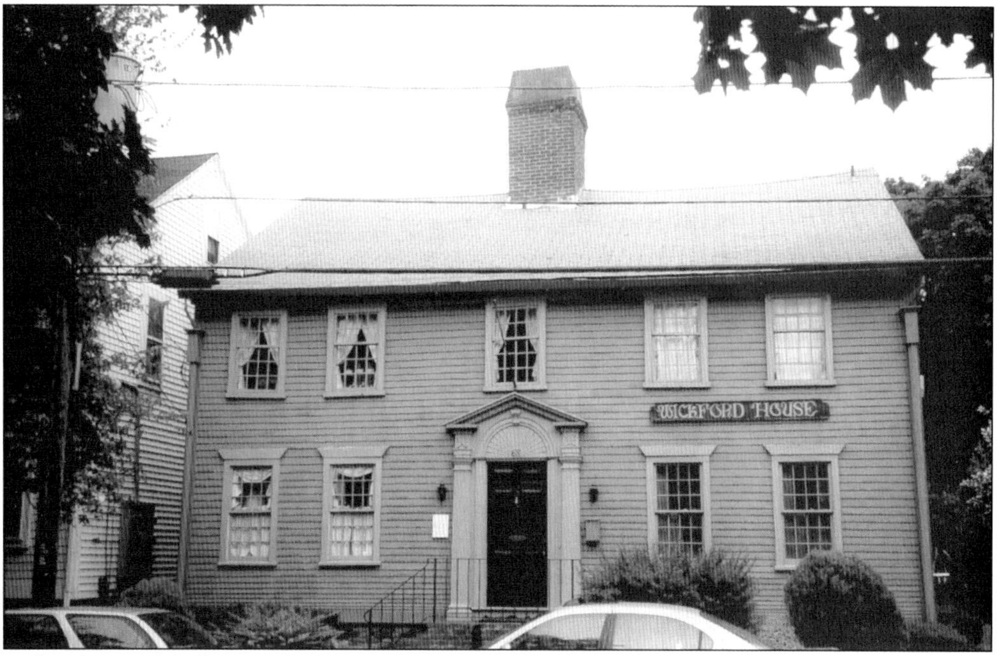

Today the Wickford House looks remarkably similar to its visage 100 years ago. The only major change to the structure has been the addition of the ornate Lt. Gov. J. J. Reynolds front door, salvaged from Reynolds's old home that was ravaged by the 1938 hurricane and subsequently demolished.

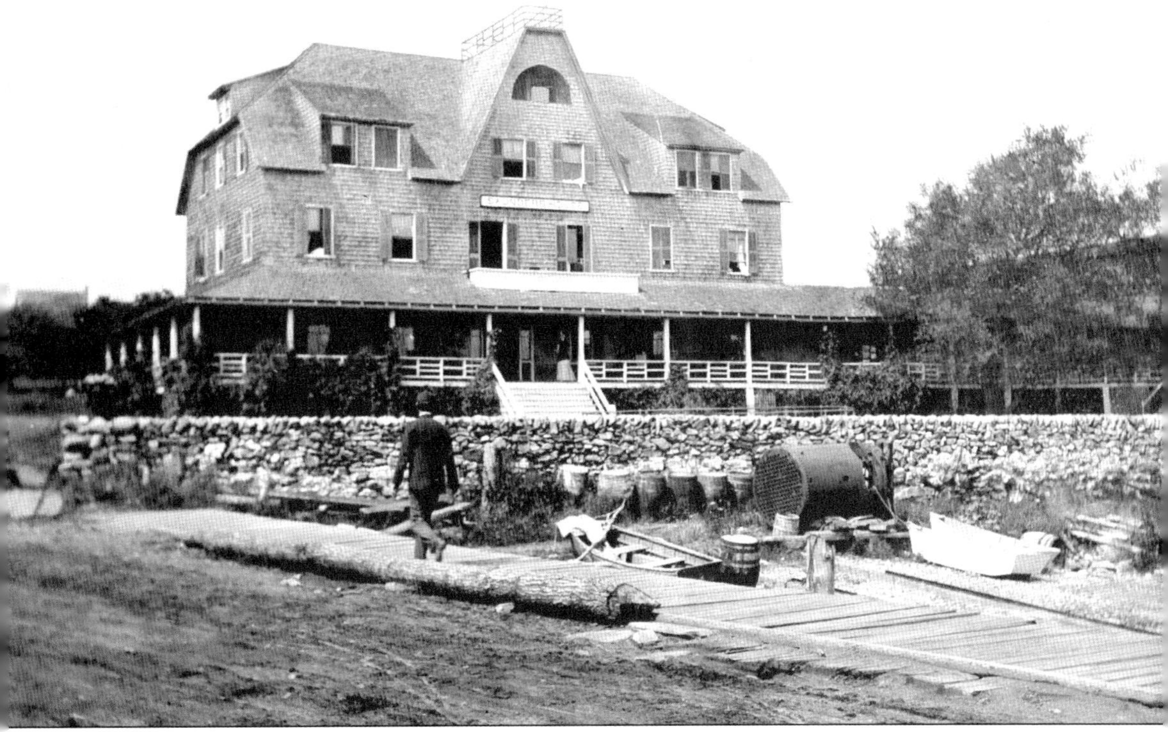

The crown jewel of the Saunderstown Village hotels was the Saunders House, located right on the beach and owned and operated by the famous ship-building Saunders family.

Built in 1889 by Stillman Saunders, it was originally constructed to take advantage of the fact that travelers often had to wait for the Saunders-owned-and-constructed Newport ferries that ran from the village.

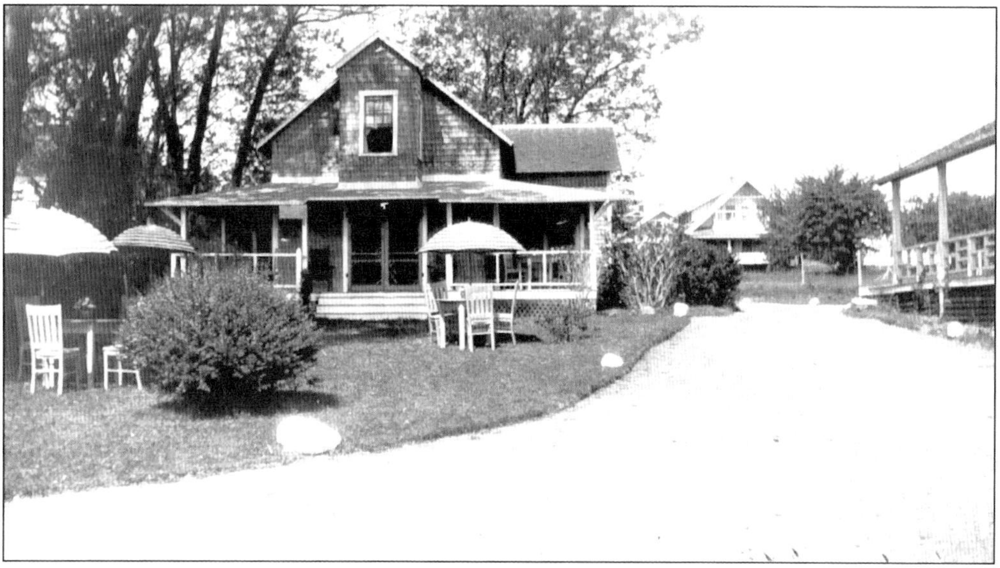

The Holiday House and the Willow Tea Cottage were two more of Saunderstown's many small inns. Teahouses were as popular then as coffee shops are today and could be found in almost every community.

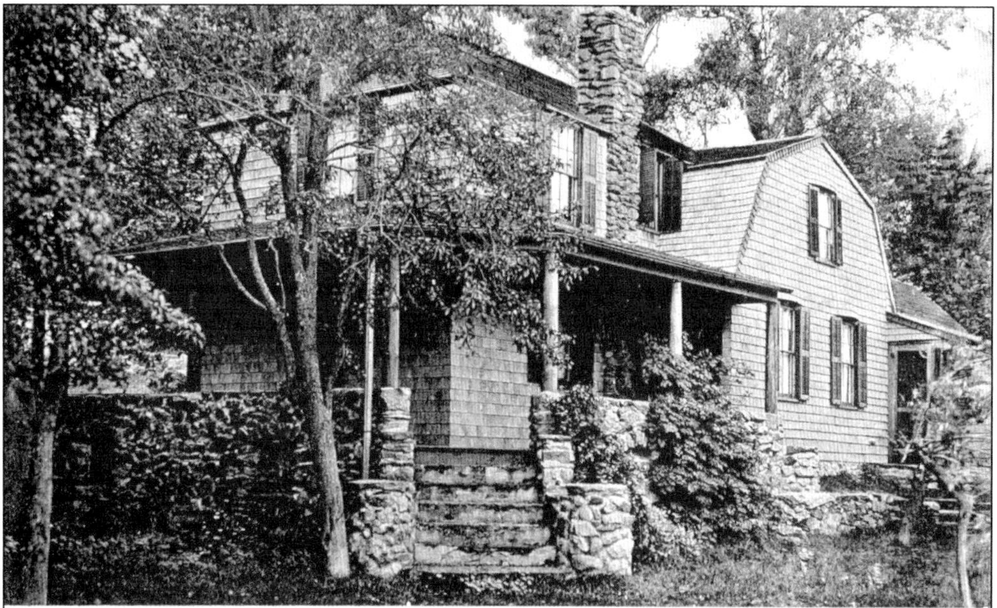

Holliday House. Barbours Heights, R. I.

Four

Tourist Destinations

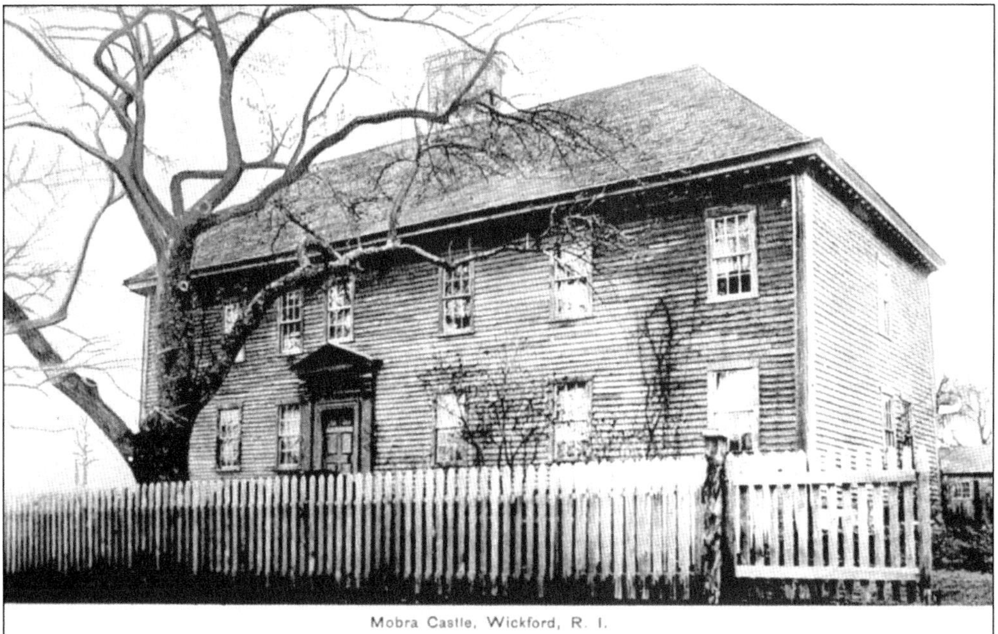

The Phillips or Mowbra Castle, located along Boston Post Road (now Tower Hill Road) adjacent to the Belleville station of the Newport and Wickford line, was a popular tourist site. The massive home included a great stone fireplace so large that a full-grown man could comfortably walk into the fire chamber. The Phillips family was among the first to settle in the area and were contemporaries of and equals to the Smiths and Updikes. Sadly, the fine home burned to the ground in 1960. The exact origin of the Phillips family–assigned name of Mowbra Castle is unknown to this day.

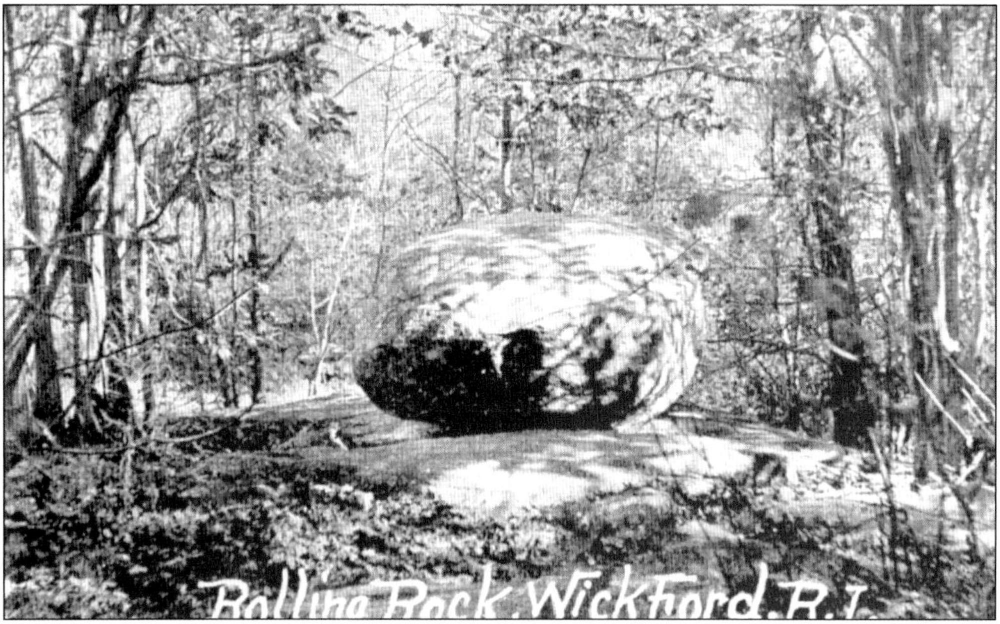

The Rolling Rock was also located off of Boston Post Road a mile or so north of Phillips Castle. It was said to date back to the time of the Narragansetts and was used to call the tribal members for important get-togethers. Two braves standing on each end of the great stone could rock it back and forth and create a sound that could be heard for miles. Unfortunately this event was recreated so many times by tourists visiting the stone that, in the 1940s, a neighbor living nearby cemented the stone down and rendered it inoperable.

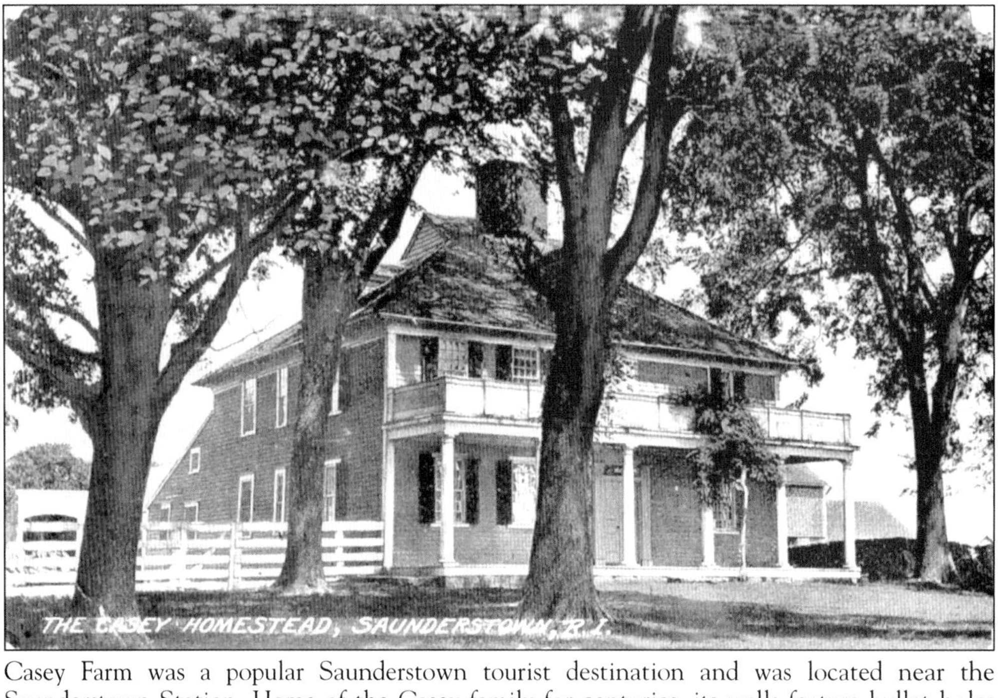

Casey Farm was a popular Saunderstown tourist destination and was located near the Saunderstown Station. Home of the Casey family for centuries, its walls feature bullet holes made during a Revolutionary War skirmish that was fought there.

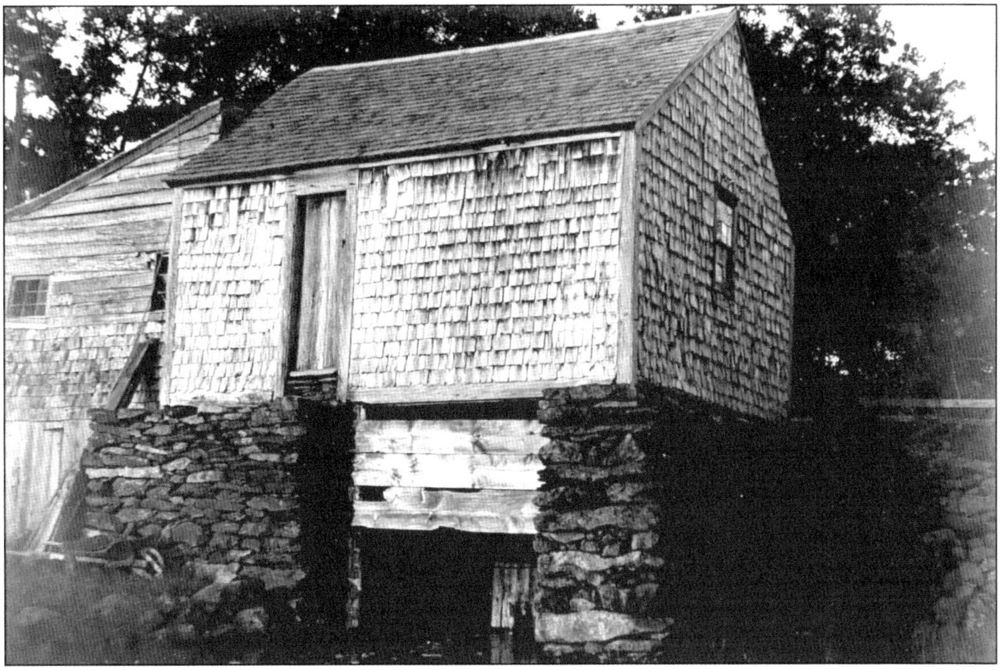

The old gristmill on Camp Avenue was another popular tourist attraction. Throughout the first third of the 20th century, corn was still being ground into meal there by members of the colorful Tourjee family. The gristmill was so historically accurate that in the 1920s, representatives of Henry Ford approached its owner to see if he could purchase the mill and move it, stones and all, to his recreated New England village planned for the outskirts of Dearborn, Michigan. The owner declined, preferring to keep it here. Unfortunately the devastating hurricane of 1938 had other ideas, and the mill was swept away. Seabees from the local base at Quonset-Davisville later filled in the millpond as a training exercise.

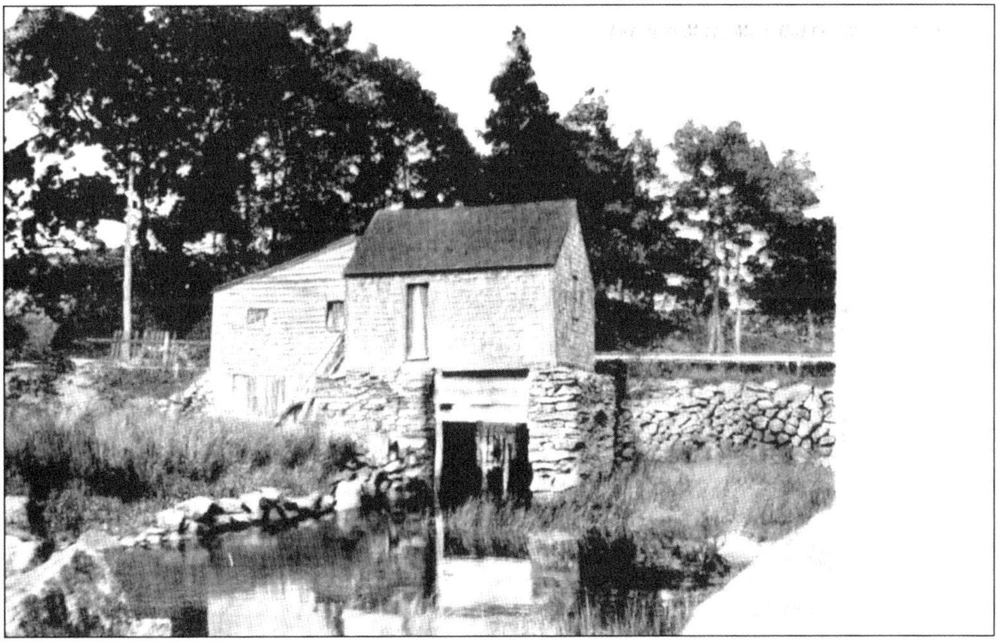

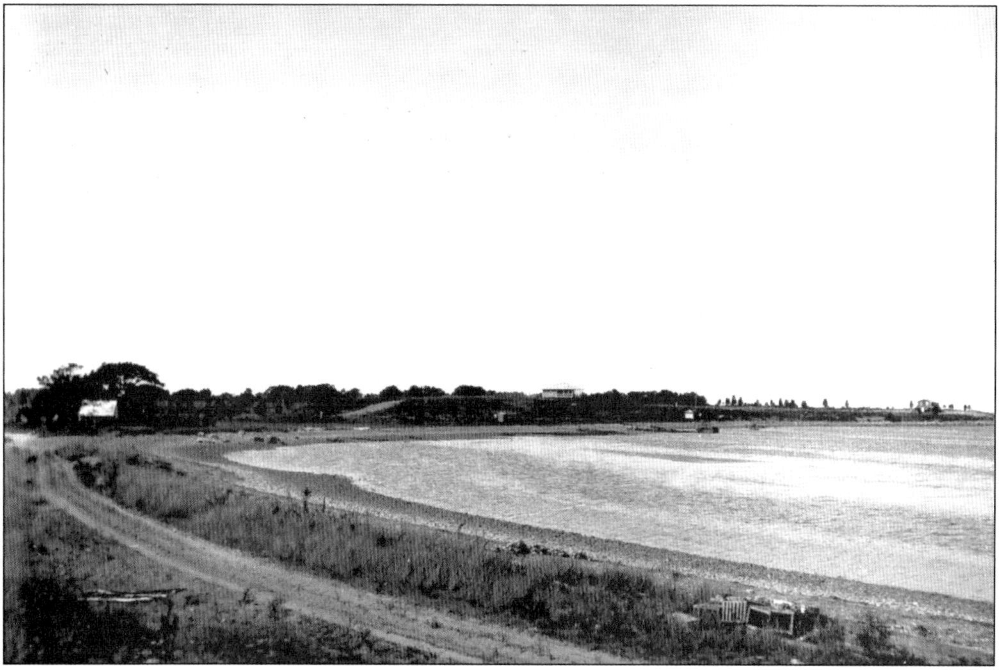

Another important tourist destination was the Hummocks, an open-air restaurant located off of Waldron Avenue, in the Hamilton section of town. The Hummocks was famous for its New England clambakes and was well known throughout the region. These photographs show the road to the Hummocks and one of the open-air dining facilities.

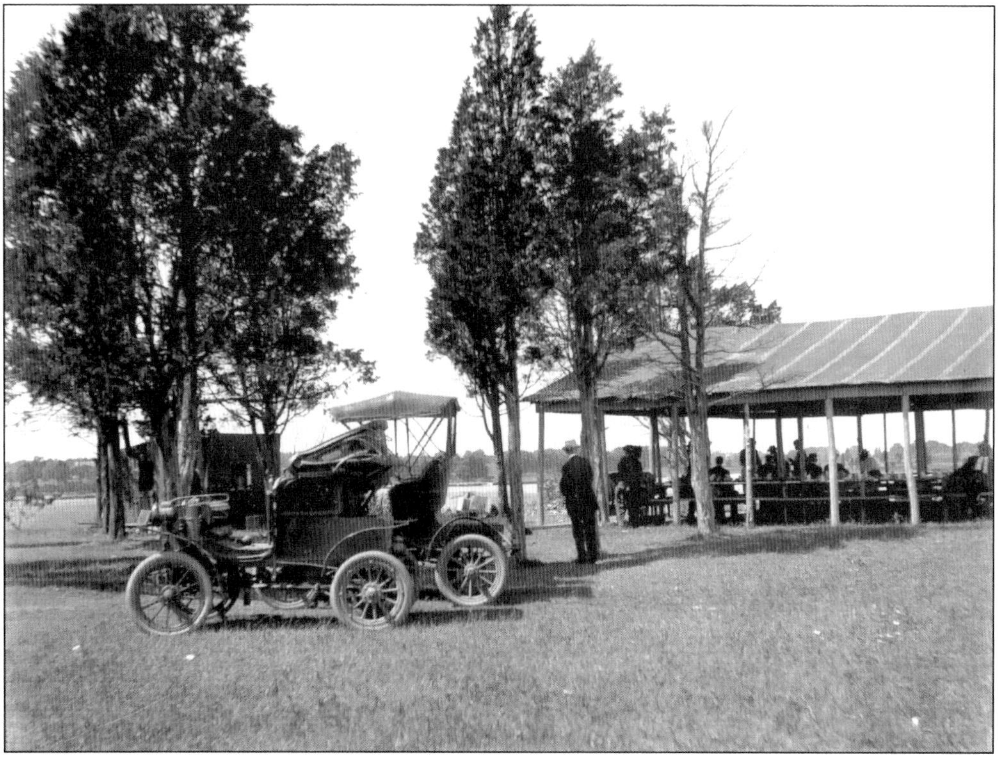

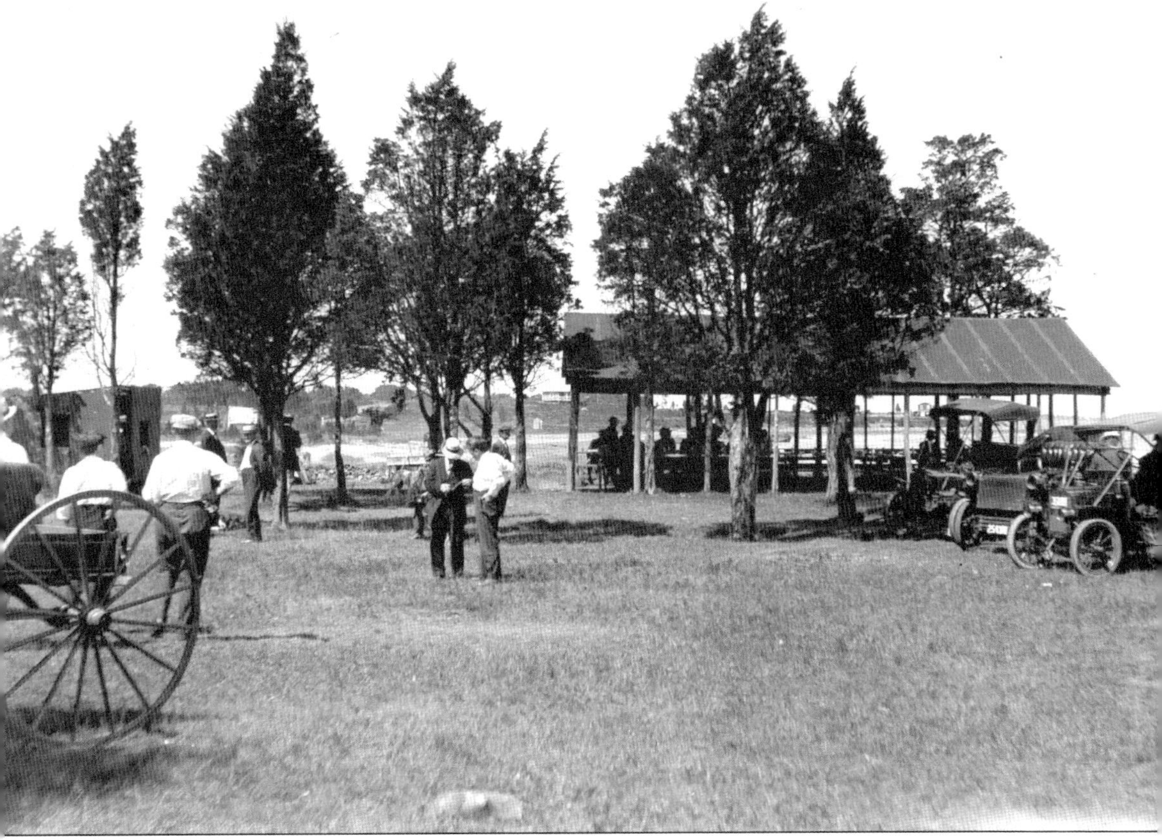

This photograph shows another view of the Hummocks during a summer get-together of the Wickford Businessmen's Association. Through license plate registration data, the center car on the right side of the photograph can be identified as belonging to Walter Rose. The car is an 18-horsepower Stevens.

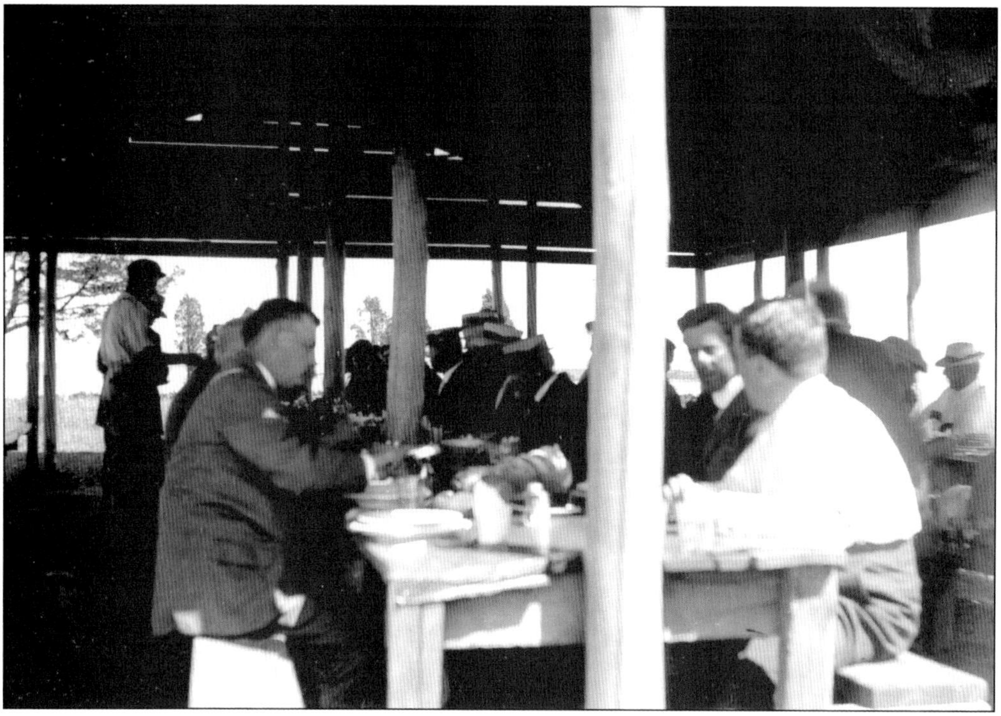

Two more views of the goings-on at the Hummocks during the Wickford Businessmen's Association outing are depicted in these photographs.

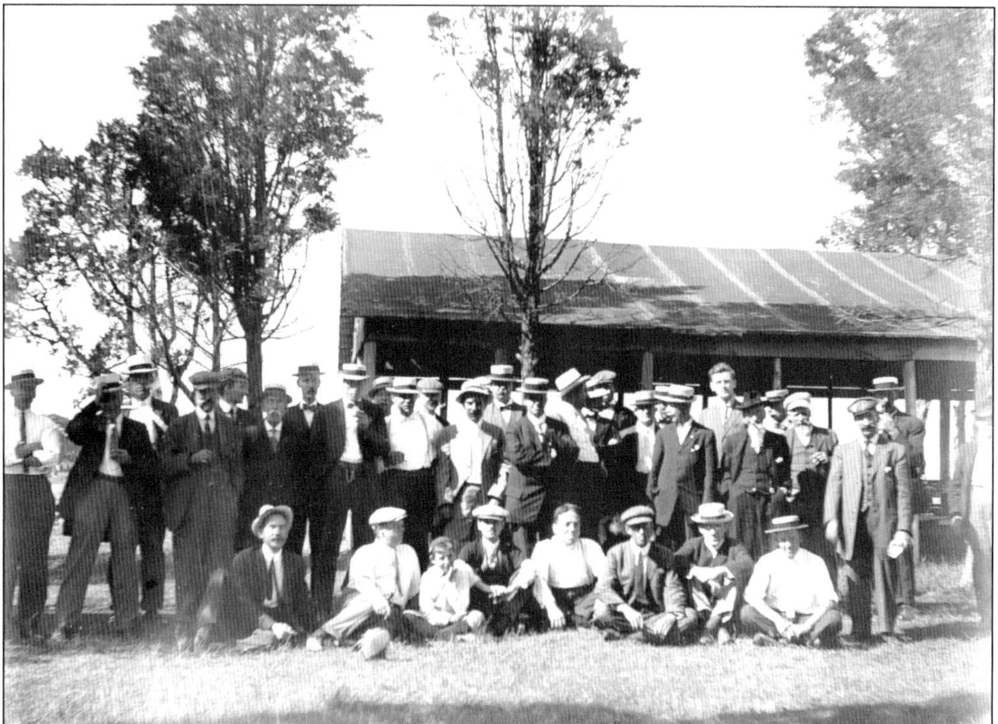

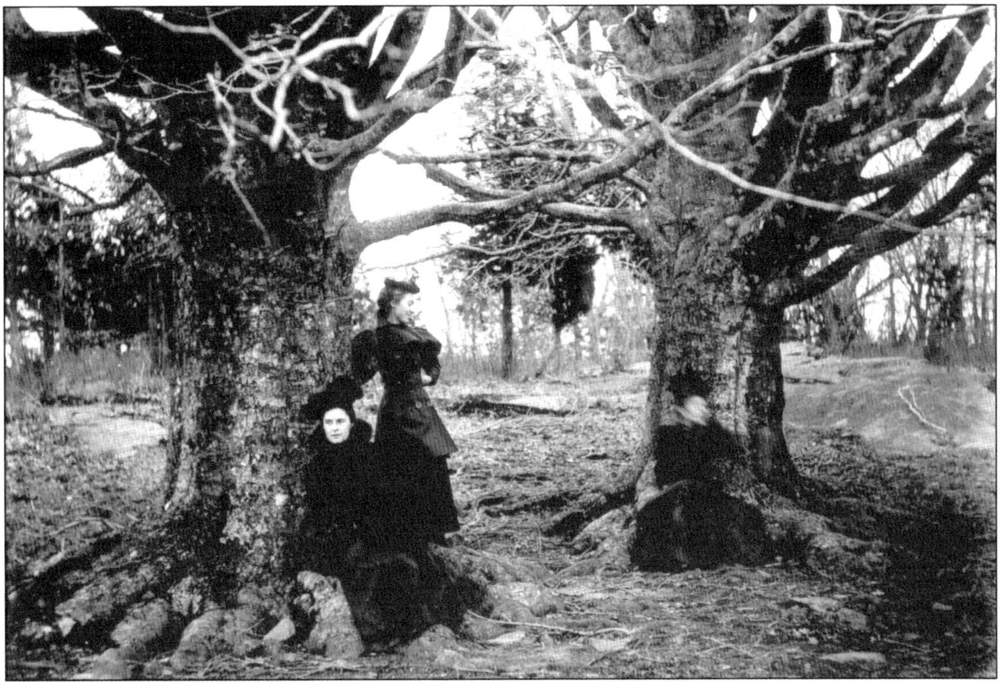

The Twin Beeches was another popular picnicking destination just south of the Wickford station ,shared by the Sea View trolley and the Newport and Wickford line. It was on property owned by Abigail Updike Reynolds, who allowed access to the spot. It was also a frequent meeting place for young couples looking for a romantic place for courting.

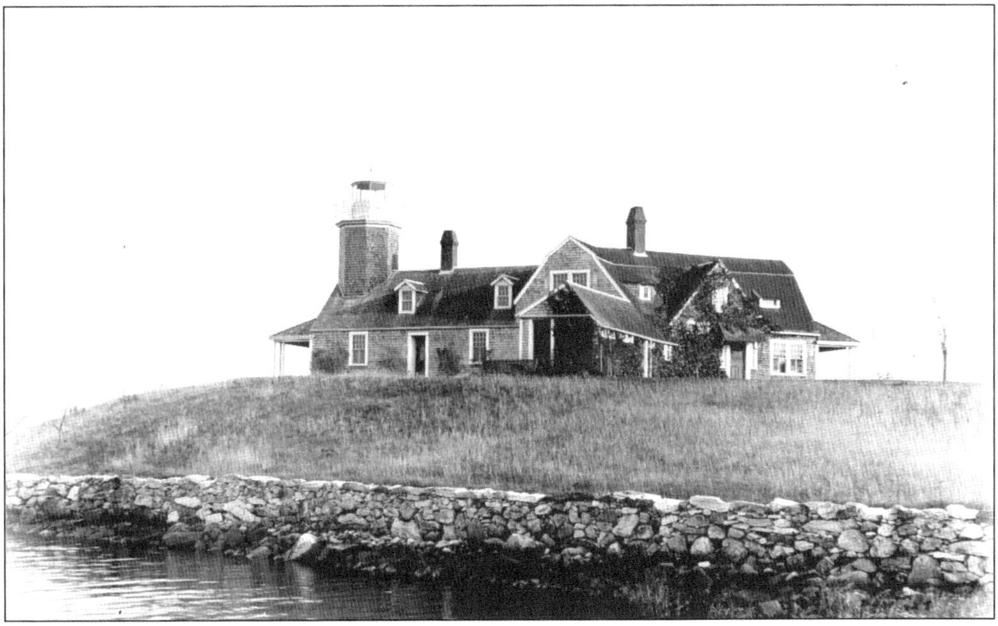

The Poplar Point Lighthouse was another location enjoyed by visitors to Wickford. It was easily visible from the deck of the *General* on its way to Newport. By that time, it was already a private home, having been replaced by the Wickford Light in 1882. It is still extant and thought to be the oldest all-wooden lighthouse in the United States.

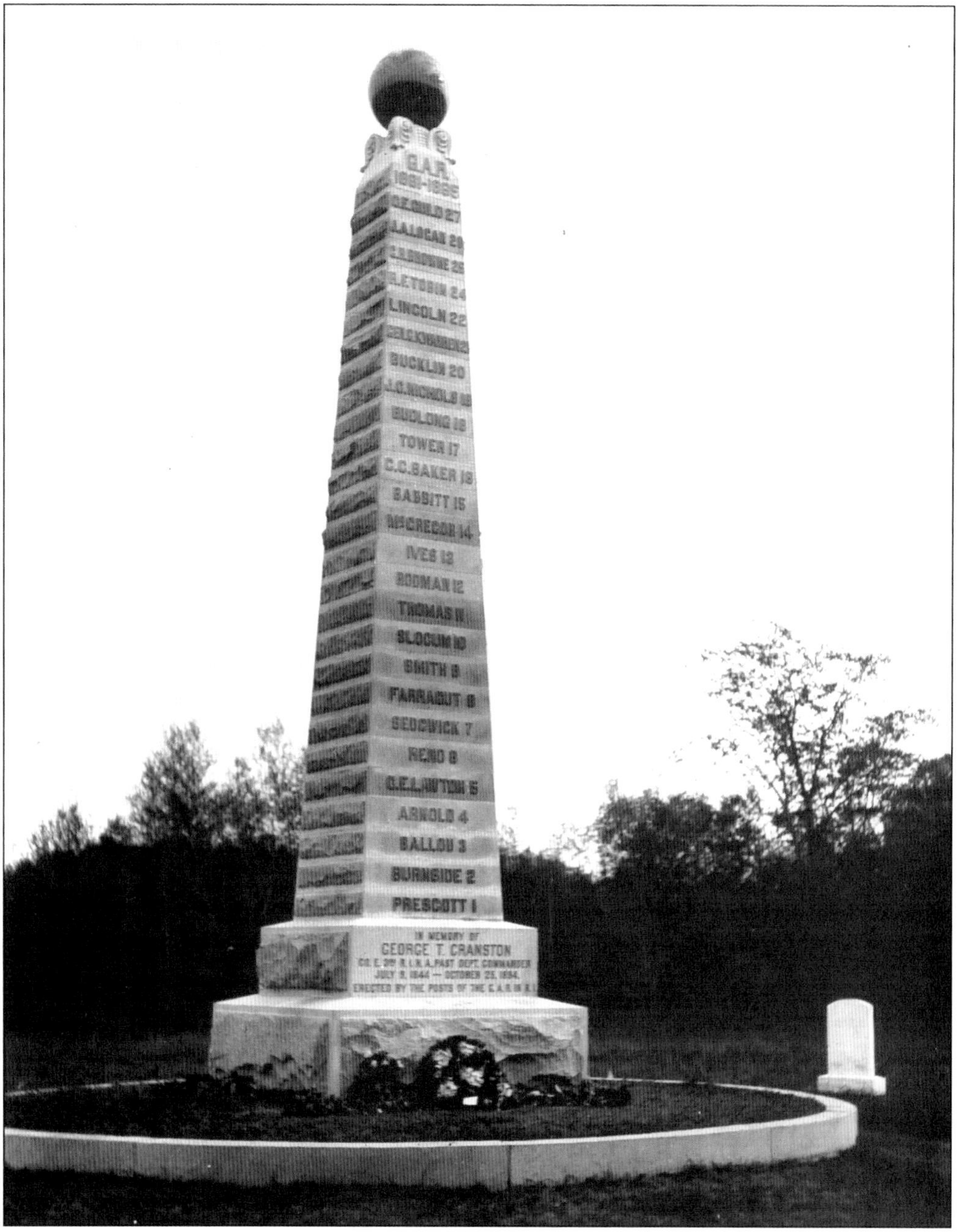

Amazingly enough, this imposing Grand Army of the Republic cemetery monument found in Elm Grove Cemetery in the village of Allenton was frequently visited by Rhode Island's many Civil War veterans. It was erected by the numerous Grand Army of the Republic posts throughout the state to honor the memory of state Grand Army of the Republic commander George Tillinghast Cranston. The names found on each granite slab in the main column correspond with the name of each of the state posts.

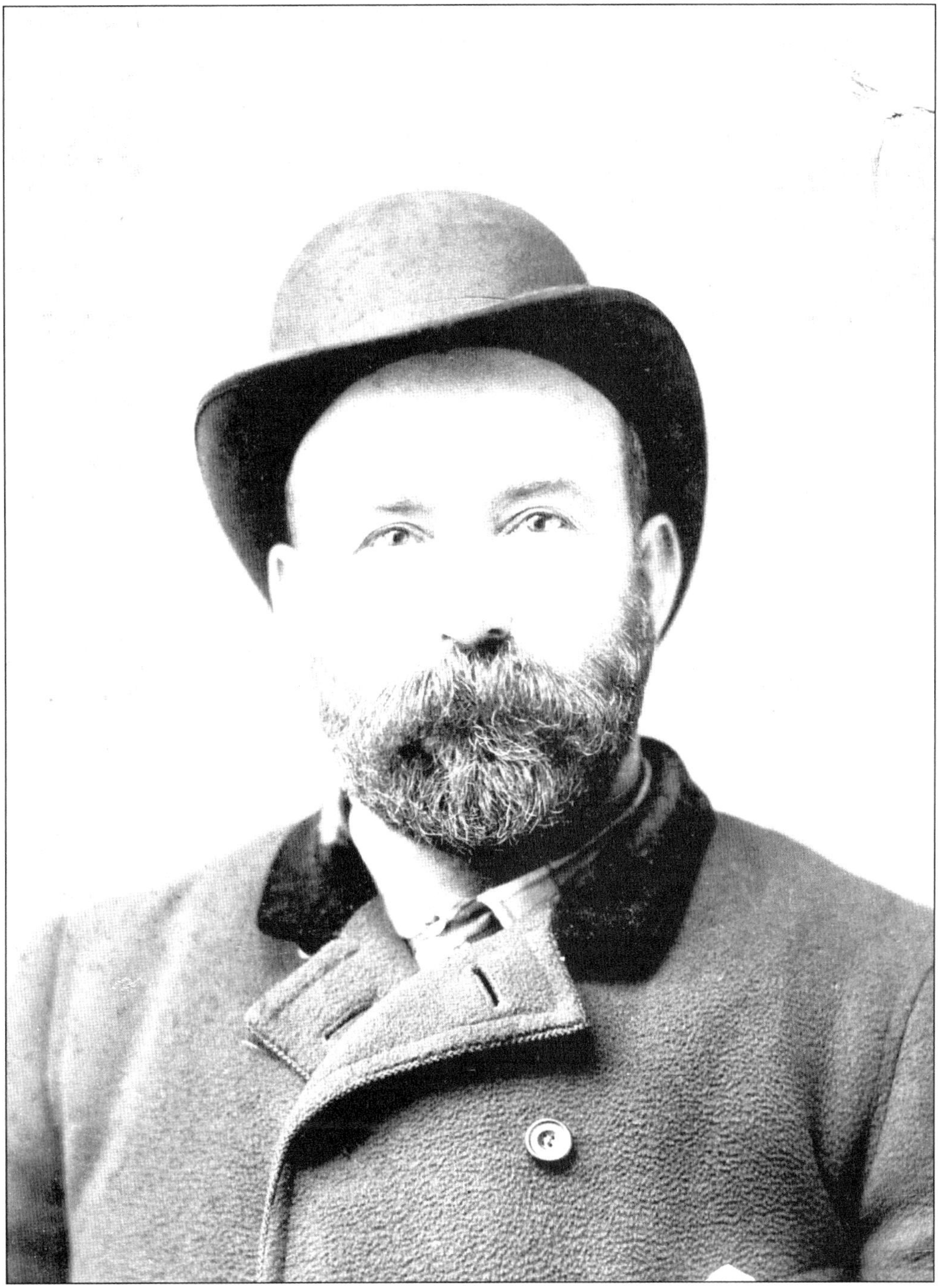

This portrait of George Tillinghast Cranston was taken around 1880. Cranston was a local farm boy who enlisted in the army at the age of 17. He fought in dozens of major battles during the war. He was captured by the Confederates but later escaped to rejoin his unit. After the war, he became a popular merchant and politician who championed veterans' rights in the state. His funeral, attended by well over 5,000 veterans and politicians, is still considered among the largest ever held in the region.

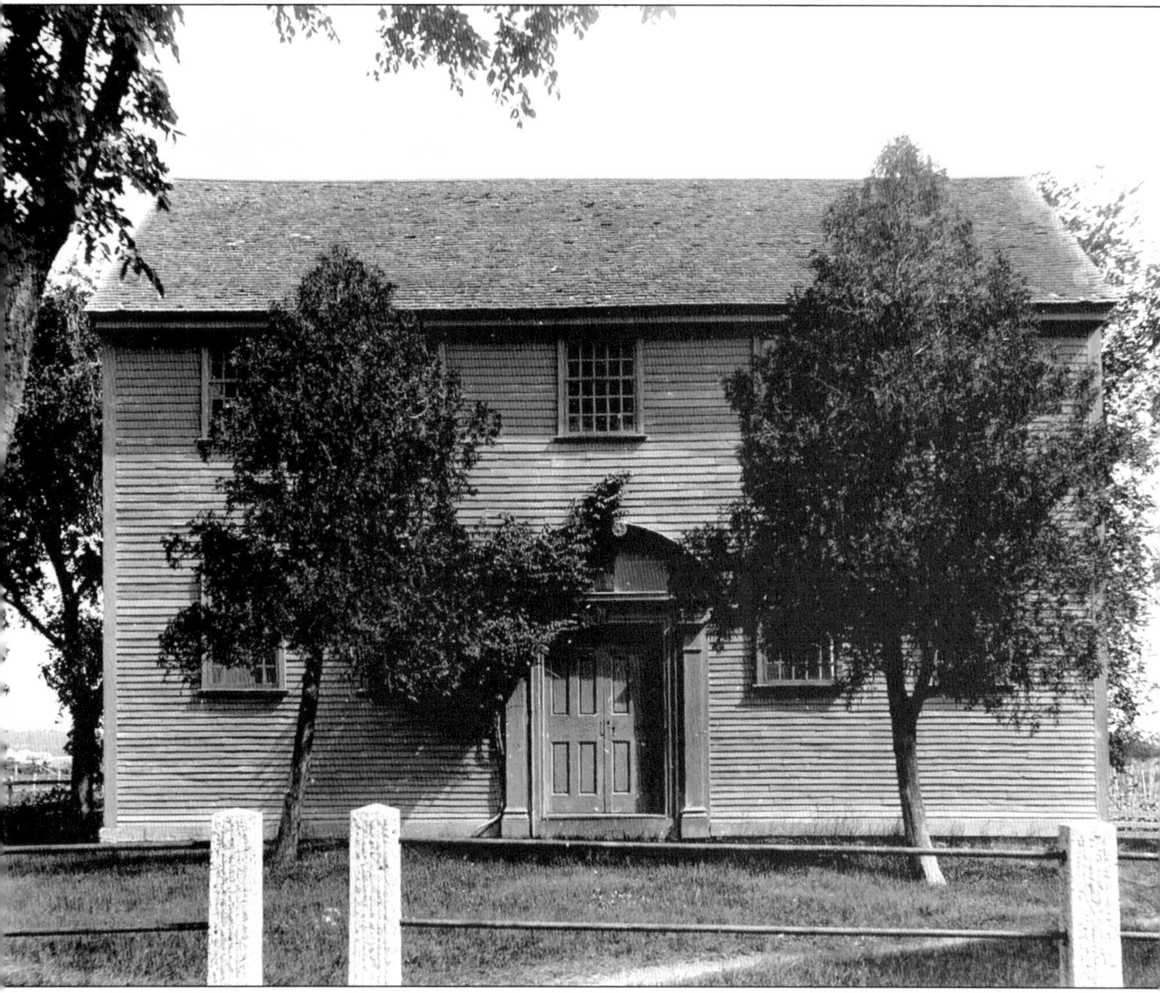

The Old Narragansett Church, located in Wickford proper, dates back to 1707 and once stood out amidst the great plantations of the old Narragansett County in the Shermantown region of North Kingstown. It is said to be the second oldest church building east of the Potomac River.

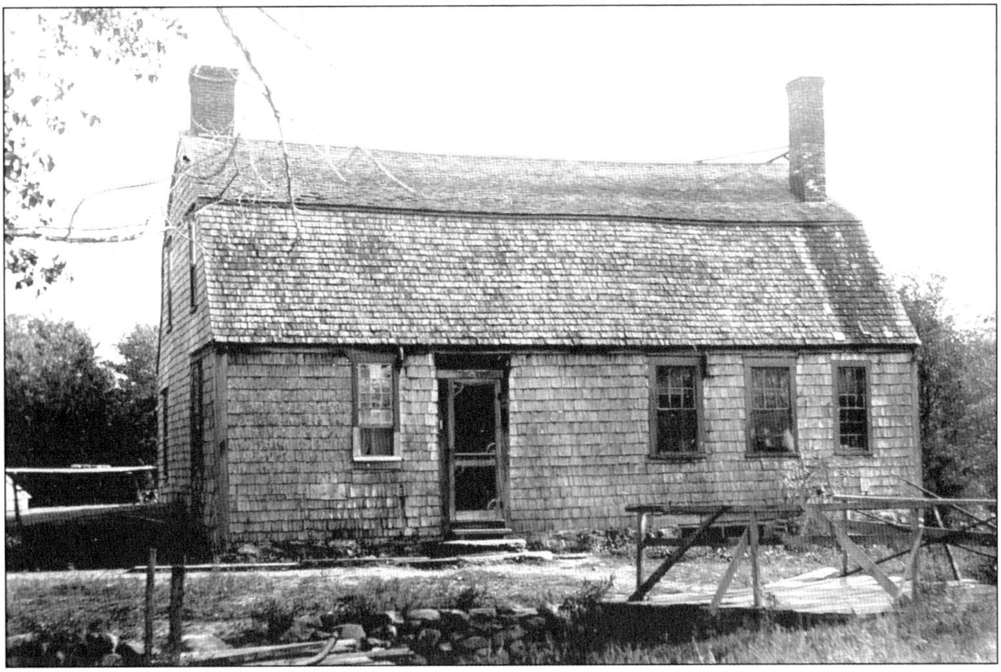

Even in Doc Young's time, well before its subsequent renovation, the Gilbert Stuart Birthplace was a popular destination for visitors to the region. A gifted 18th-century painter, Stuart's most popular work, a portrait of George Washington, can be found on every dollar bill in the United States. This photograph was taken by Young in the late 19th century.

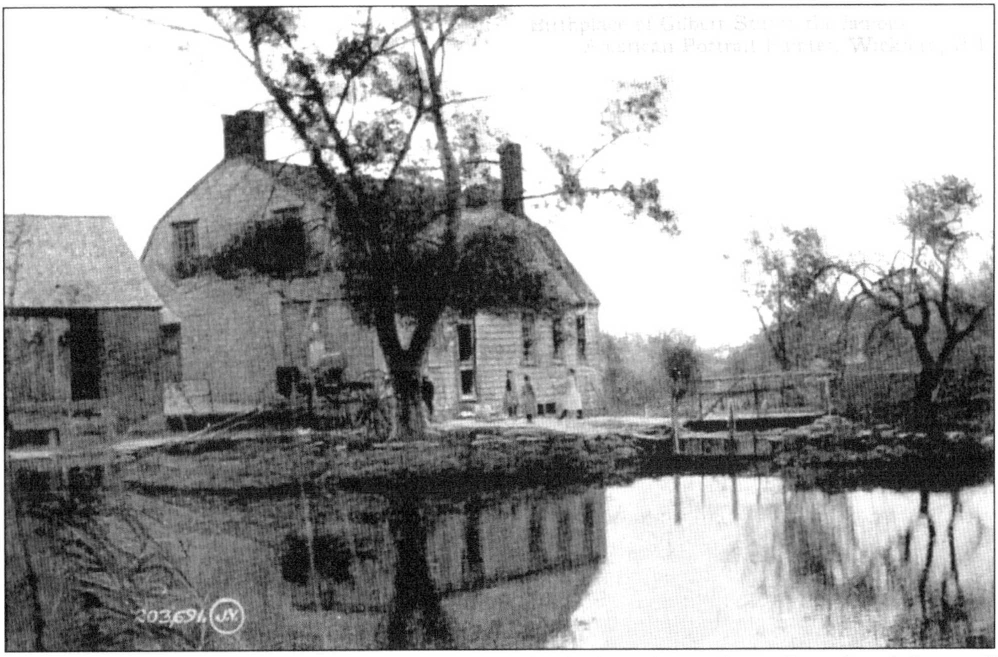

This early-20th-century postcard view of Stuart's birthplace shows the millpond and the snuff mill building.

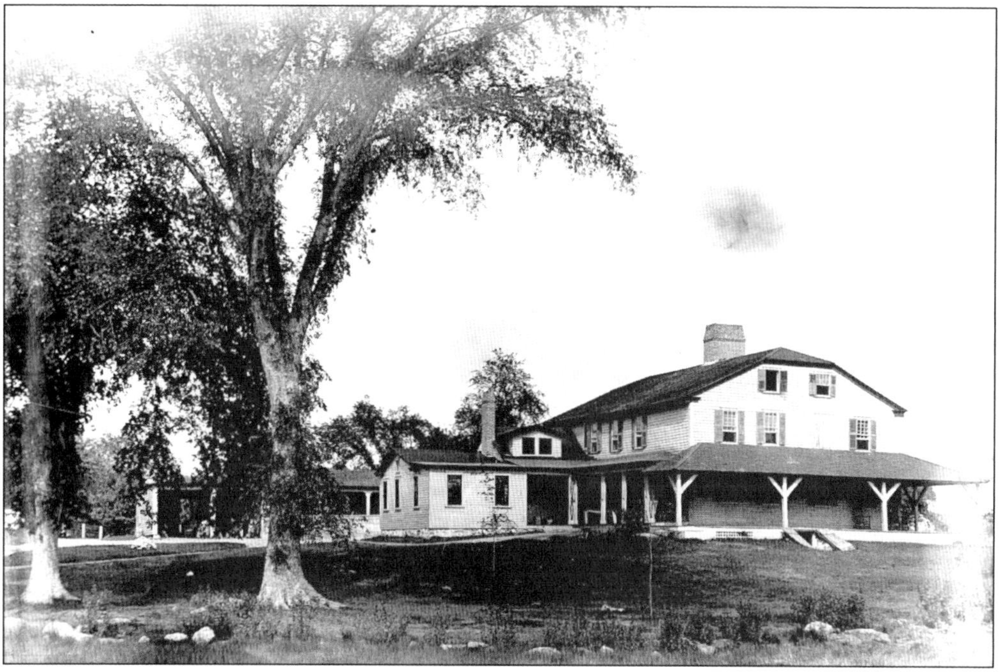

This image of the Richard Smith Blockhouse was also taken by Doc Young in the late 19th century. The Blockhouse, now more commonly known as Smith's Castle, dates back to 1678 and was a private home at that time. A short walk from the Sea View trolley line, it was popular with day-trippers coming into town.

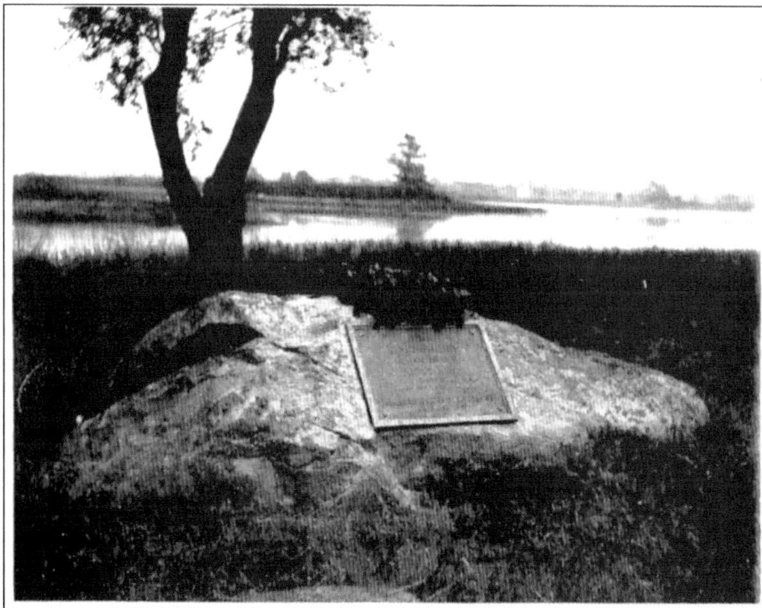

"GREAT GRAVE," Wickford, R. I., containing remains of 42 heroes of Great Swamp Fight, Dec. 1675.

This Doc Young postcard features the Great Grave found on the grounds of the Blockhouse. It purportedly contains the remains of 42 of the colonial soldiers killed at the Great Swamp Fight during the King Phillips War of 1675.

Five

The Harbor and the Bay

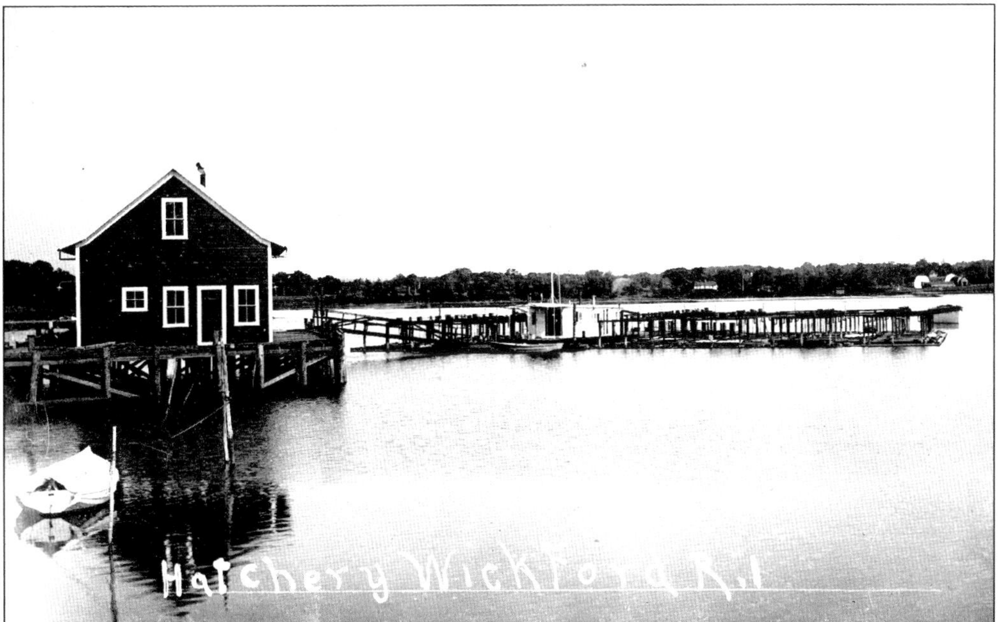

This postcard features the Rhode Island State Lobster Hatchery, which was located at the end of Fowler Street in Wickford.

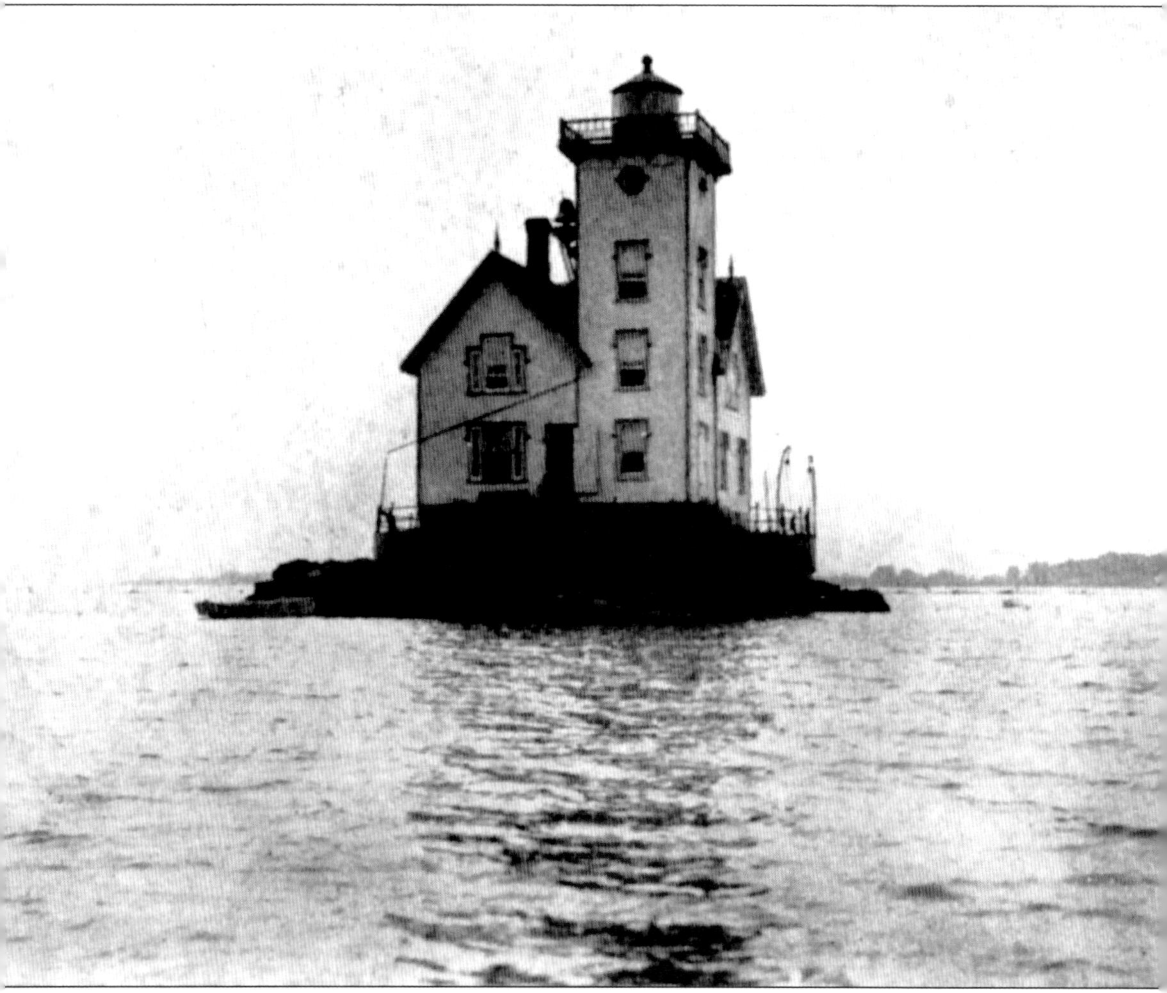

This Doc Young postcard shows the picturesque Wickford Light, formerly located at the entrance to the harbor. This lighthouse was both a welcome sight to the many mariners who called Wickford home and a popular feature of the harbor to those who were only coming for a visit.

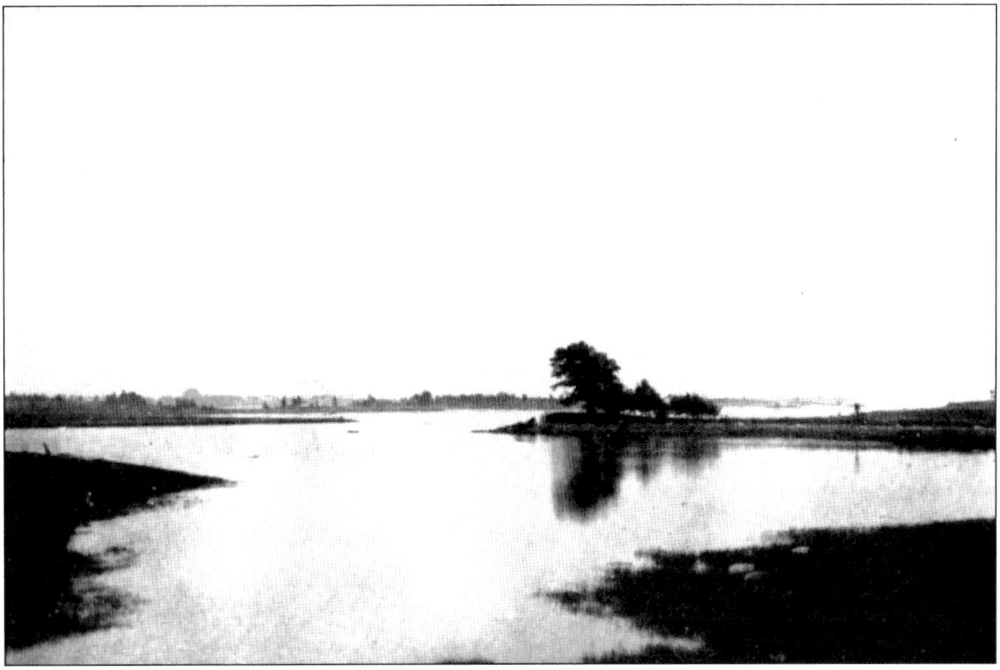

A peaceful view of the Mill Creek area of the harbor is seen in this Doc Young postcard.

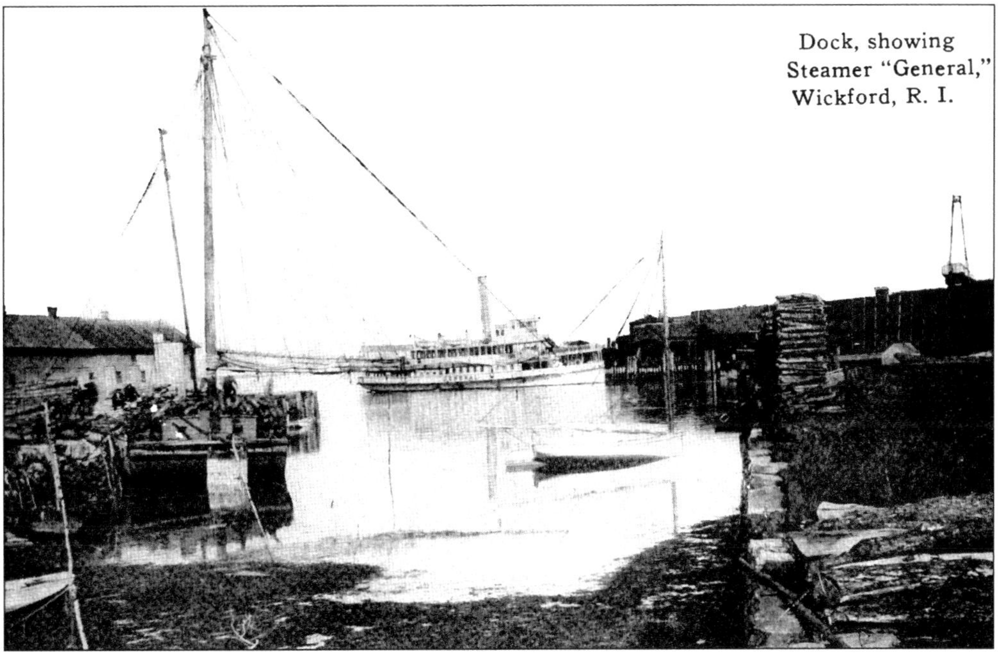

This postcard shows the *General* entering its berth at Poplar Point. It was taken from just in front of the Baker coal yard at the end of Main Street. Also visible on the left is a vessel being loaded with lumber, bound eventually for Newport. The loading of firewood for shipments into the city by the sea were a frequent sight at the Wickford docks.

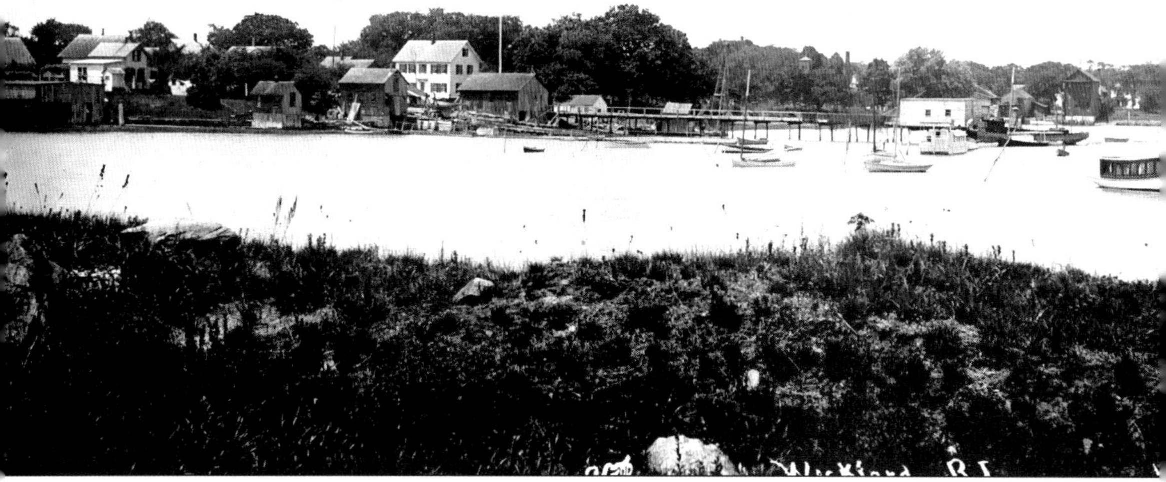

This view of the docks, at the end of what is now known as Reynolds Street, features some of the small warehouse facilities that were found there and showcases a variety of different small vessels that were typically seen on the harbor.

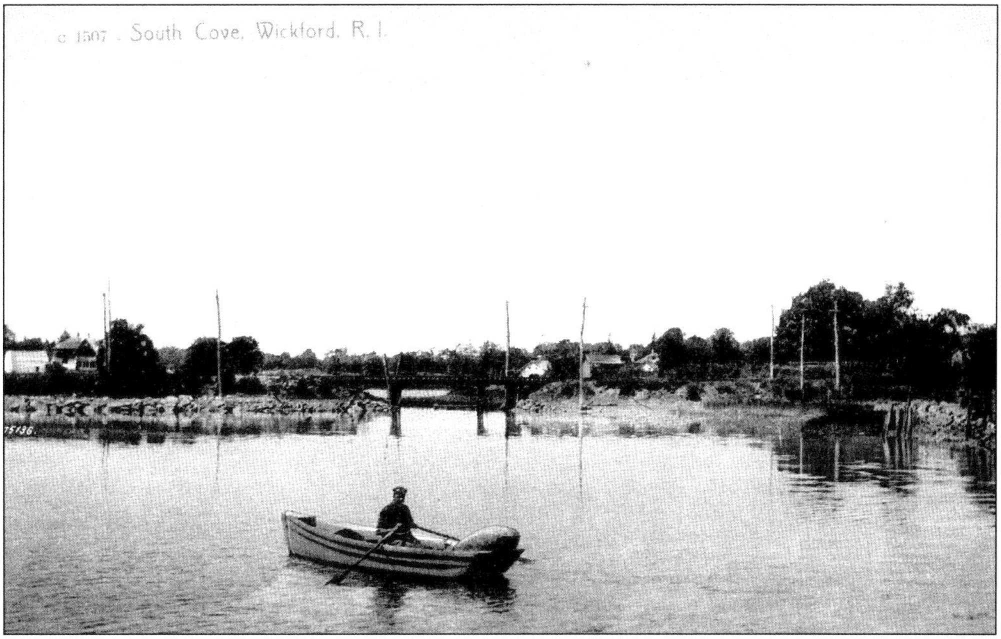

This postcard view of Wickford's south cove was taken from the Hamilton Bridge, the predecessor to the Hussey Bridge. One of the trestles and the power lines of the Sea View trolley line as it heads towards the Wickford Station can be seen.

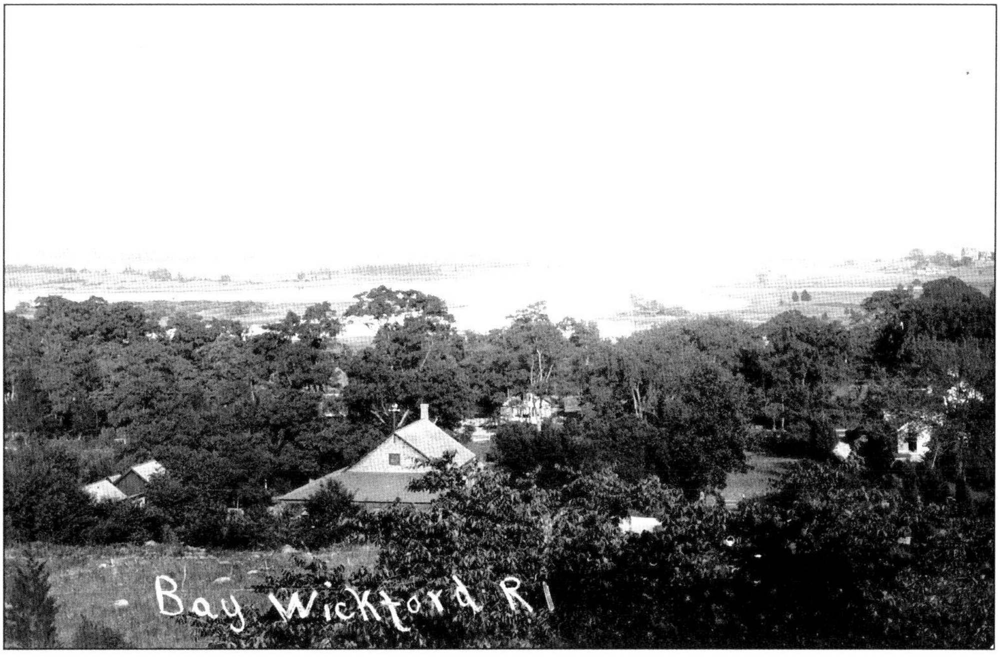

Taken from Hall's Rock, a location west of Post Road, this is a view of the Mill Creek and Mill Cove portions of the harbor. Rabbit Island and Cornelius Island are also visible.

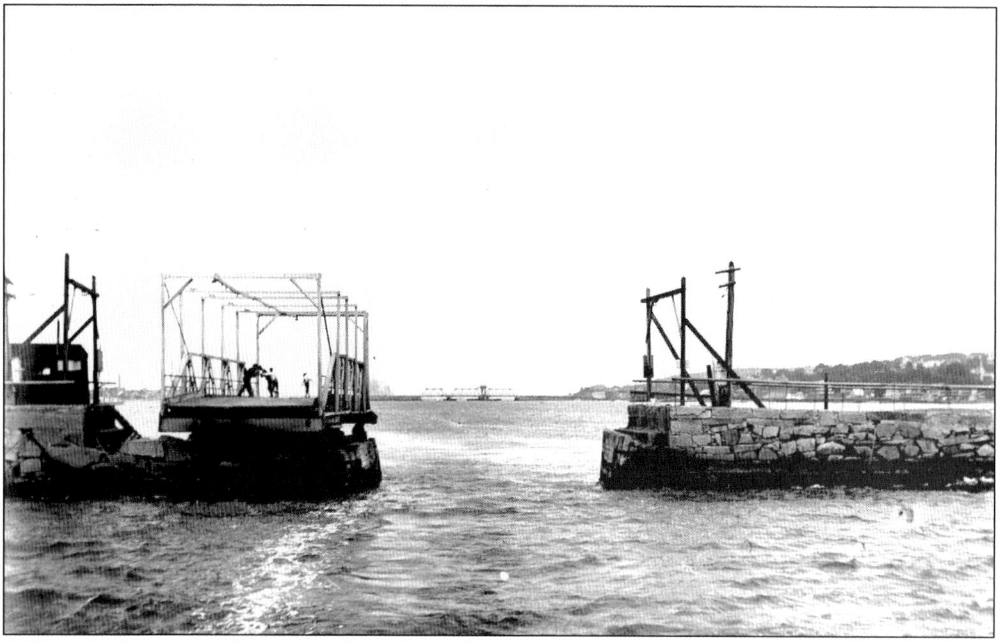

Although this manually operated swing bridge was not located in North Kingstown, it was a popular destination for the many excursion boats that left the landing at Poplar Point for a day trip. This photograph of the Stonebridge landmark was taken by Doc Young on just such a trip.

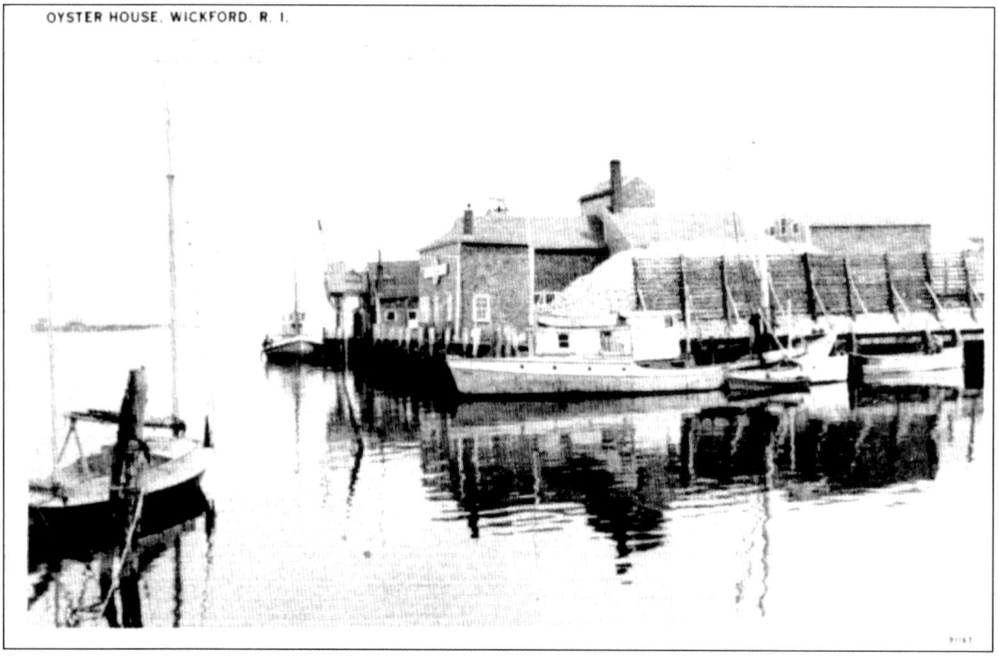

Oysters were an important industry in Rhode Island from 1880 to 1920. Long predating present-day aquaculture concerns, oyster farming was deliberate here in the bay, and the oysters were famous across the region. The entire industry was wiped out by the 1938 hurricane. This oyster company was located at the end of Pleasant Street.

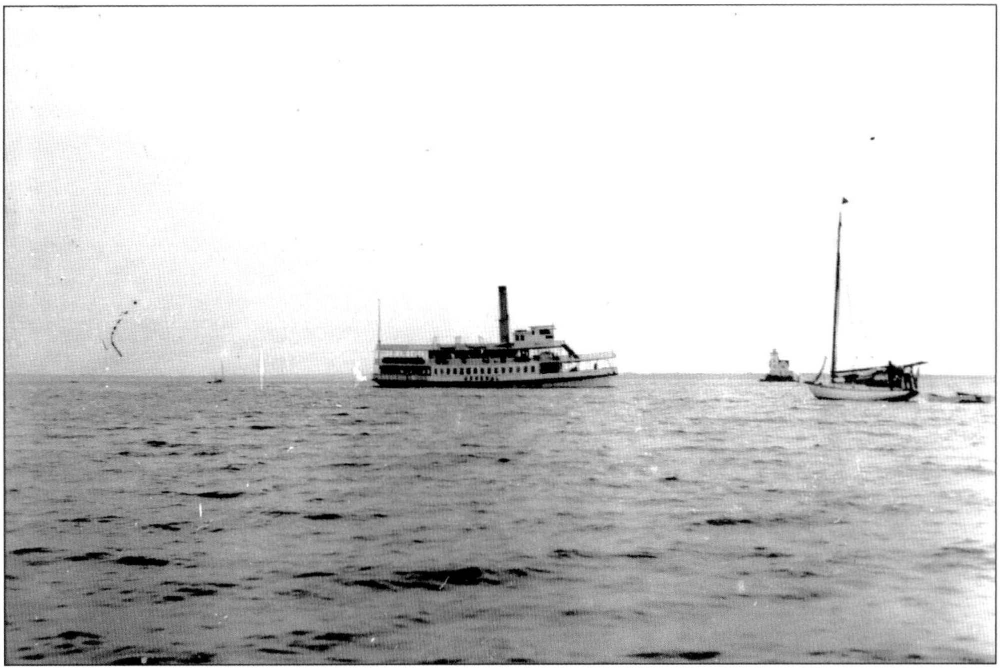

The *General* is leaving the harbor on its way to Newport in this Doc Young photograph. The Wickford Light can be seen off in the distance.

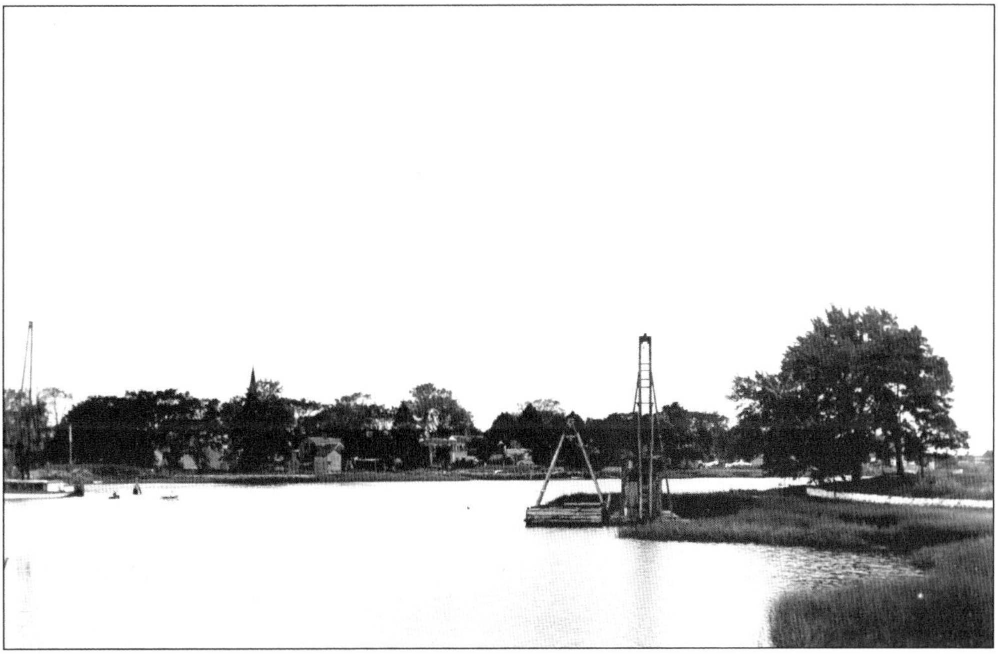

Taken from the Hamilton Bridge, this view looks back toward the village. A pile-driver barge can be seen to the right, and C. Prescott Knight's steam-powered launch can just be made out to the left. Knight was a powerful textile baron whose company eventually became the Fruit of the Loom Company.

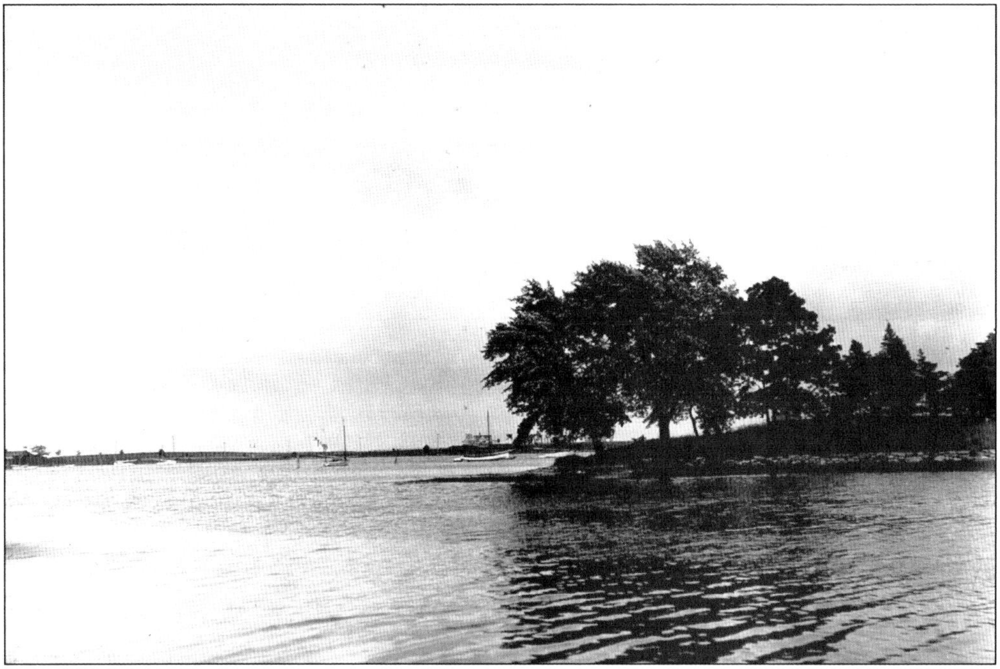

Both Wickford lighthouses can be discerned in this photograph taken from the Hamilton side of the South Cove.

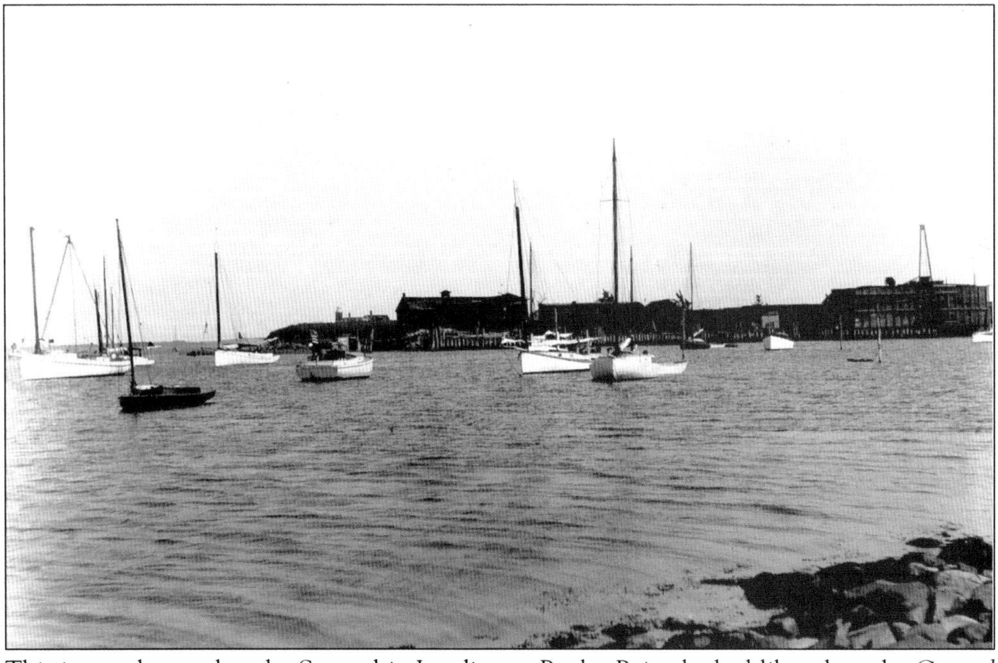

This image shows what the Steamship Landing at Poplar Point looked like when the *General* was not present. A number of railcars are parked at the landing.

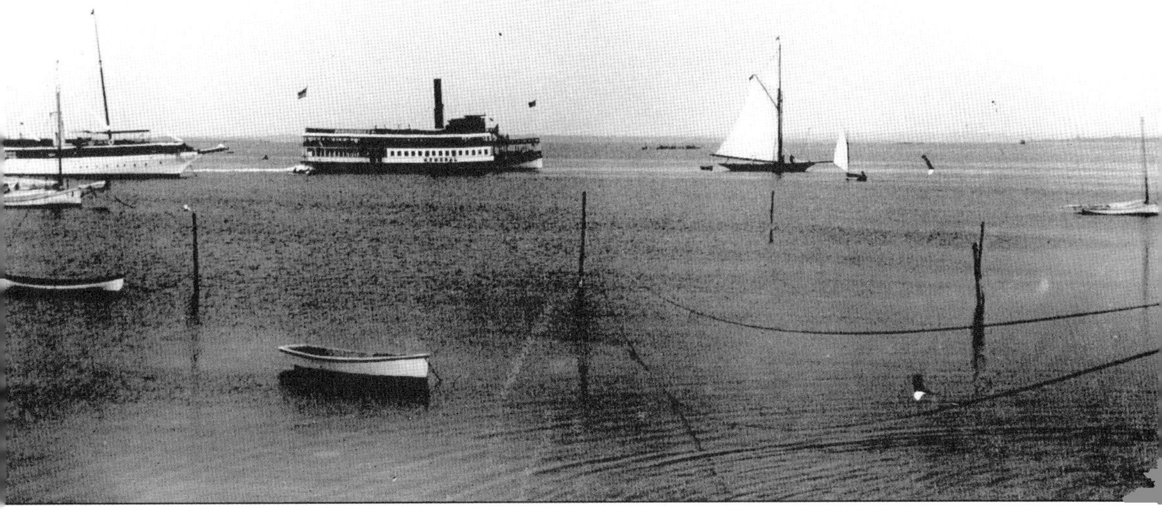

The *General* passes the anchored *Hiawatha*, the elegant yacht of the Fleischman family. A local sailor captained the magnificent vessel for the Yeast King, and the Fleischmans often summered here in Wickford.

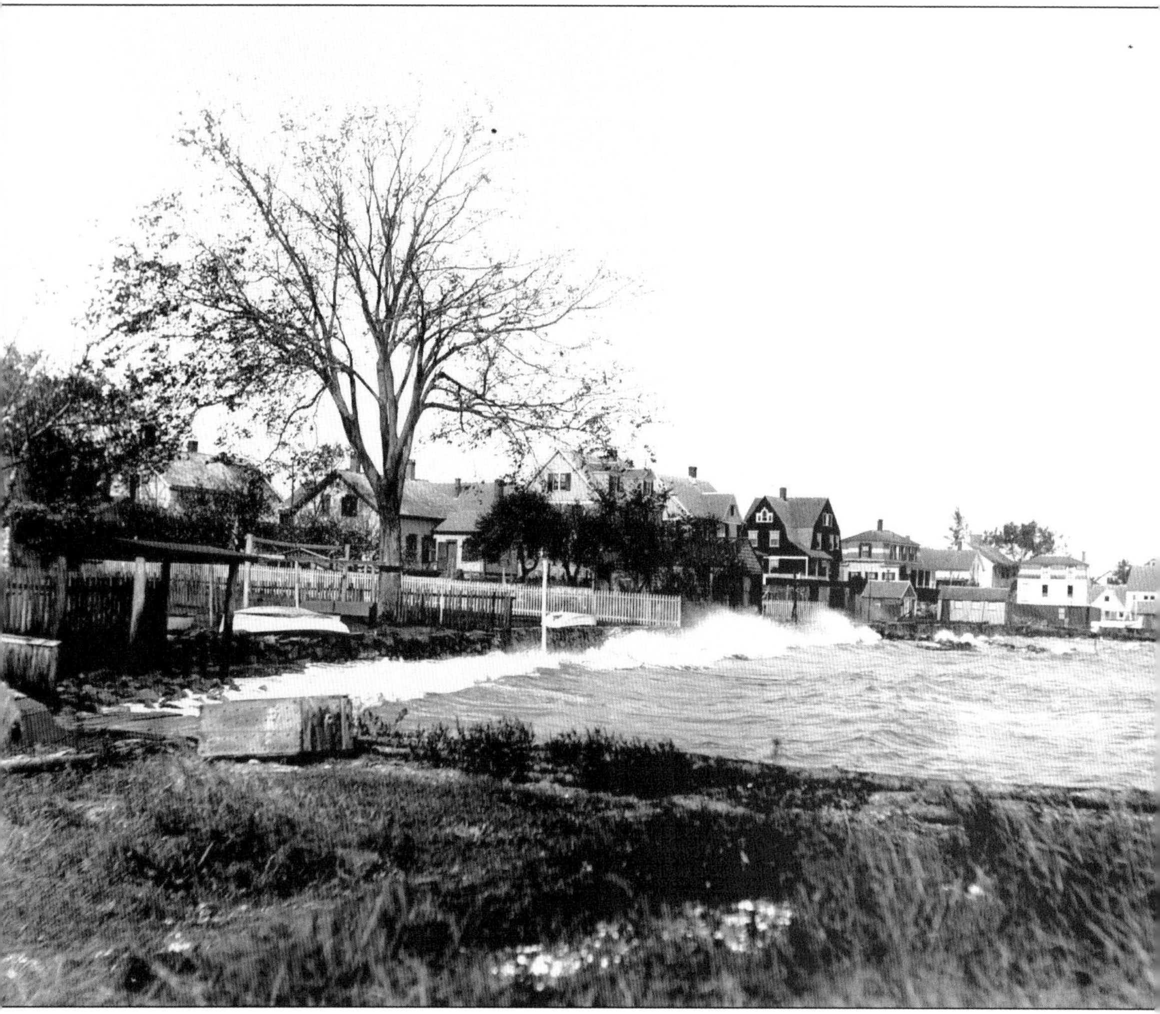

The seas crash against the Pleasant Street shoreline. Nearly all of these fine homes still exist today.

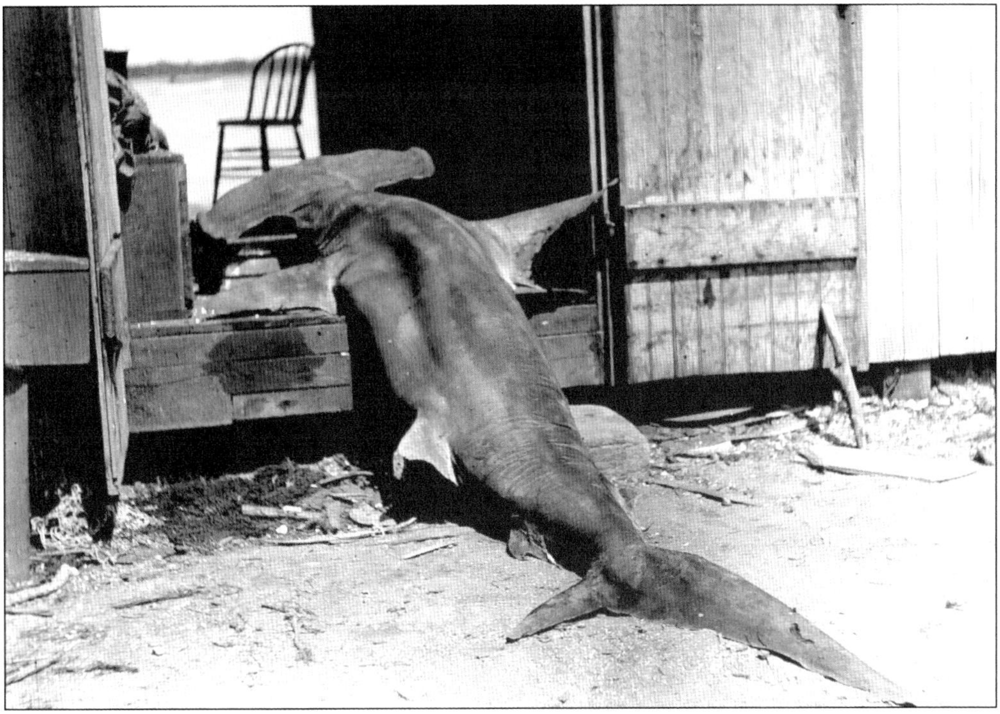

This great hammerhead shark was photographed by Doc Young at what is now Gardner's Wharf and probably ended as fertilizer in a farmer's field.

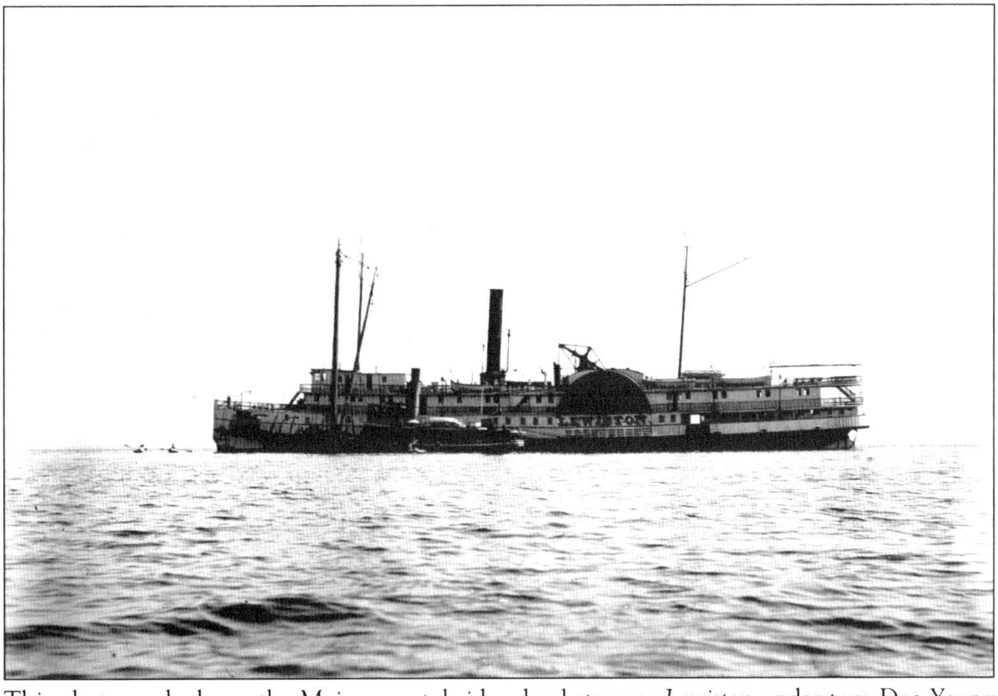

This photograph shows the Maine coastal side-wheel steamer *Lewiston* under tow. Doc Young was never known to have left Rhode Island, so it may be that the *Lewiston* was being towed into Providence for repairs.

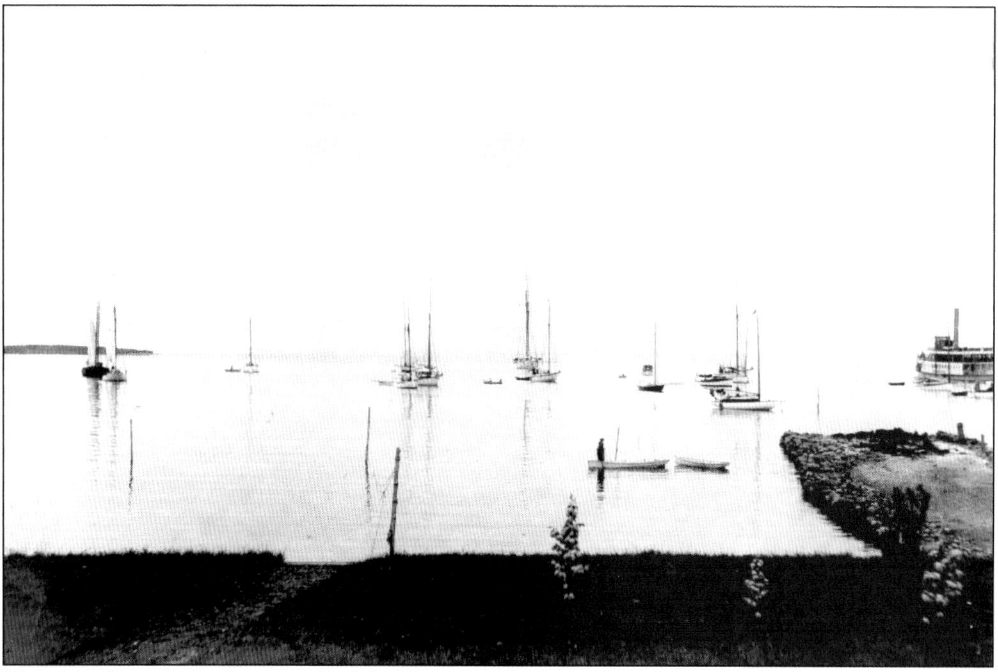

This bucolic scene photographed by Doc Young from the Pleasant Street shoreline has an almost artistic quality to it. The *General* is bound for Newport, passing by a number of anchored pleasure craft.

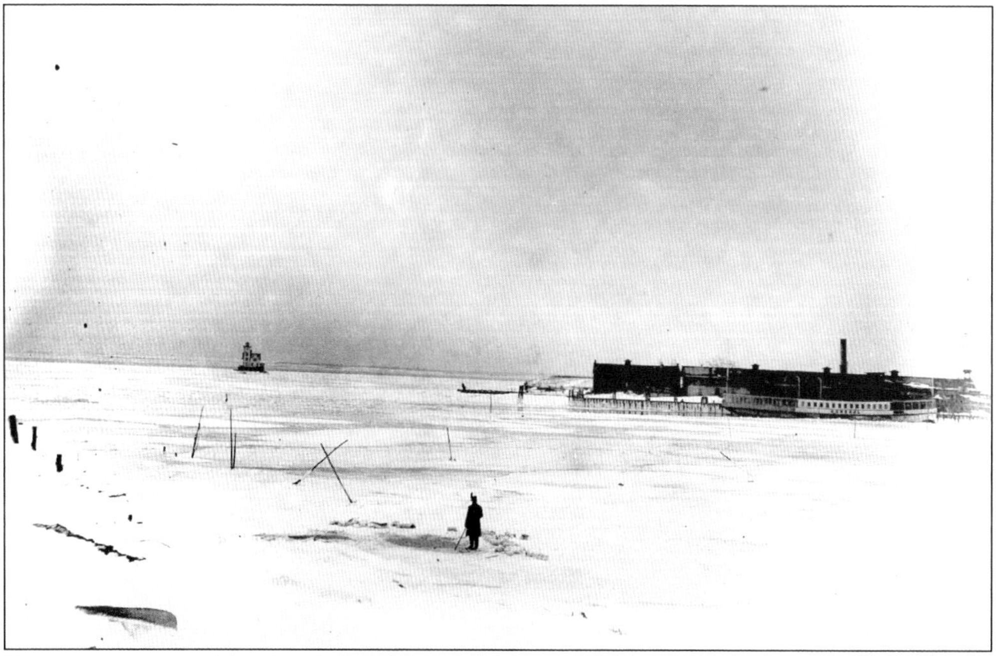

This winter view is also taken from the Pleasant Street shoreline. One can see the *General* iced-in at its berth and the ice surrounding Wickford Light. This was most likely shot during the winter of 1908. In that year, the Narragansett Bay froze up so thoroughly that townsfolk were able to walk safely out to the lighthouse.

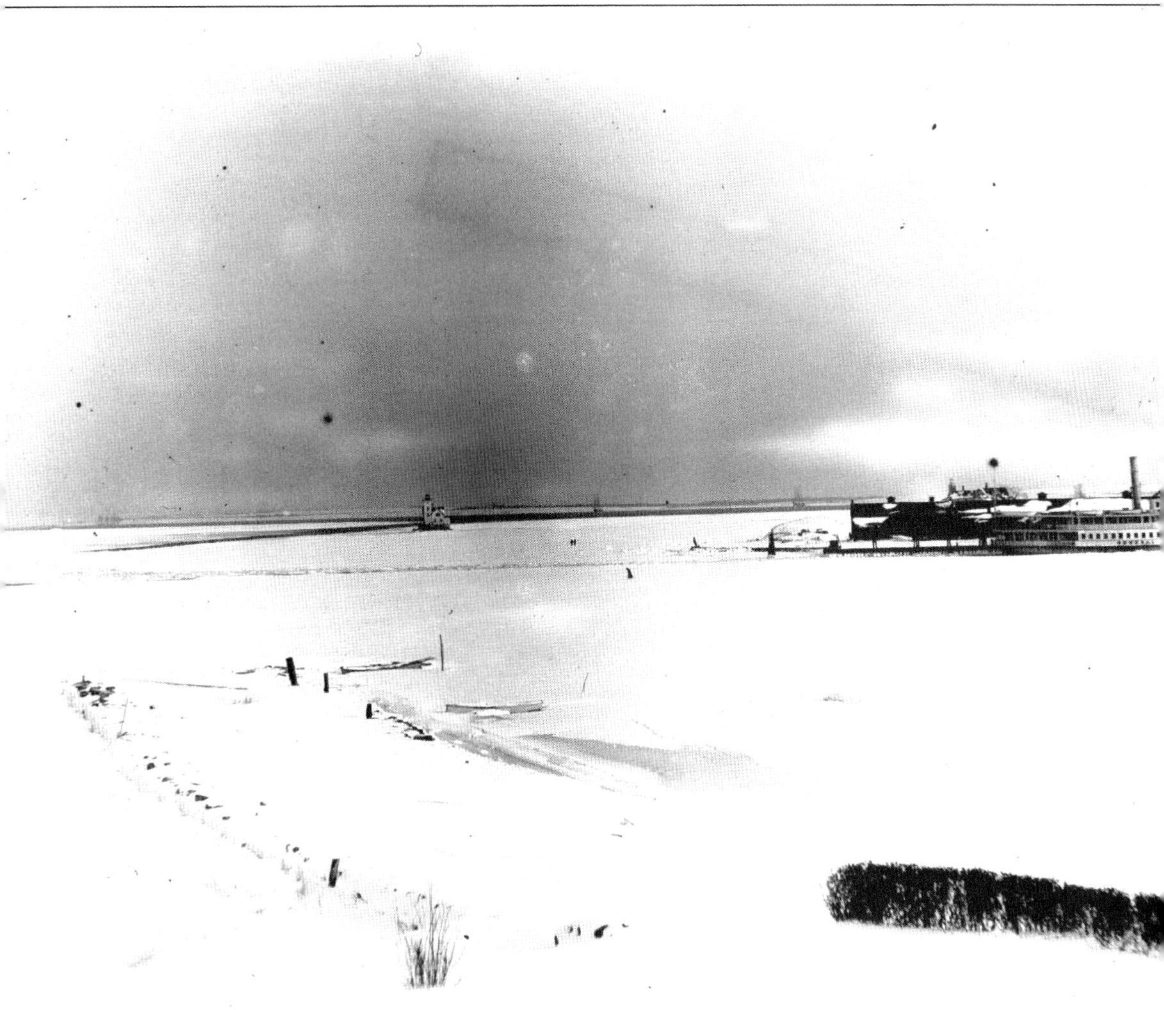

Taken during the winter of 1908, this view shows numerous three-masted schooners out on the bay waiting for a break in the harbor ice.

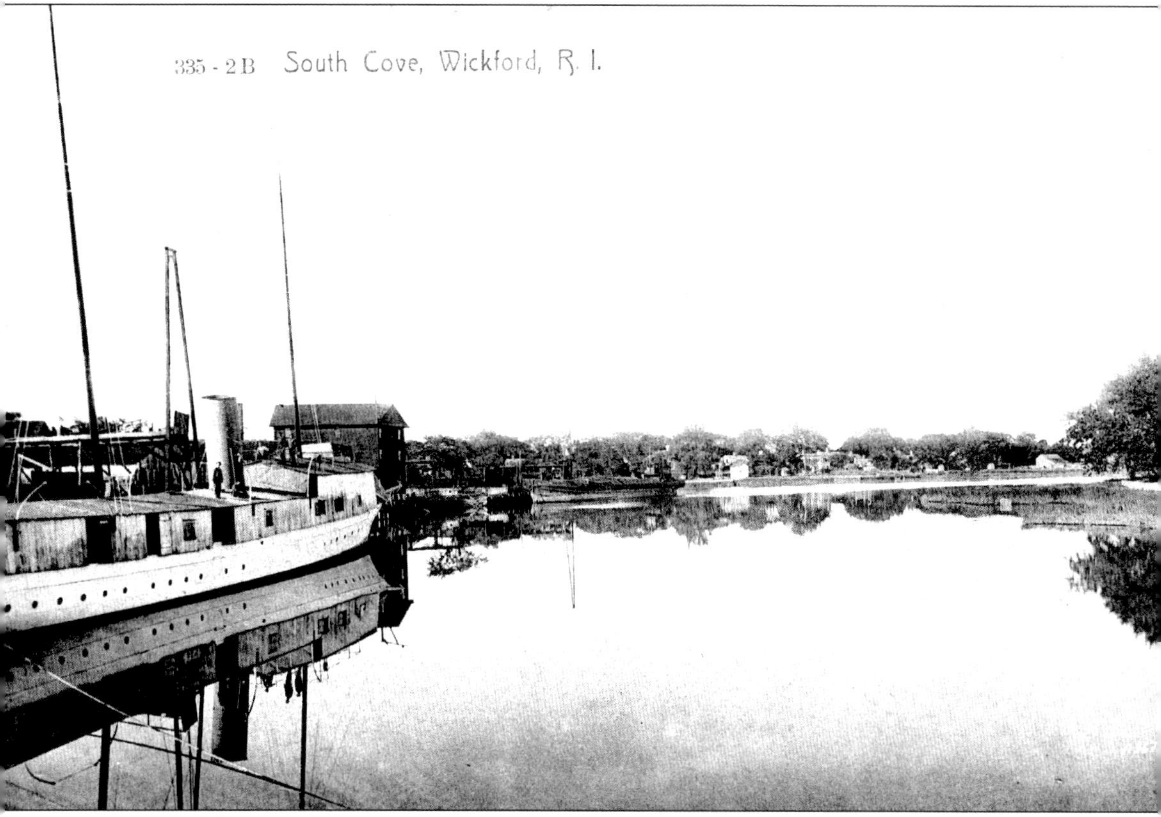

Two coal ships can be made out in this postcard view from the Hamilton Bridge, looking back at the village of Wickford. The one in the foreground is tied up at the coal yard utilized by the Gregory Textile Mill, which was located right in the village. The ship seen off in the distance is going to off-load at the Hamilton Web coal yard. Coal was then brought to the Hamilton Web Mill on a special freight run that utilized the tracks of the Sea View trolley line. This system was also utilized to supply coal to the Sea View power plant located very close to the Hamilton mill village. The Rodman mills also had a coal yard along the waterfront in the village, as did the Baker family. Their coal yard was primarily used to supply coal for home-heating purposes.

Six

Street Scenes from Bygone Days

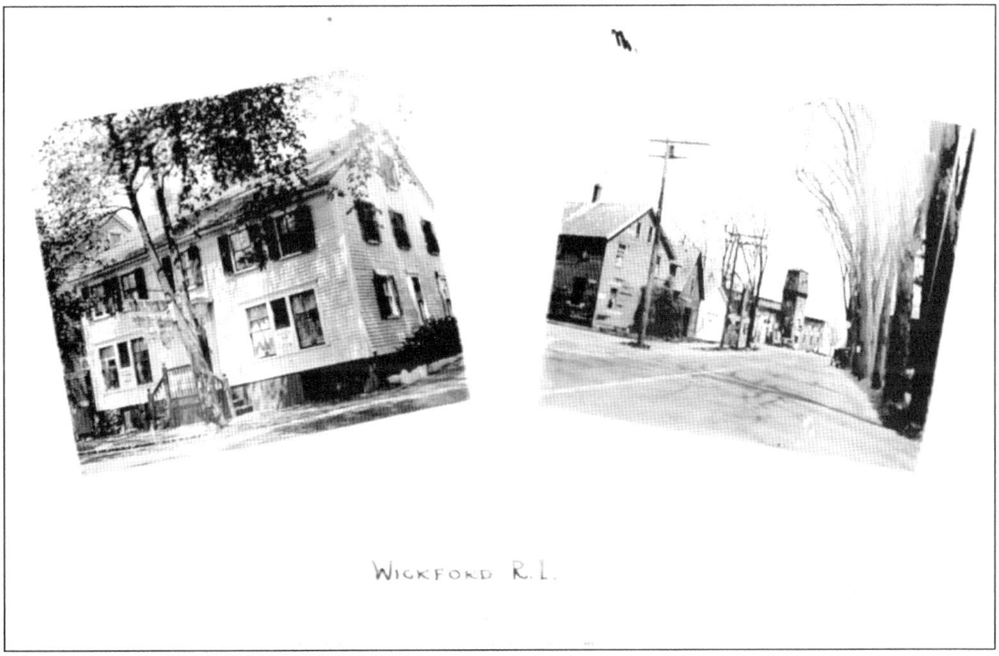

This typical Wickford postcard depicts a view of the Wickford House run by Mother Prentice and a look down Phillips Street toward the Gregory Textile Mill that is off in the distance.

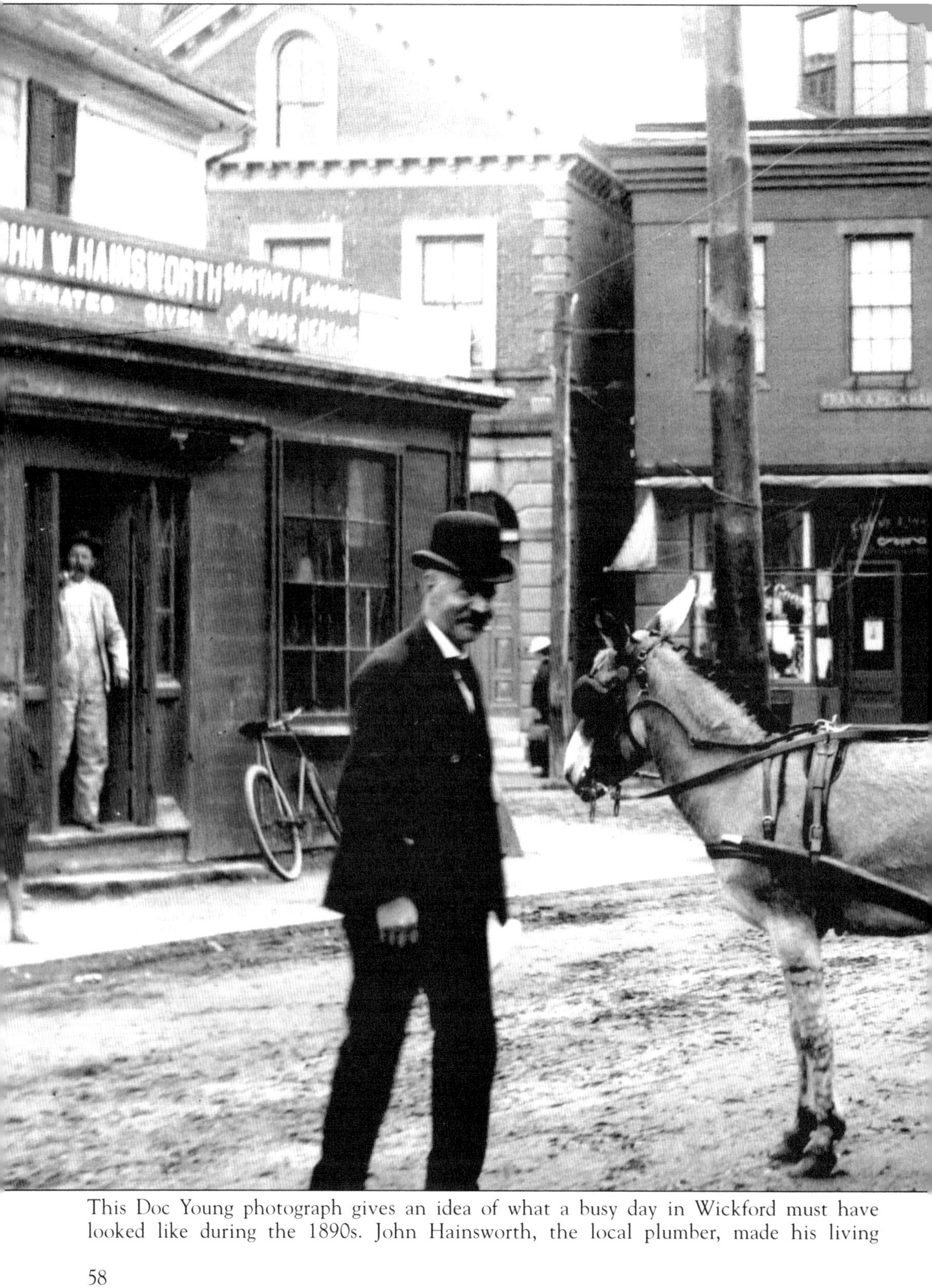

This Doc Young photograph gives an idea of what a busy day in Wickford must have looked like during the 1890s. John Hainsworth, the local plumber, made his living

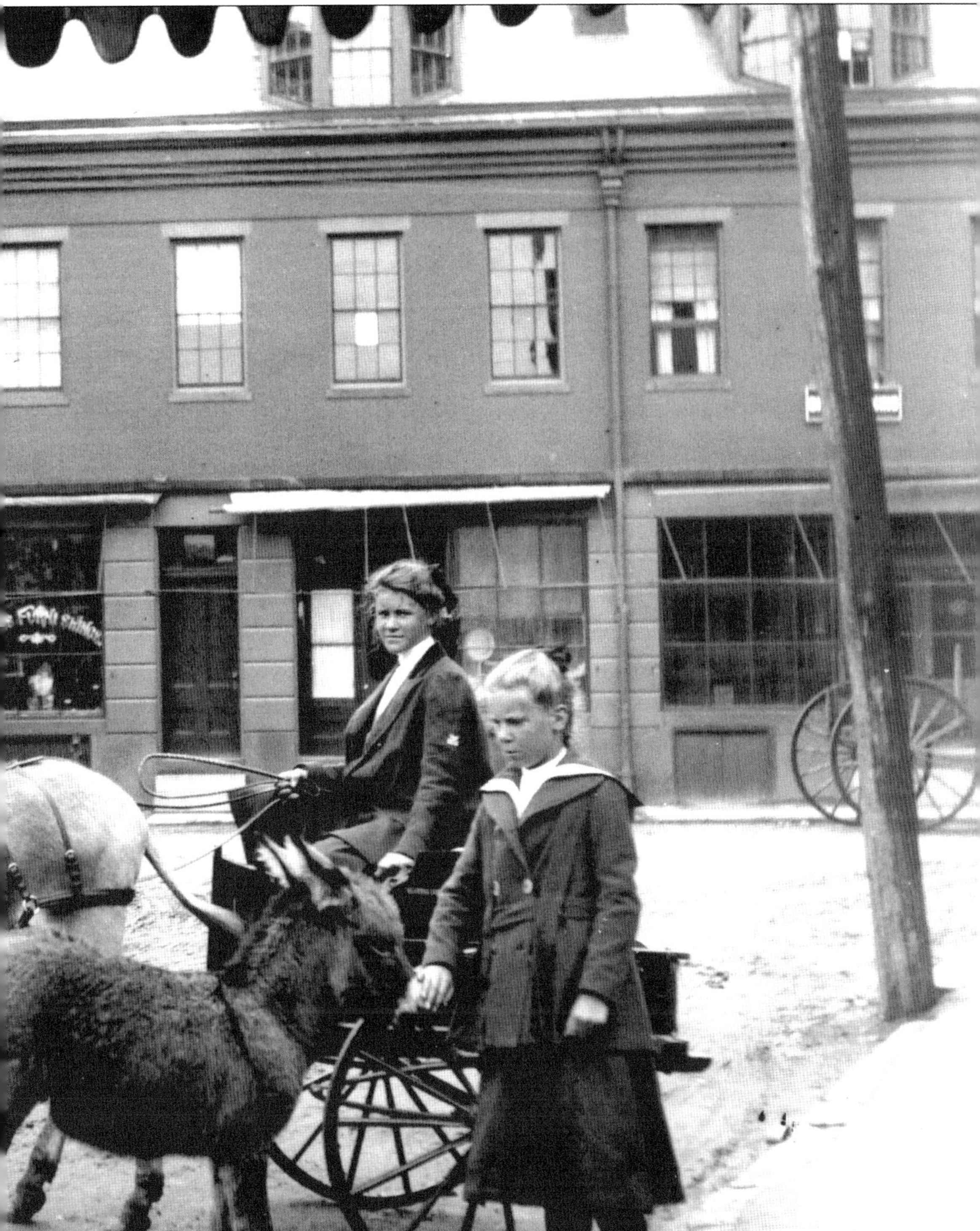

primarily by updating the older homes in the area with indoor plumbing and central heat.

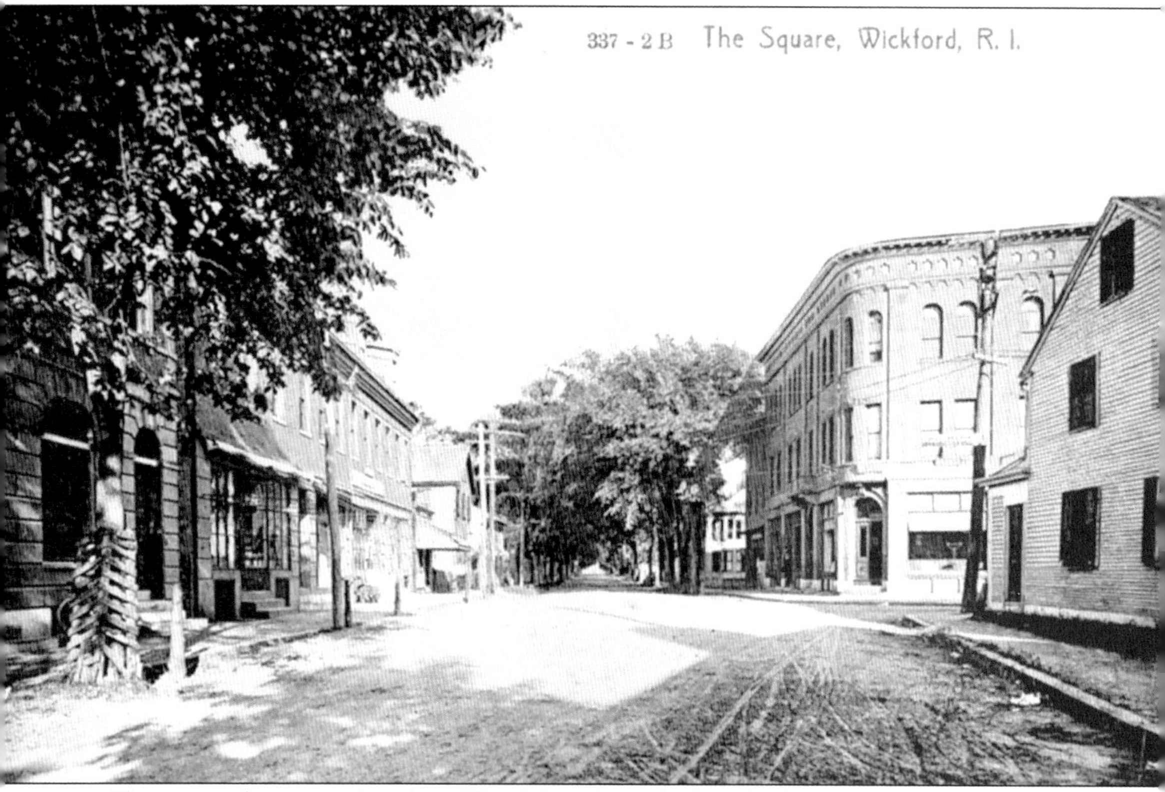

This postcard view is taken from West Main Street looking back toward its intersection with Brown and Main Streets. The wooden guards on the trees are to keep horses and mules from chewing through the tree's bark while they are tied up to the nearby hitching posts.

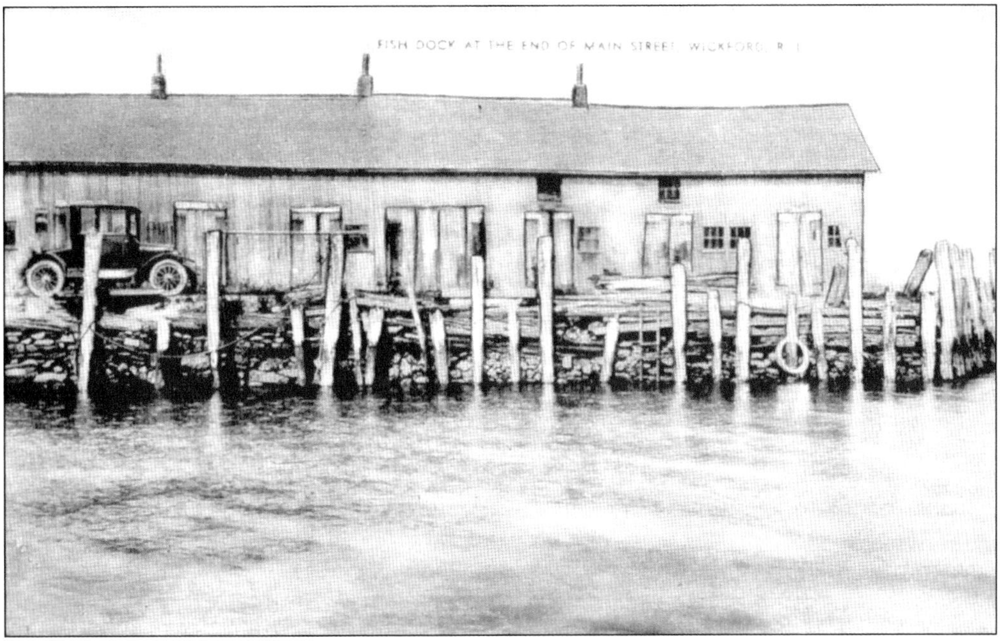

This early-20th-century postcard shows the fish dock at Gardner's Wharf at the end of Main Street.

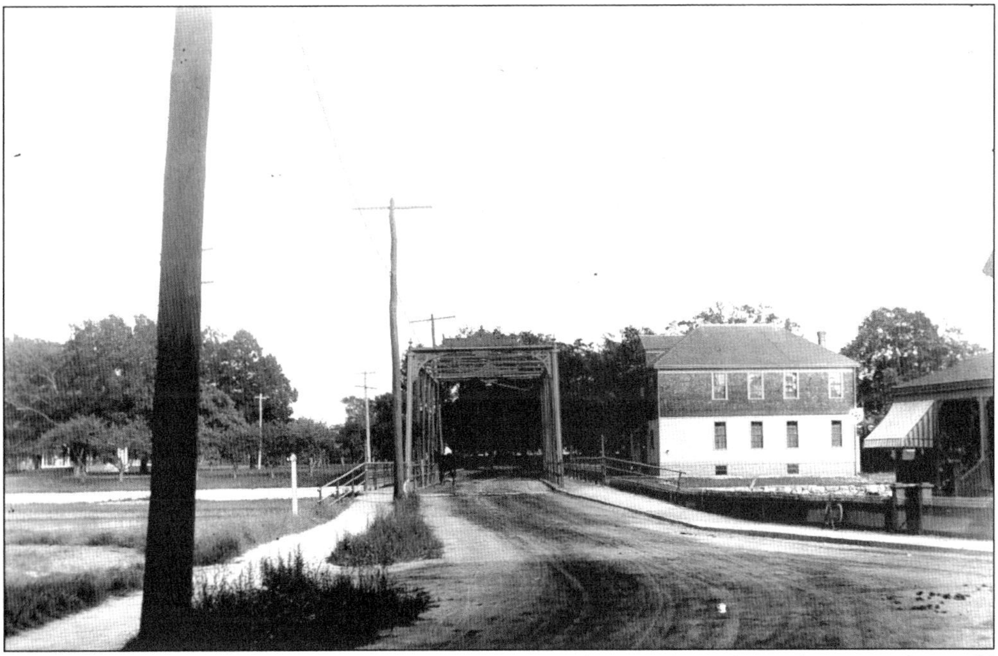

In this view, a horse and rider cross the Hamilton Bridge. To the right is the St. Paul's Guild Hall, a meeting place for the Episcopal parish that also housed the town's first public library. On the left are the grounds of Gov. William Gregory's estate, the Oaklands.

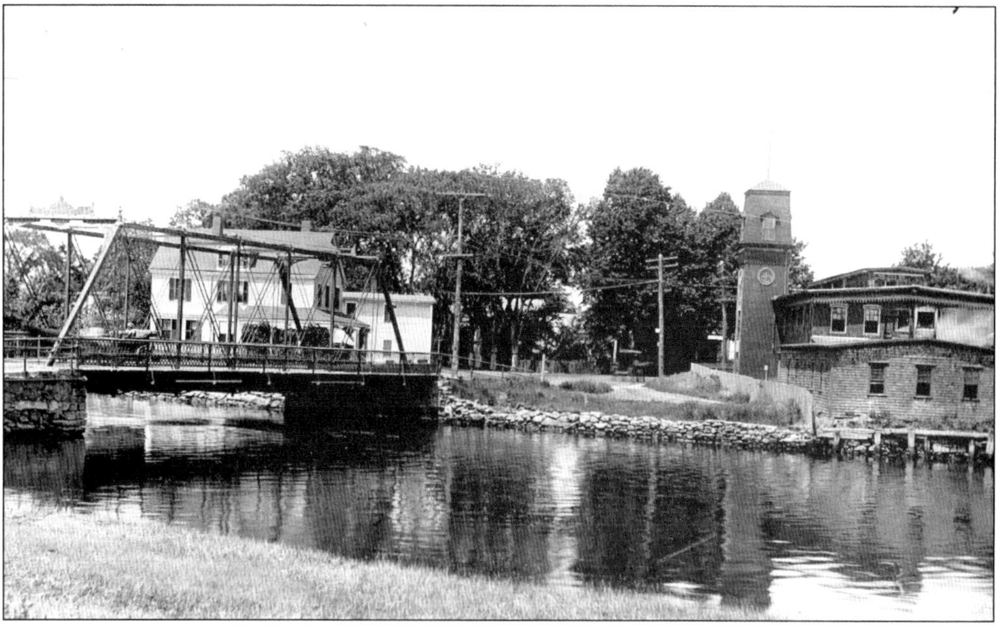

Here is a view taken from the lawn of the expansive Gregory estate, the Oaklands, looking back at the Hamilton Bridge and the Gregory Woolen Mill.

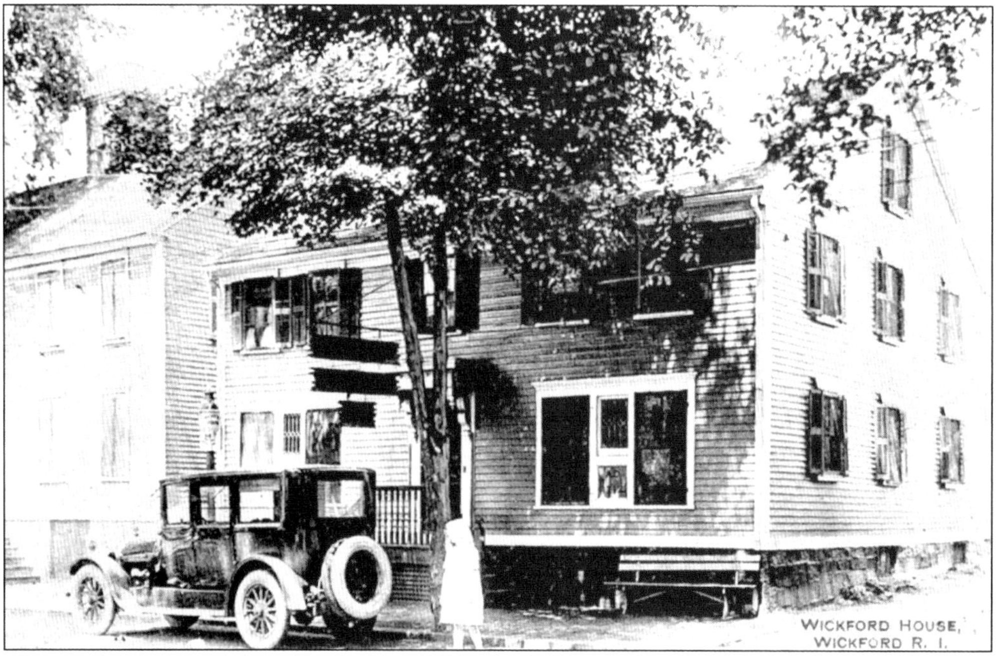

This postcard view of the village's most famous eatery, Mother Prentice's Wickford House, was produced for Frank Peckham to be sold in his dry goods store.

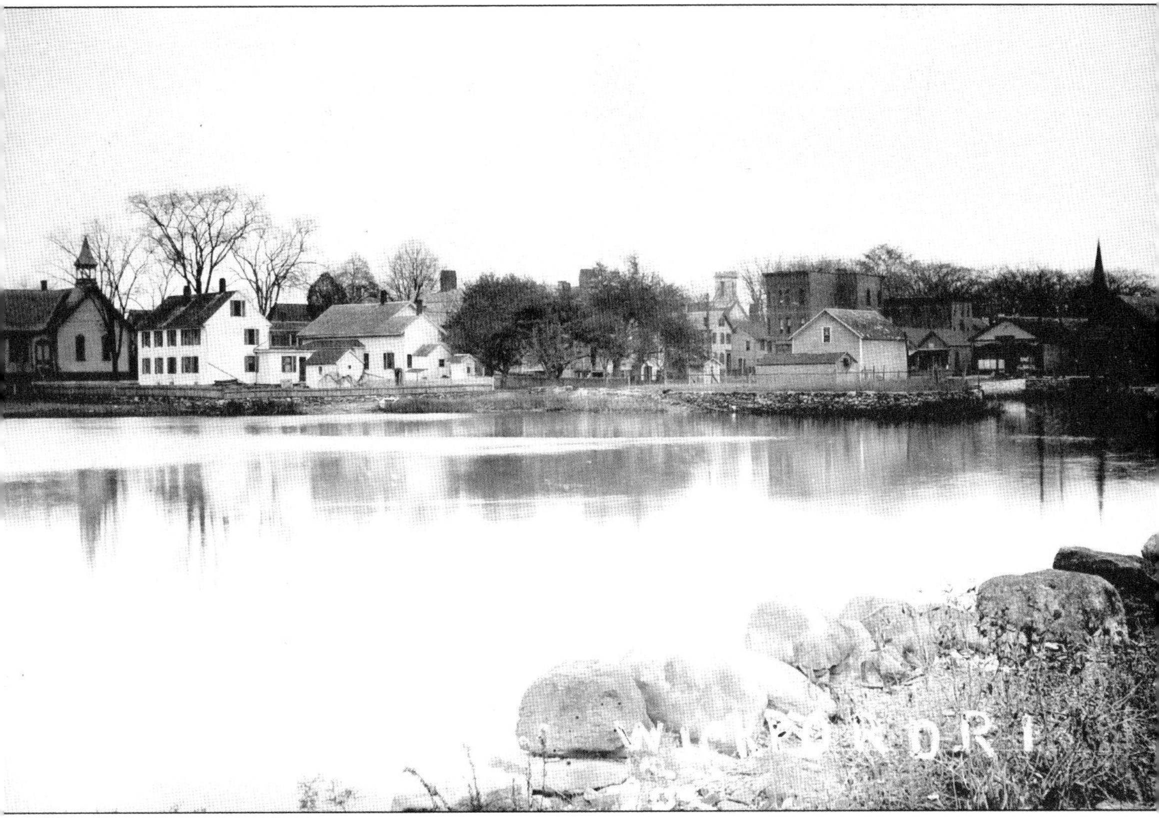

This photograph looks across the cove at the lower West Main Street area. To the extreme left stand the Wickford Methodist Episcopal Church and its rectory. Both buildings now house retail shops. The steeples of the Baptist and Episcopal churches can also be discerned in the distance.

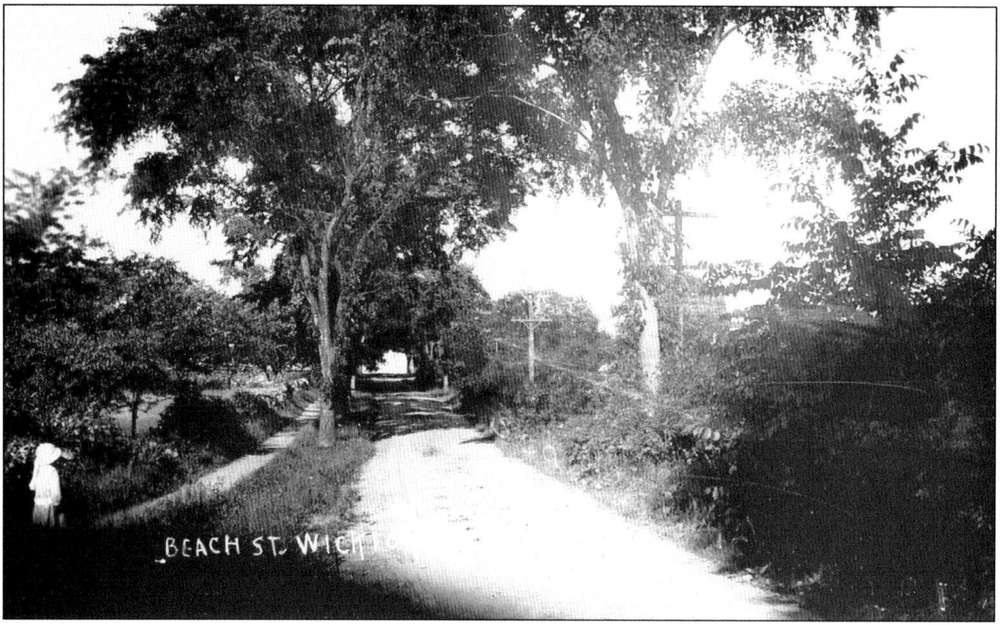

This is a view looking up from Beach Street toward what is now Boston Neck Road. The three summer hotels, the Cold Spring House, the Beachwood, and the Bayview Manor, were accessed via this lane.

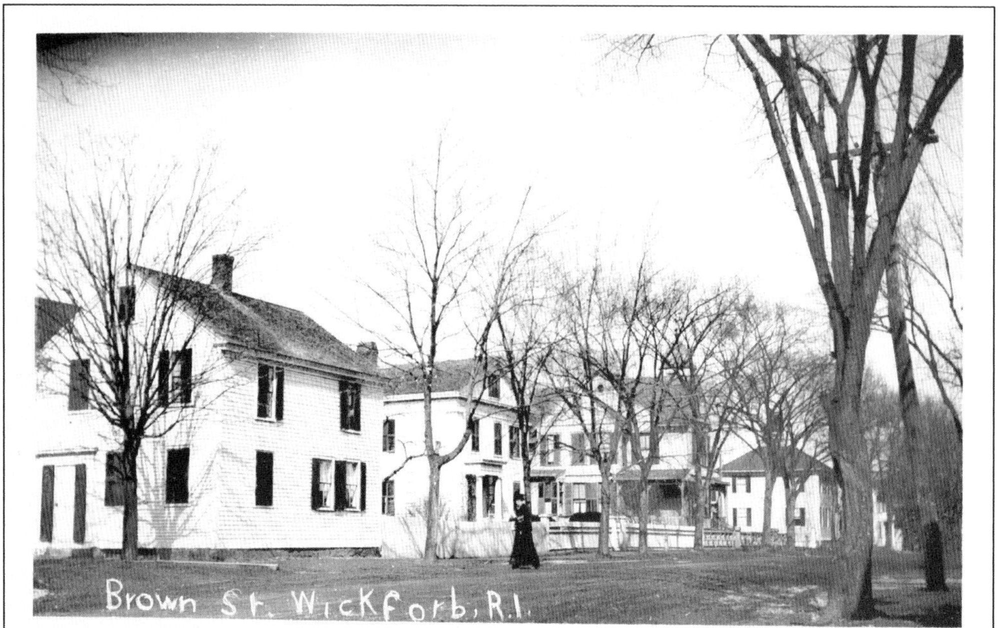

A local woman strolls down Brown Street. Most of this area, known then as Elamsville, was still residential at the start of the 20th century. All four of these fine homes still exist today and have been converted into commercial properties.

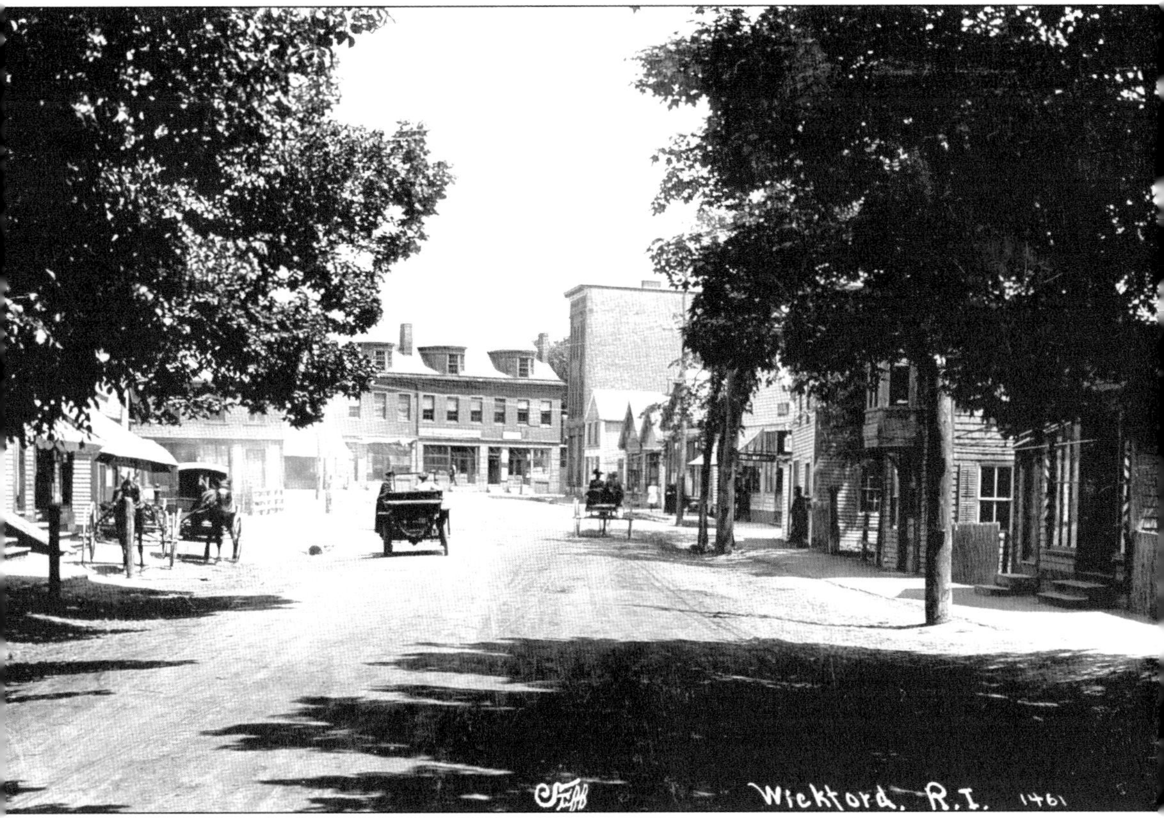

Taken at the start of the 20th century, this view highlights the other end of Brown Street. Most of the buildings to the right are long gone and replaced by the drugstore and adjacent parking lot. The first visible building on the left is Ryan's Market.

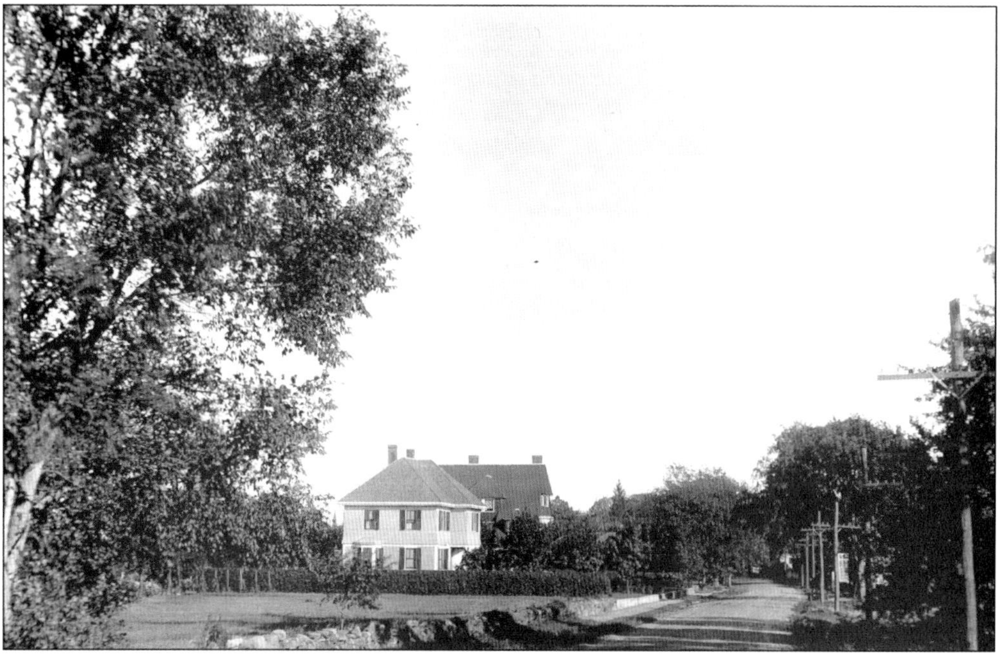

This photograph spotlights the upper portion of West Main Street, an area that was known as Quality Hill. The two houses shown can still be found on West Main Street today. They were owned by two of the Lewis brothers, members of a family of locally well-known fishermen.

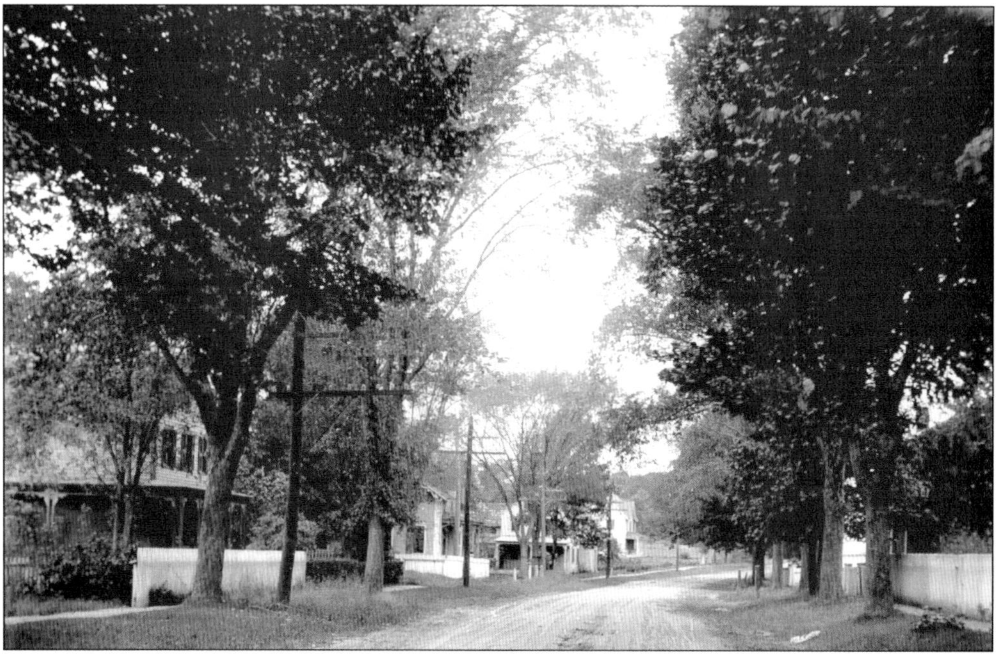

Here is another view of the Quality Hill area of Wickford. Most of these homes, too, are still intact, although the last home on the left burned down in a dramatic early-20th-century fire. At that time, it was known as the Elms and served as a summer guesthouse. A florist shop now sits on the site once occupied by the Elms.

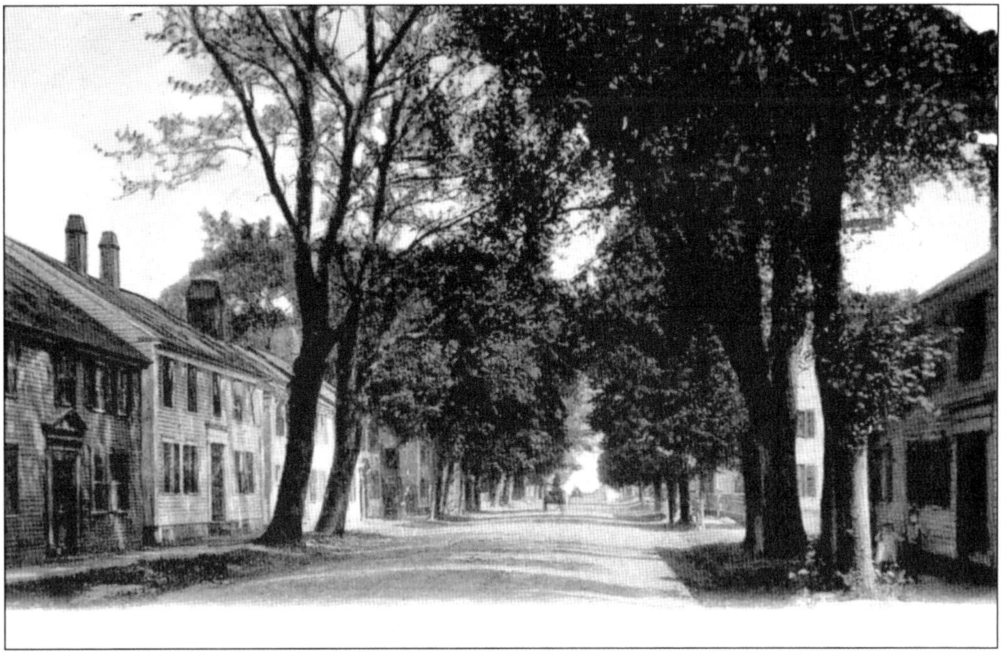

This postcard view looking down Main Street in the heart of the old village was printed for sale in Sealey's Drugstore, Doc Young's primary competitor at the time.

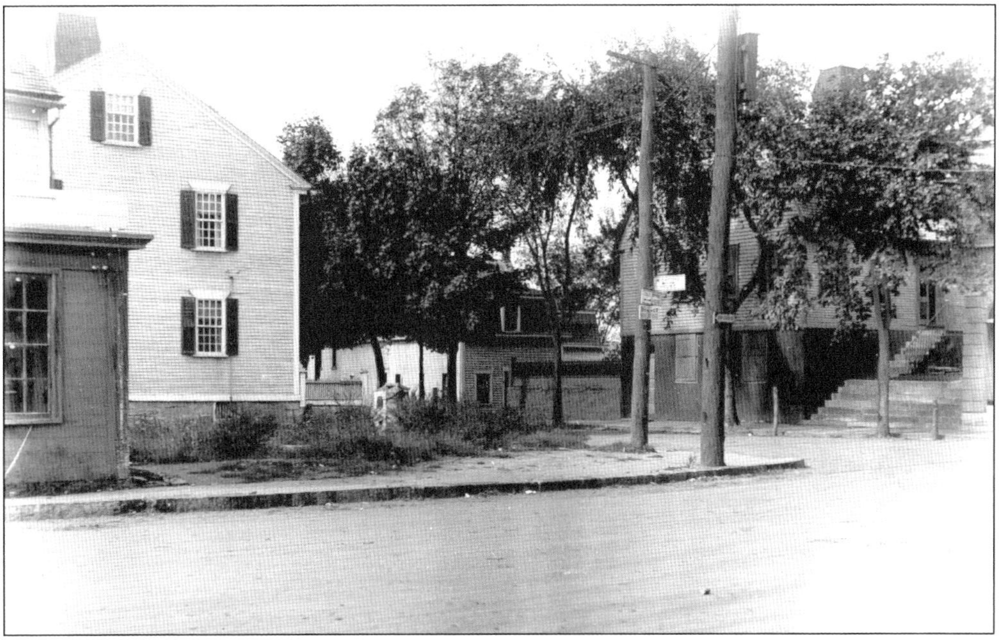

This photograph features the corner of Brown and Main Streets. Centered in the shot, but somewhat obscured by the foliage, is one of the town wells. The town installed these wells for residents who were not fortunate enough to have their own well. It, like all other wells in Wickford proper, was forever fouled with saltwater by the hurricane of 1938. When the town converted the property into a park later in the century, a walk-through gate shaped like a well house was added as a way of remembering the old town wells.

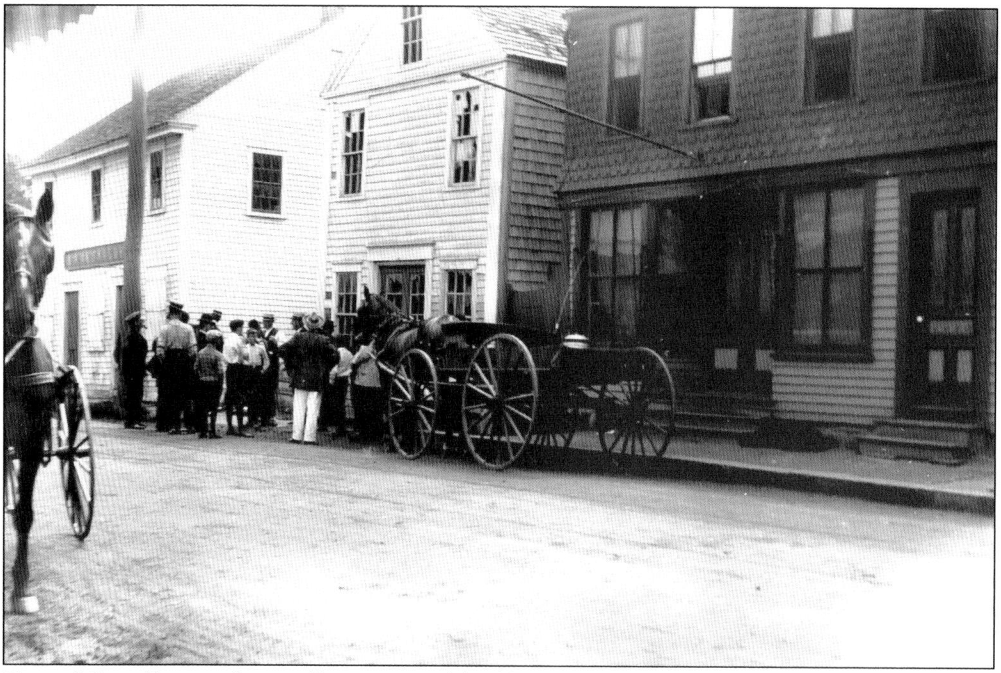

Townsfolk mill around a small commercial building that had suffered a fire. It was eventually demolished. Horatio Reynolds's store can be seen just past the crowd.

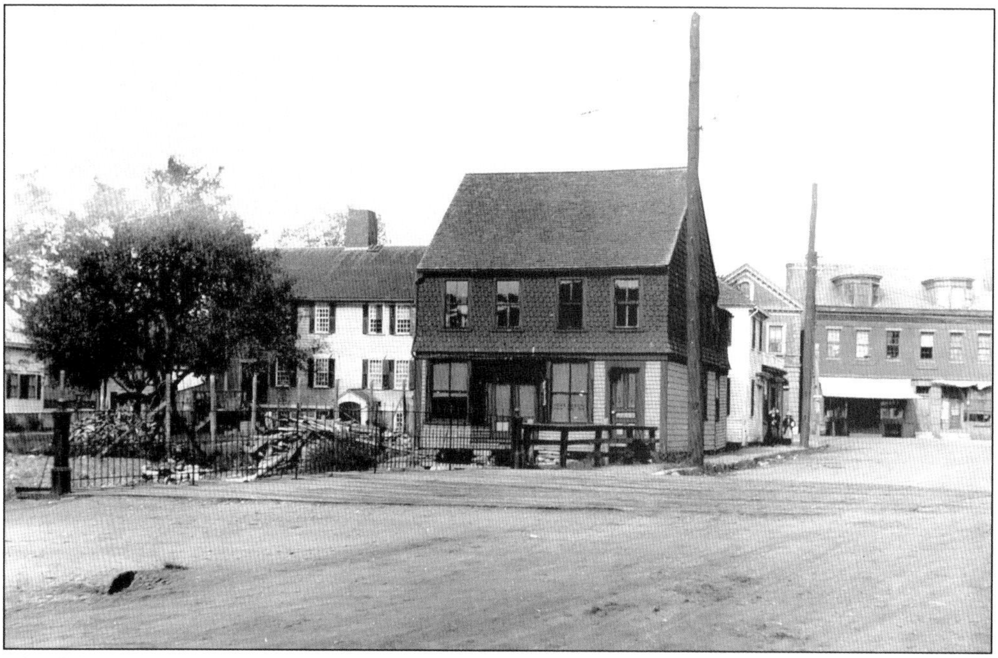

The debris from the building's demolition can be seen in this photograph. The Reynolds store was demolished as well. The two buildings fronting Brown Street were eventually sold and relocated within the village. The nearer building was moved up to the Quality Hill area of town and the farther one was relocated to a spot just west of the Odd Fellows Hall. The lots were then transformed into the small park that exists at this location today.

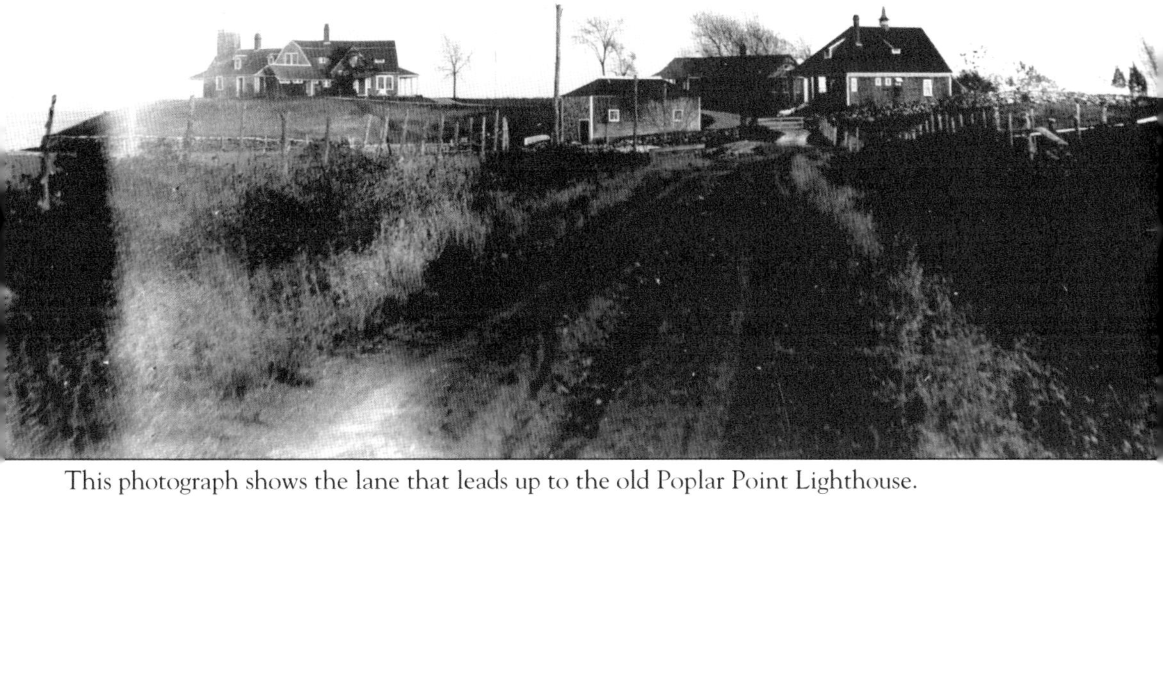

This photograph shows the lane that leads up to the old Poplar Point Lighthouse.

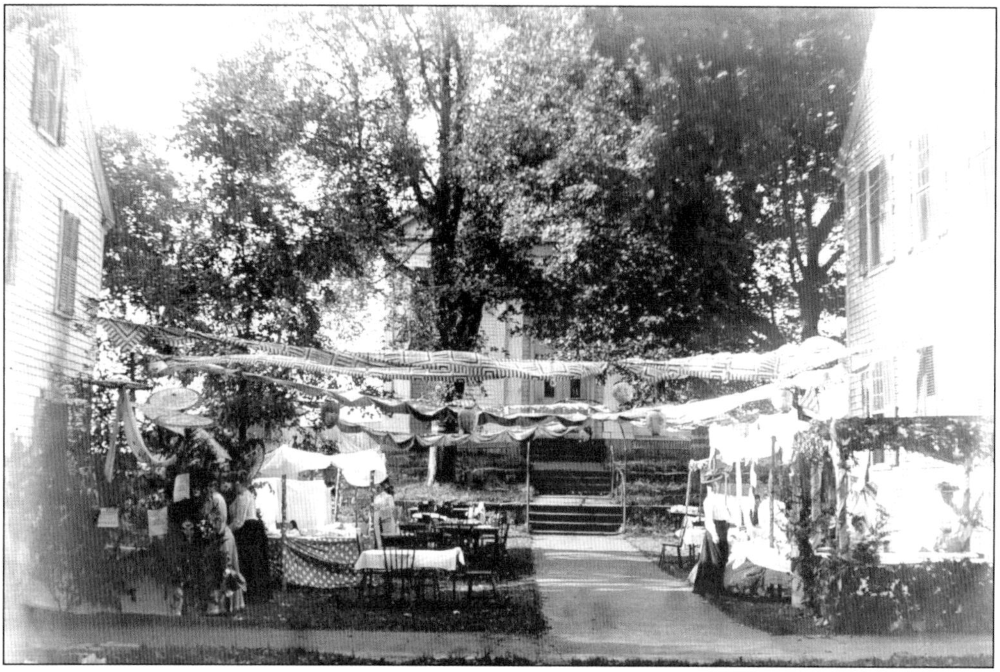

A small village fair is being put on by the ladies of the Wickford Baptist Church towards the end of the 1890s.

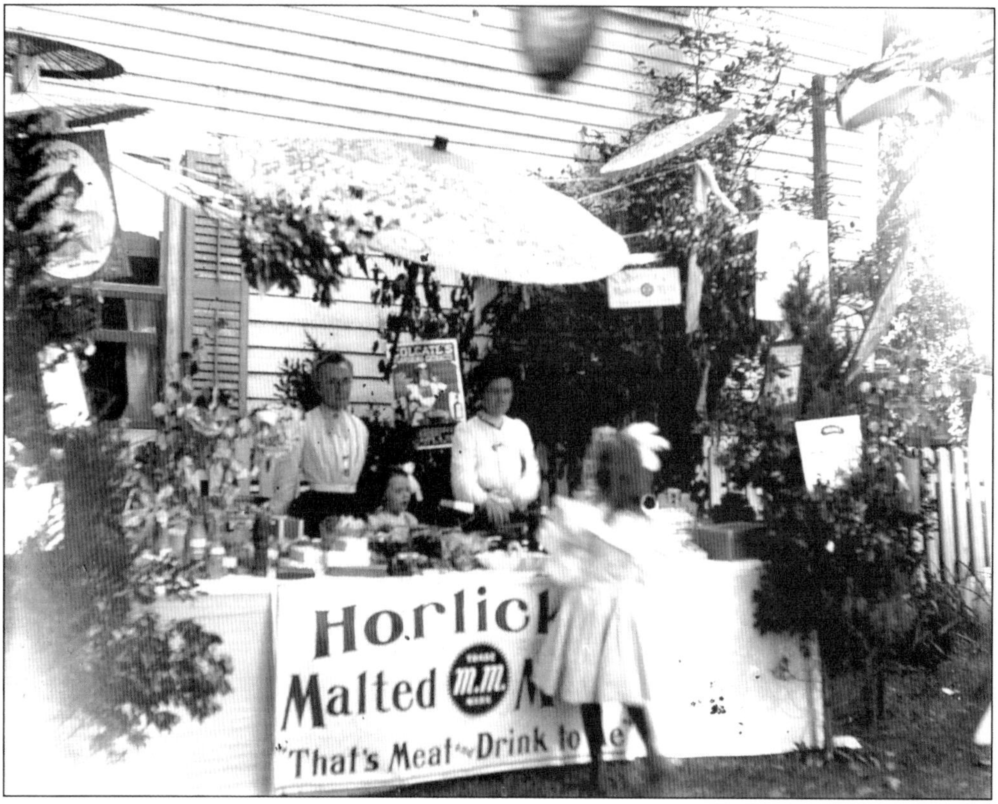

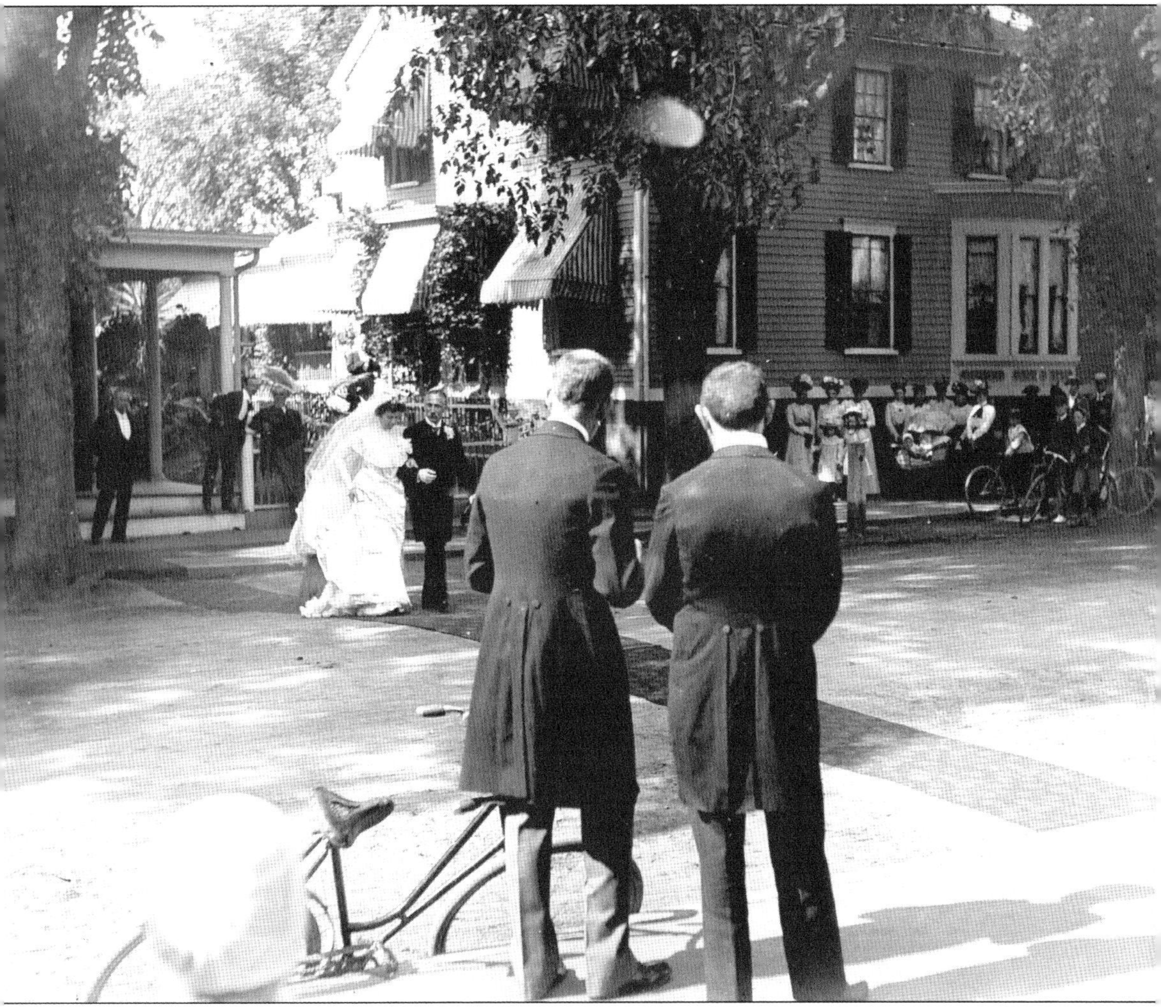

A wedding was a big event in a small, tightly knit community like Wickford. Members of a wedding party can be seen crossing Main Street from the Allen Mason Thomas House over to St. Paul's Episcopal Church just across the street.

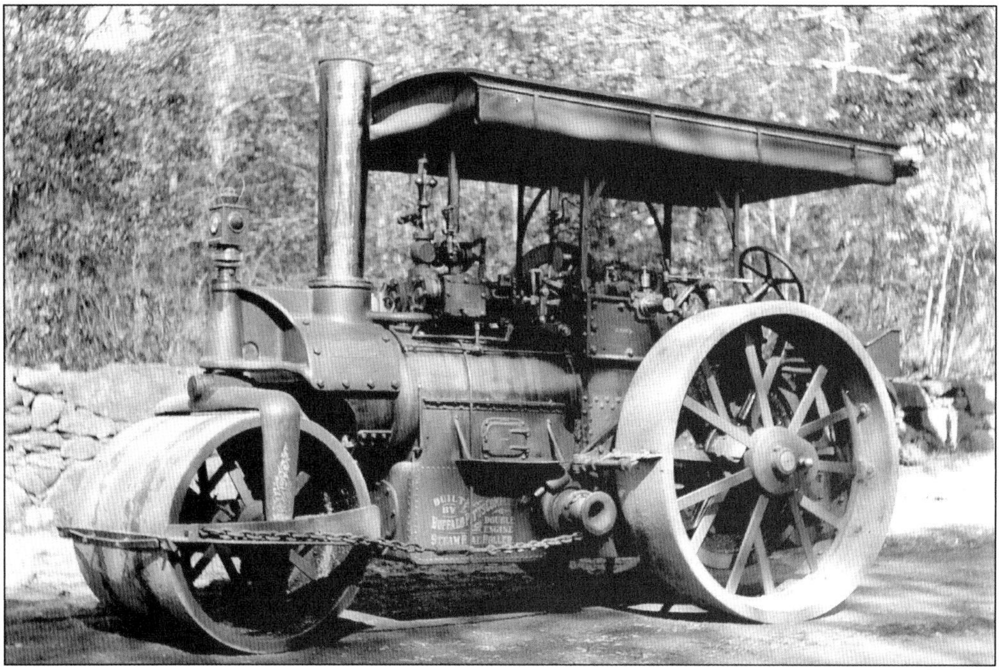

The sight of the state of Rhode Island's steam road roller was a welcome one after a long winter and a muddy spring. In an age before paved roadways were commonplace, most local roads were a rutted, muddy, nearly impassable mess by May or June. After a good work over by one of these steamrollers, things could begin to get back to normal.

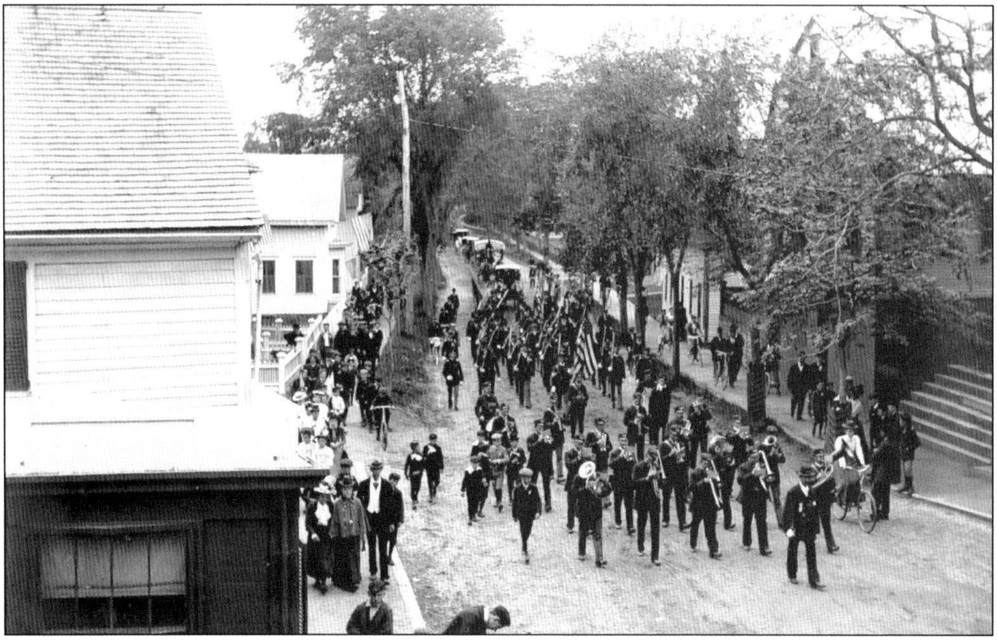

Decoration Day was an important holiday for a nation that had only recently begun to heal the wounds inflicted by the great Civil War. This *c.* 1880 photograph, taken at the intersection of Brown, Main, and West Main Streets, shows North Kingstown's parade celebrating the contribution of their local Civil War veterans. The holiday was later renamed Memorial Day.

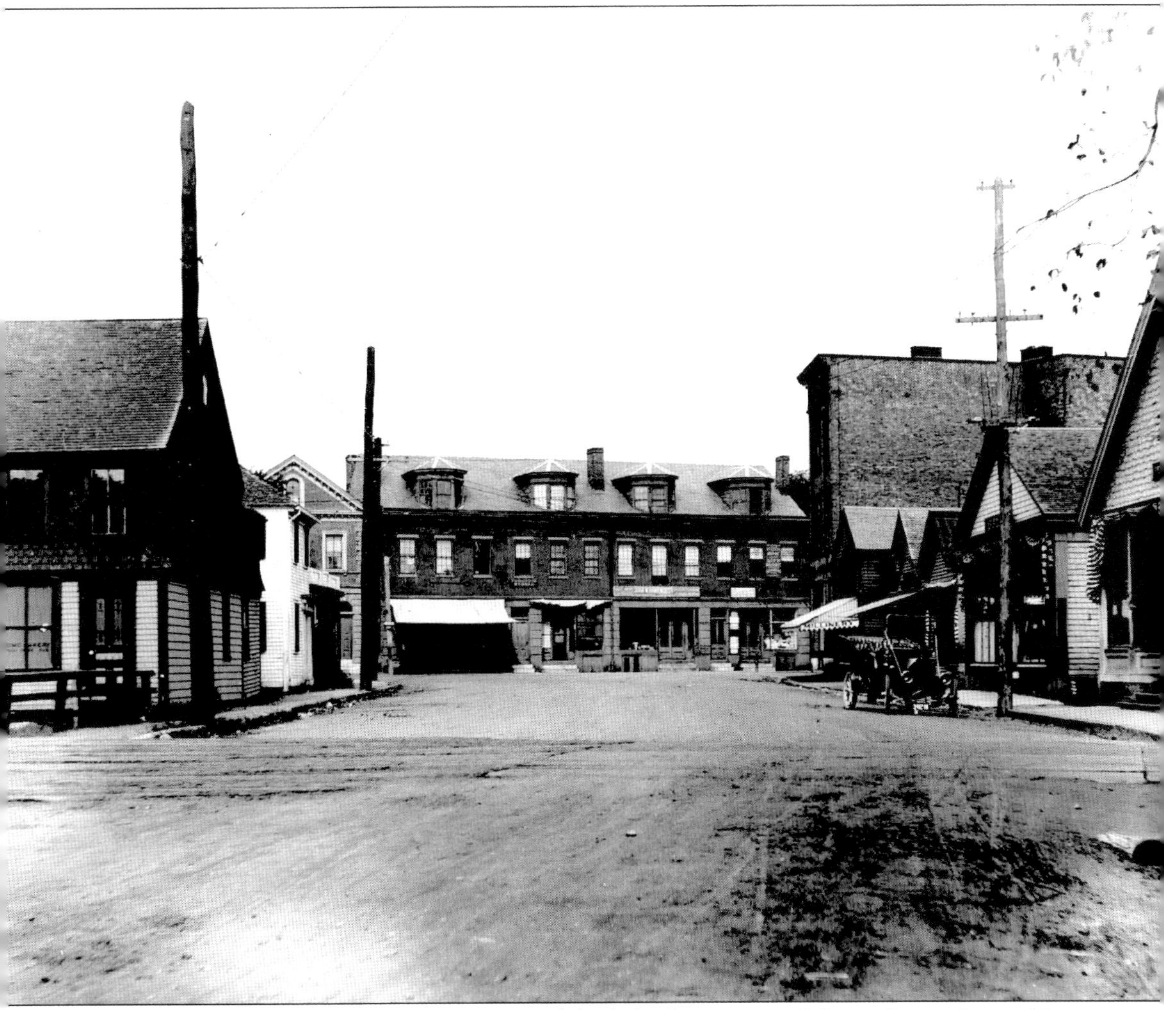

On this quiet morning on Brown Street in Wickford, the lone automobile on the road is an 18-horsepower Stevens registered to Frank Holloway, a resident of the village. To the extreme right, the village billiard hall and bowling alley can be seen.

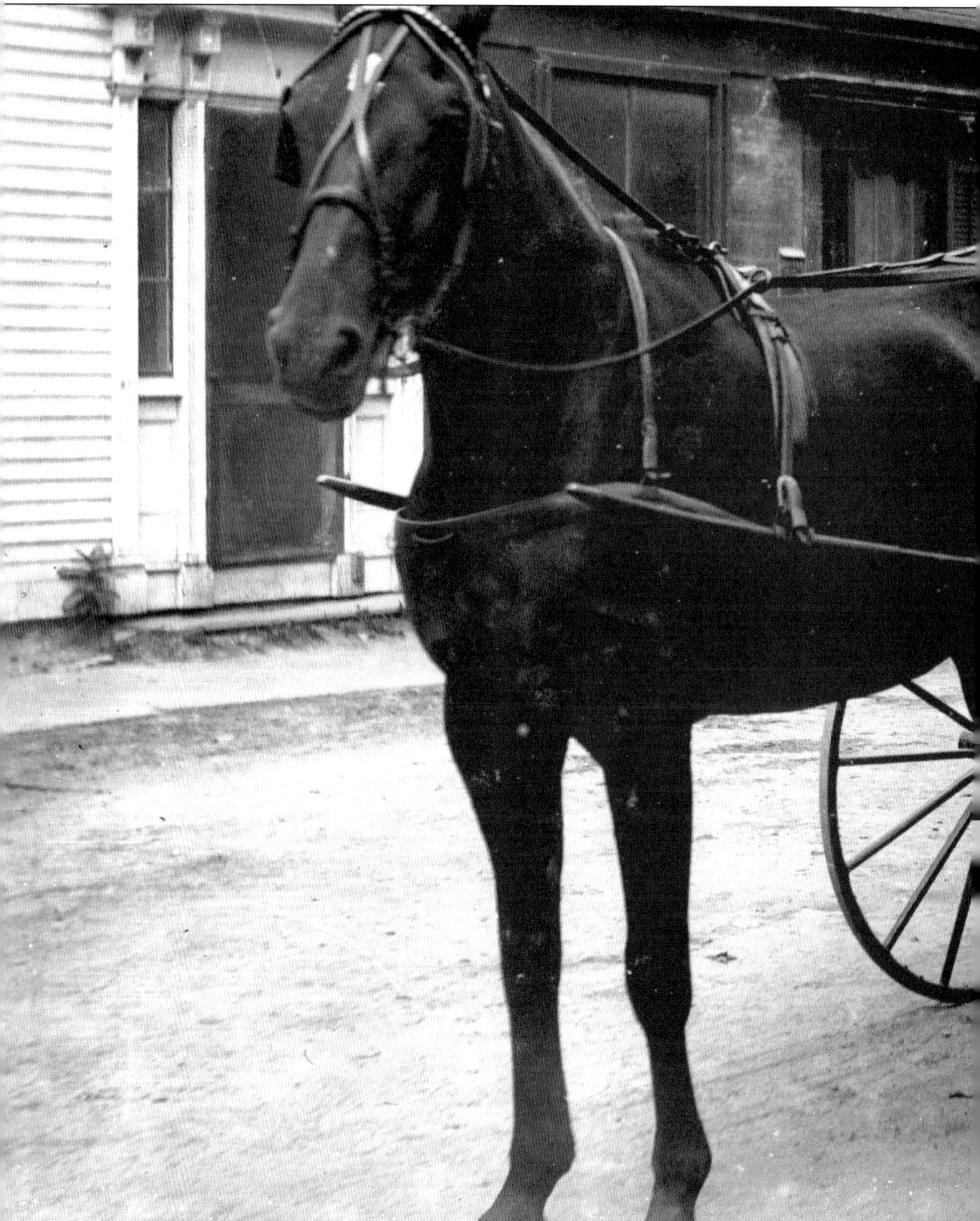

This *c.* 1910 photograph features John Hainsworth and his two children, Albert and Ethel, in their horse and buggy outside his plumbing establishment. The Hainsworths lived in a home situated

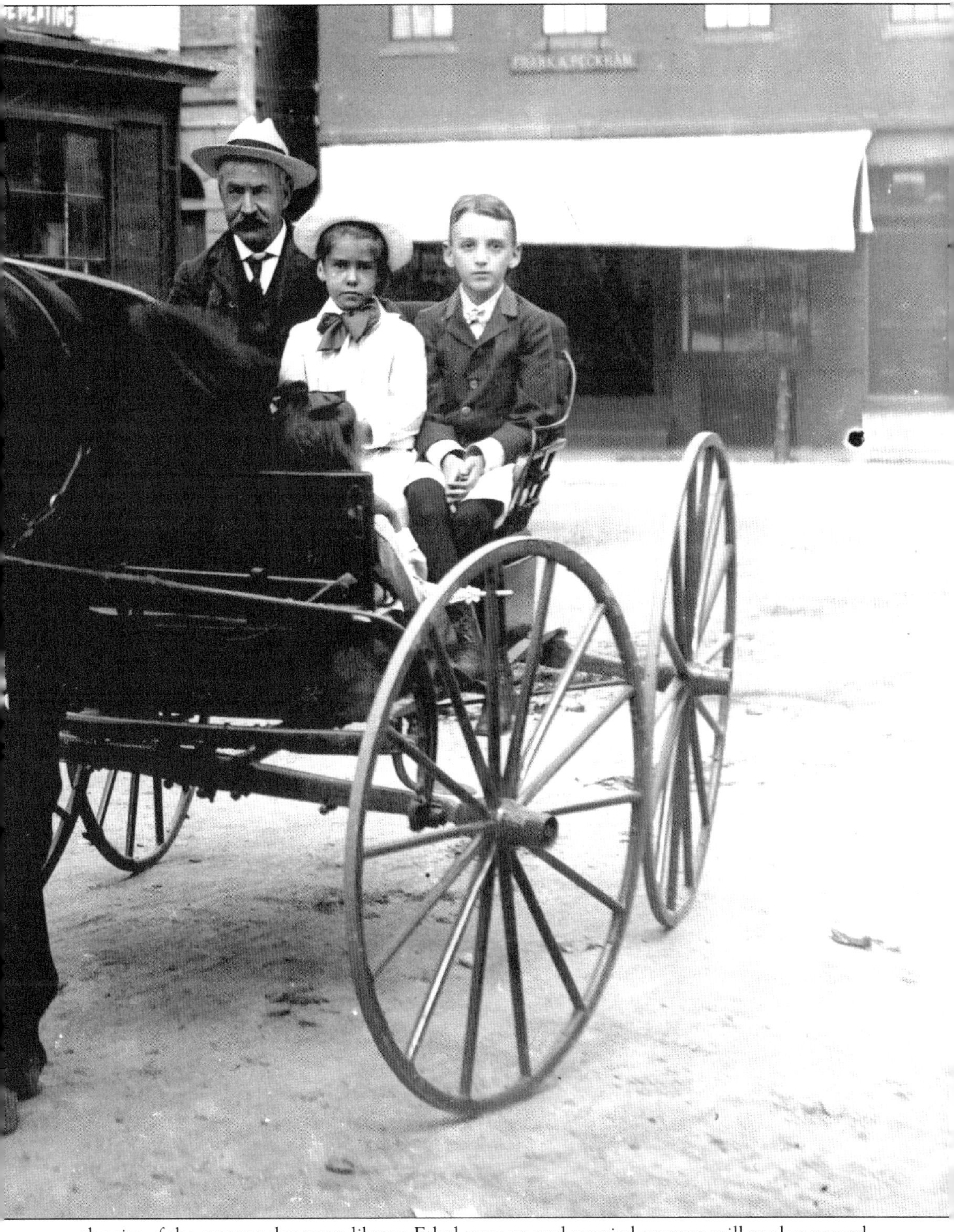

on the site of the present-day town library. Ethel grew up and married a young mill worker named Skitty Wilson. Together they founded the well-known clothing store Wilson's of Wickford.

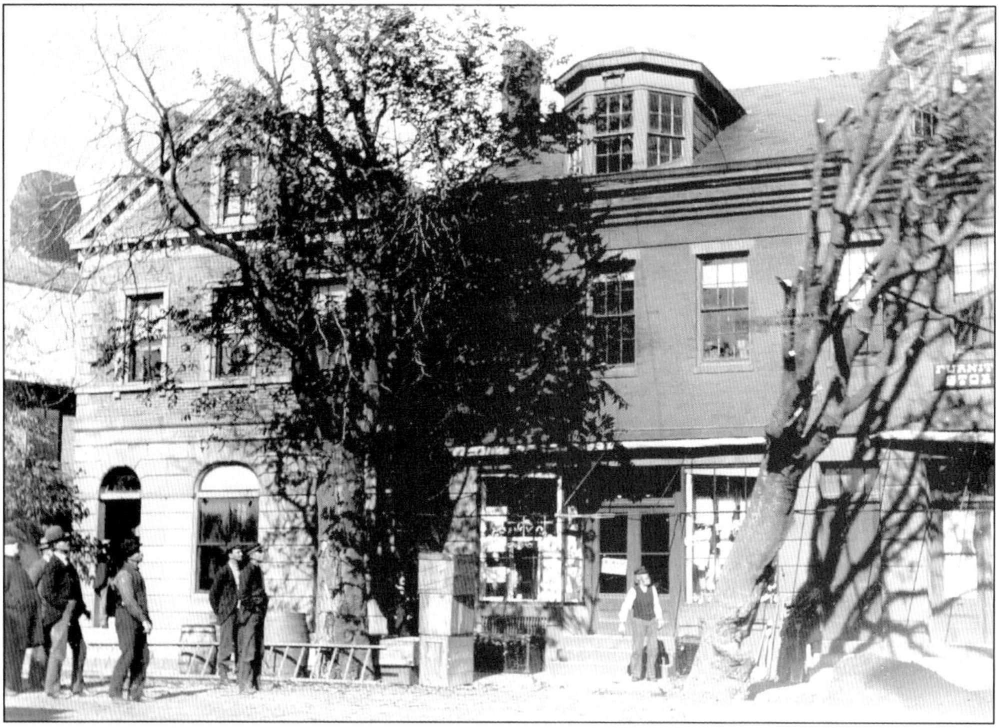

In these two photographs, townsfolk and workers mill around, contemplating the removal of two dying trees adjacent to the Wickford National Bank (now the home of the *Standard Times* newspaper). The work is accomplished utilizing a farm tractor, which can be seen pulling the tree down in the photograph below.

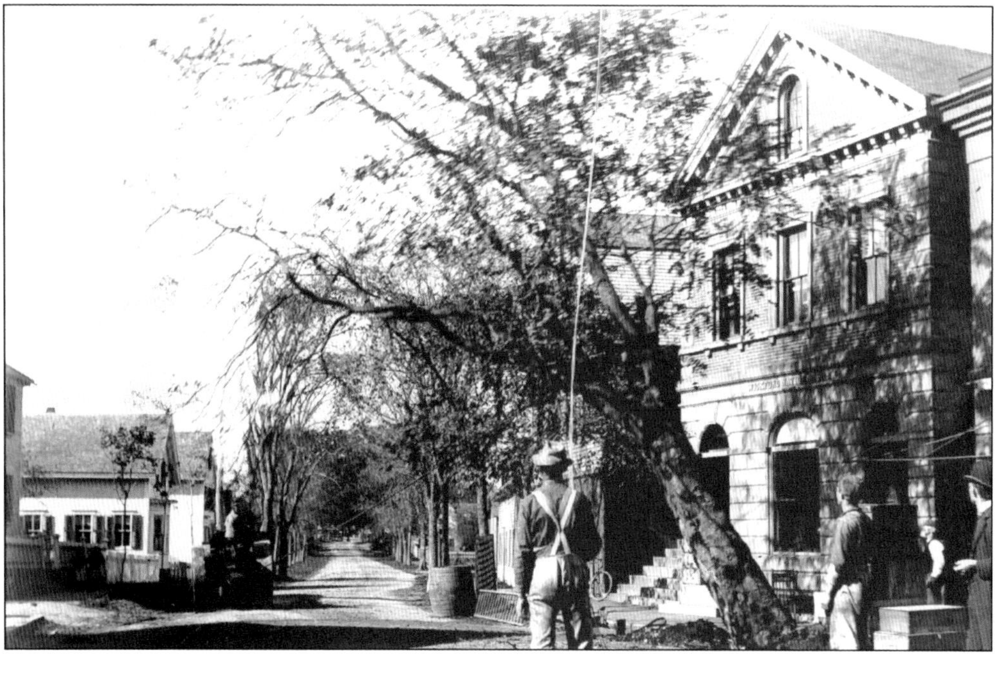

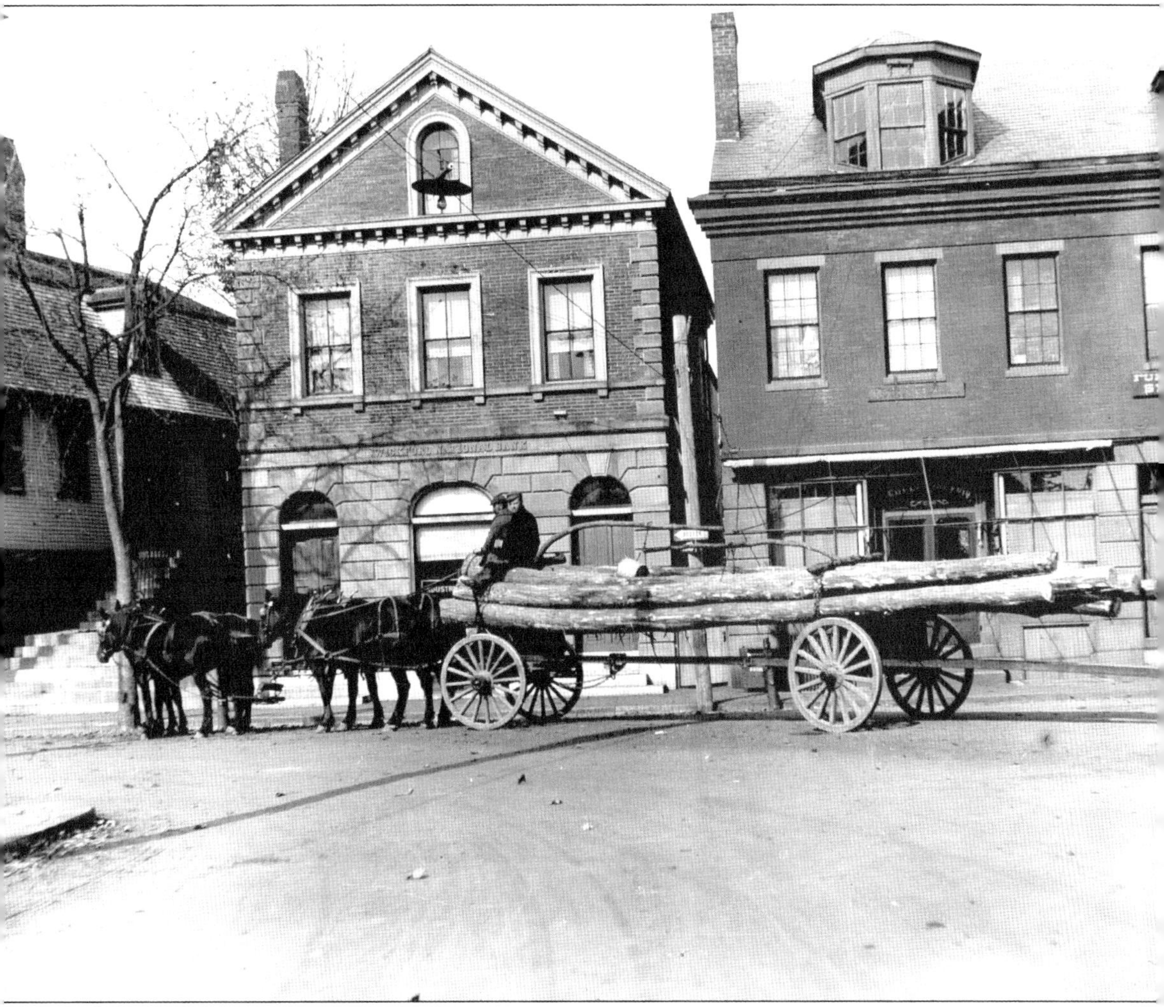

A load of lumber, bound for the dock at Gardner's Wharf and eventually Newport, is hauled through the village. The unique wagon, with its long lower frame and set of back wheels that can be slid back and forth into any position, allows for different lengths of lumber to be loaded. It is stopped in front of Frank Peckham's dry goods store.

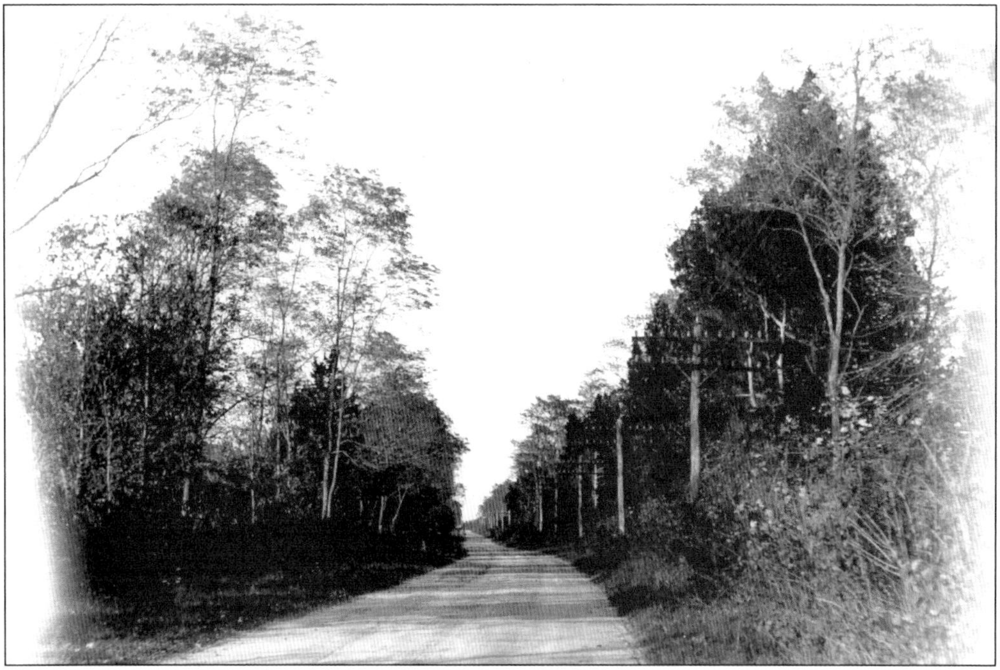

Here an 1890s photograph, and the postcard it was made into, give a feel for Post Road as it was more than 100 years ago. This photograph was taken in the area adjacent to where the North Kingstown Chamber of Commerce is now located.

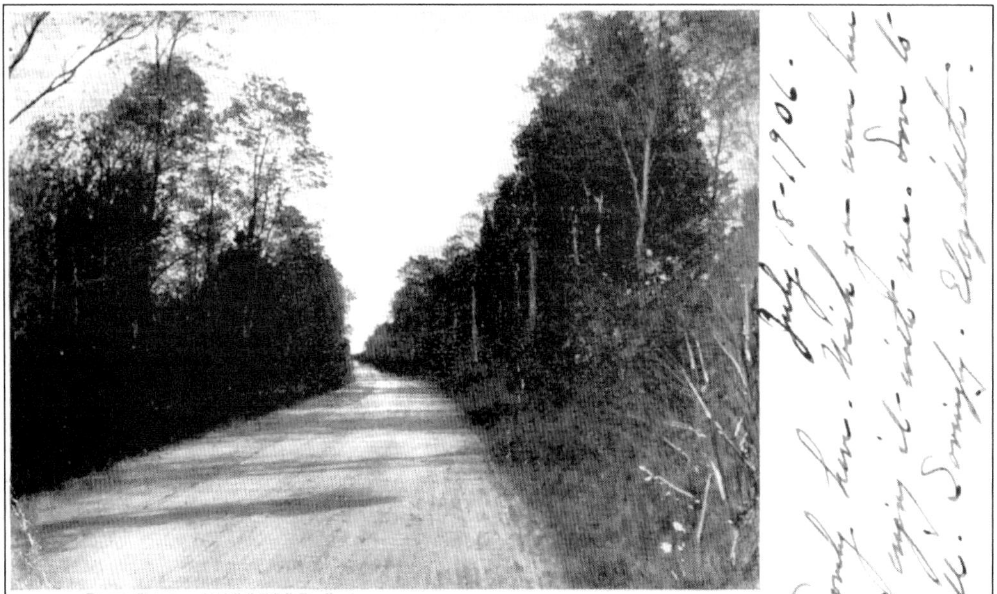

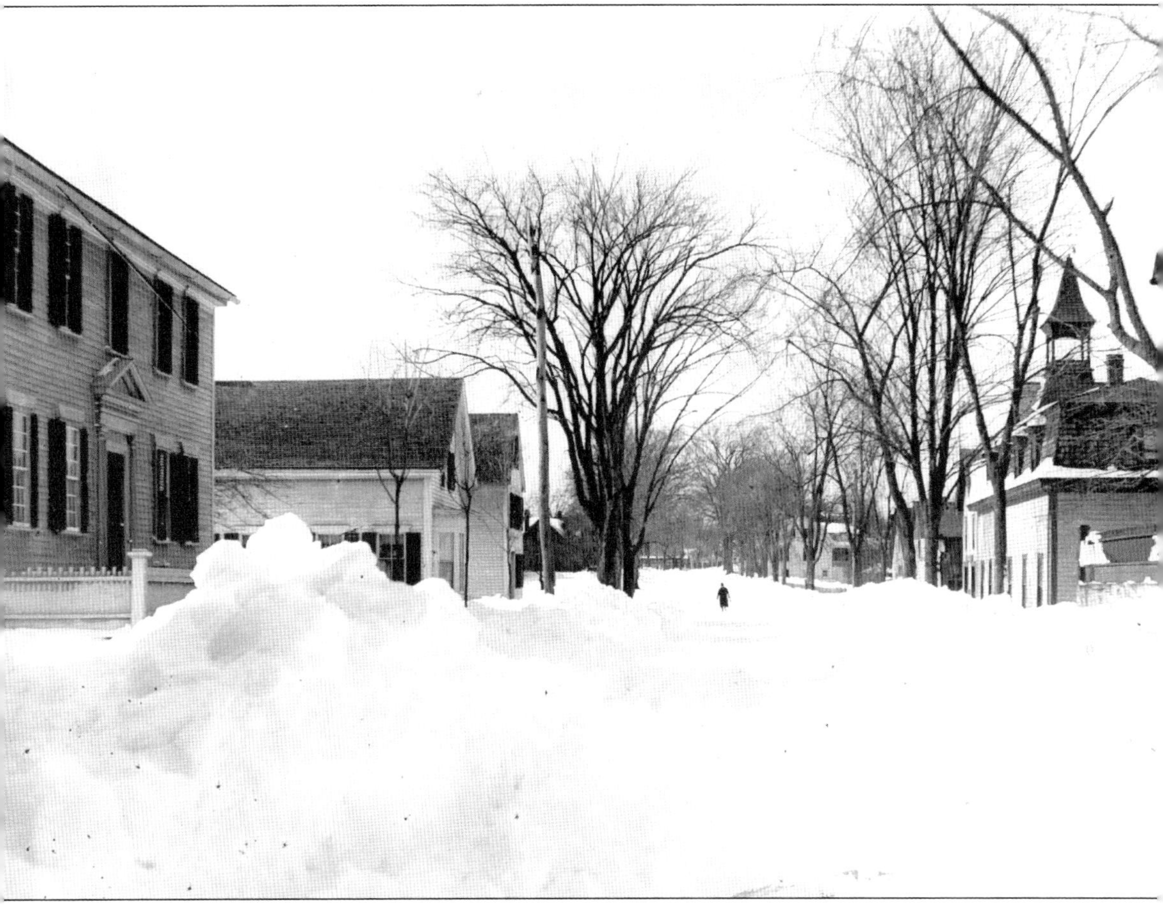

This is a view up West Main Street after a big snowstorm. A lone soul walks down the road into the village. The bell tower of the Wickford Methodist Episcopal Church can be seen on the right.

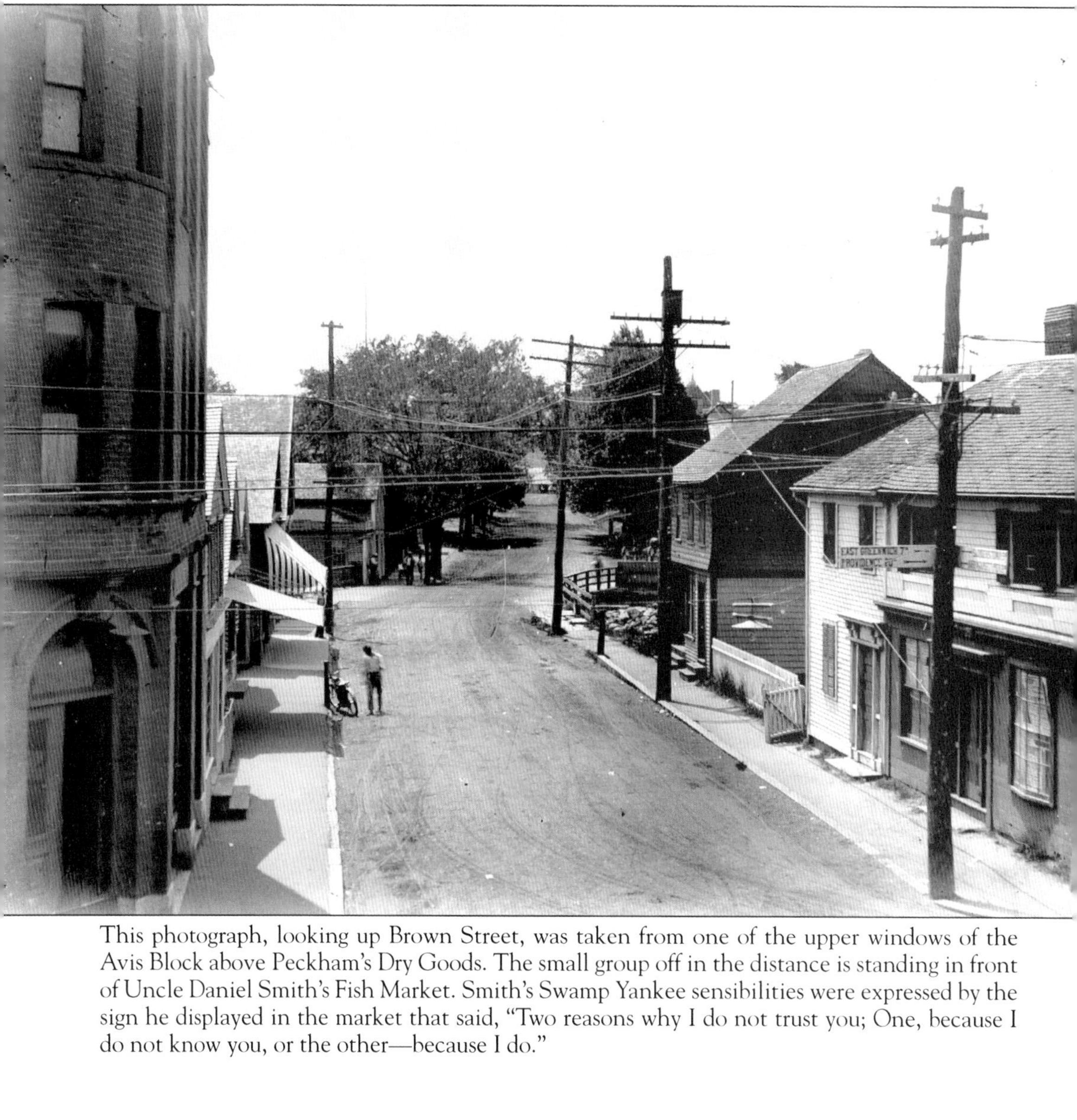

This photograph, looking up Brown Street, was taken from one of the upper windows of the Avis Block above Peckham's Dry Goods. The small group off in the distance is standing in front of Uncle Daniel Smith's Fish Market. Smith's Swamp Yankee sensibilities were expressed by the sign he displayed in the market that said, "Two reasons why I do not trust you; One, because I do not know you, or the other—because I do."

Seven

CHURCHES, SCHOOLS, AND PUBLIC PLACES

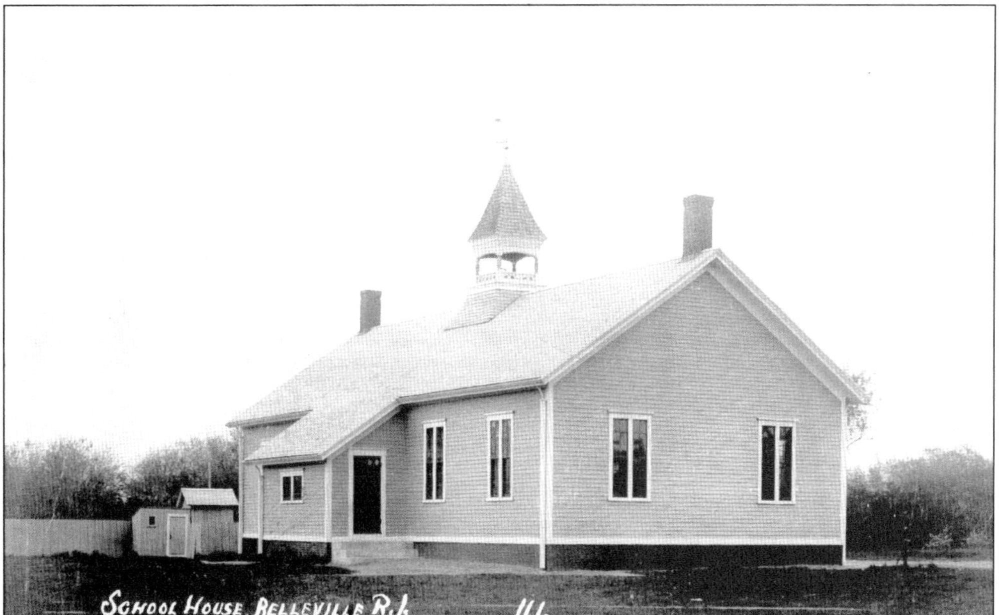

The Belleville schoolhouse was located within a stone's throw of the massive brick Belleville Woolen Mill. It was considered an architectural gem when it was constructed.

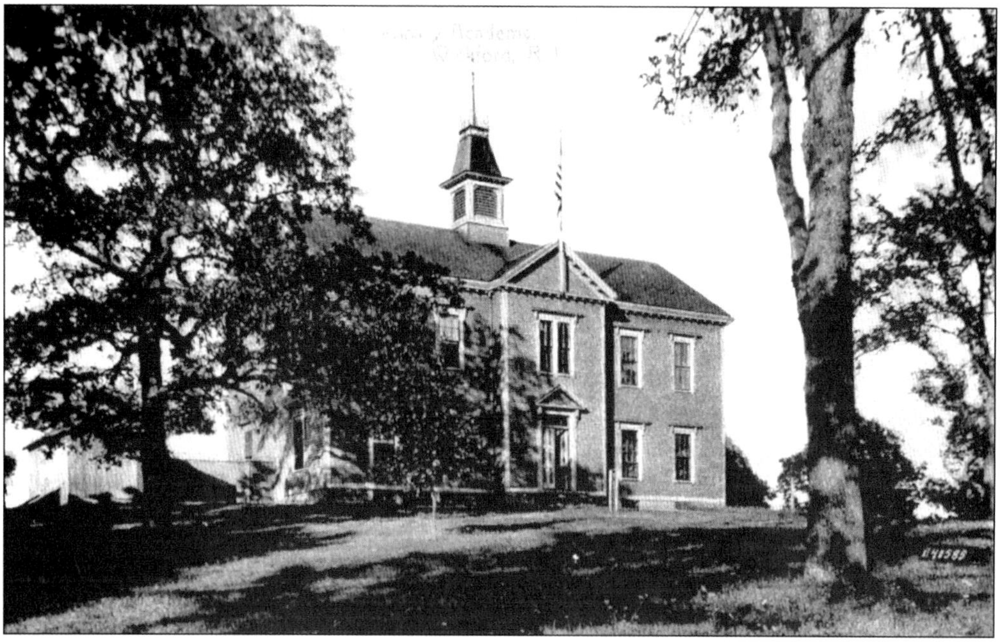

The Wickford Academy was constructed to replace the *c.* 1802 Washington Academy, which had been destroyed by fire. The building housed first through eighth grade for all of the children of Wickford, Elamsville, and Quality Hill.

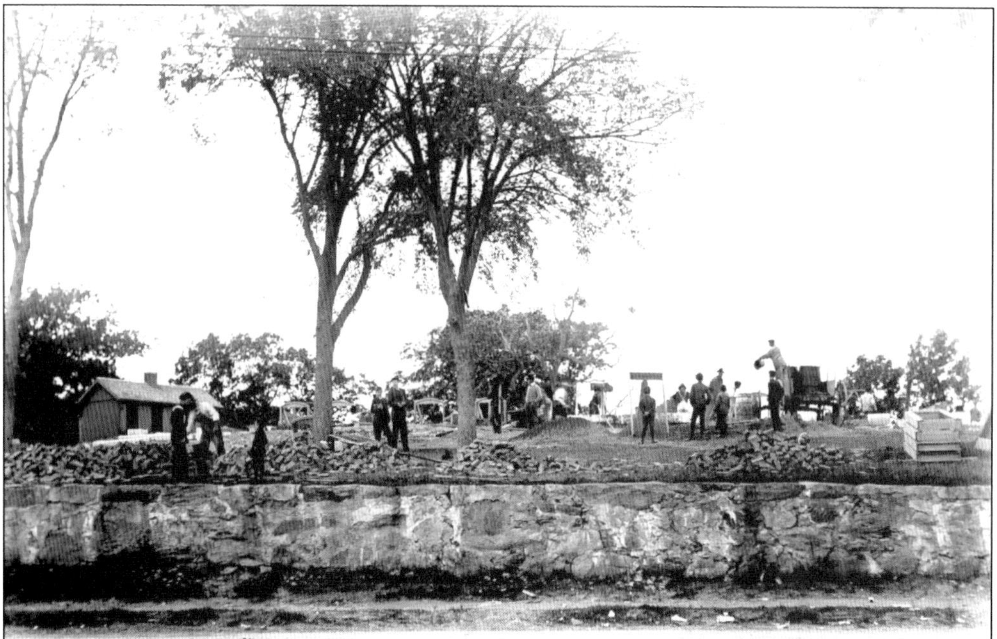

Sadly, in 1907, the Wickford Academy also burned to the ground, with only the large outhouse surviving the blaze. In this photograph taken by Doc Young, workers are hard at work rebuilding the schoolhouse.

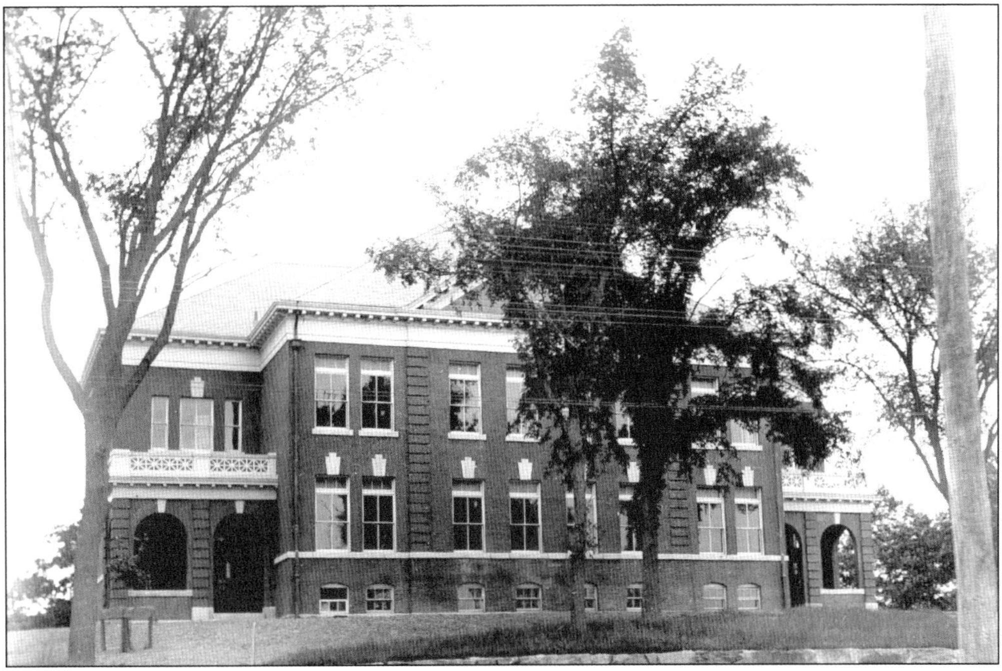

The new school building was completed just one year later. Built this time from brick, the handsome structure was also sized to fit the fledgling North Kingstown High School classes as well. It was renamed Wickford Grammar School.

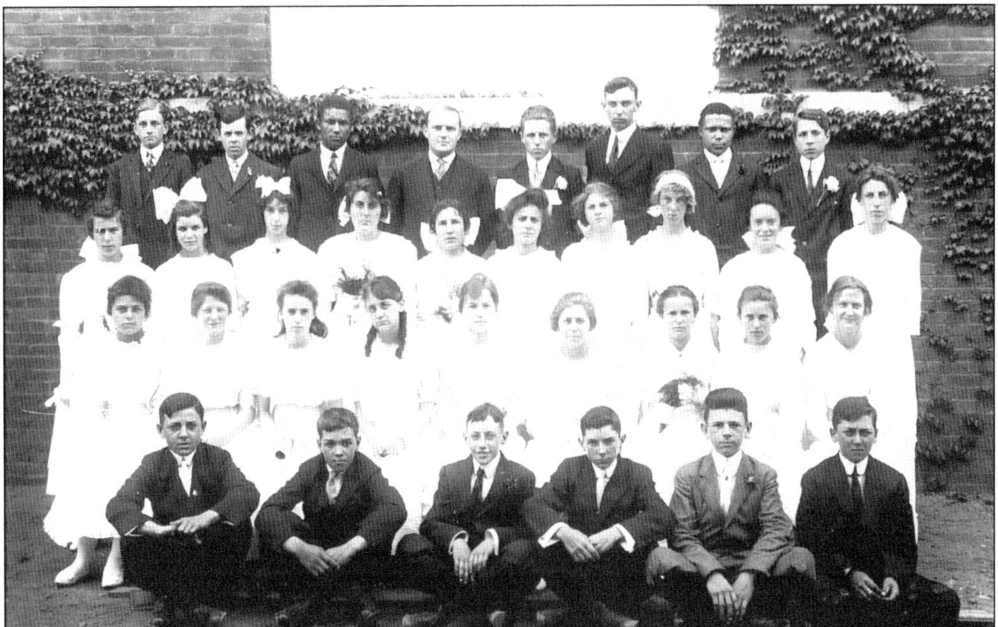

This is a typical end-of-the-year photograph of the students of Wickford Grammar School, an institution that housed children in grades one through twelve..

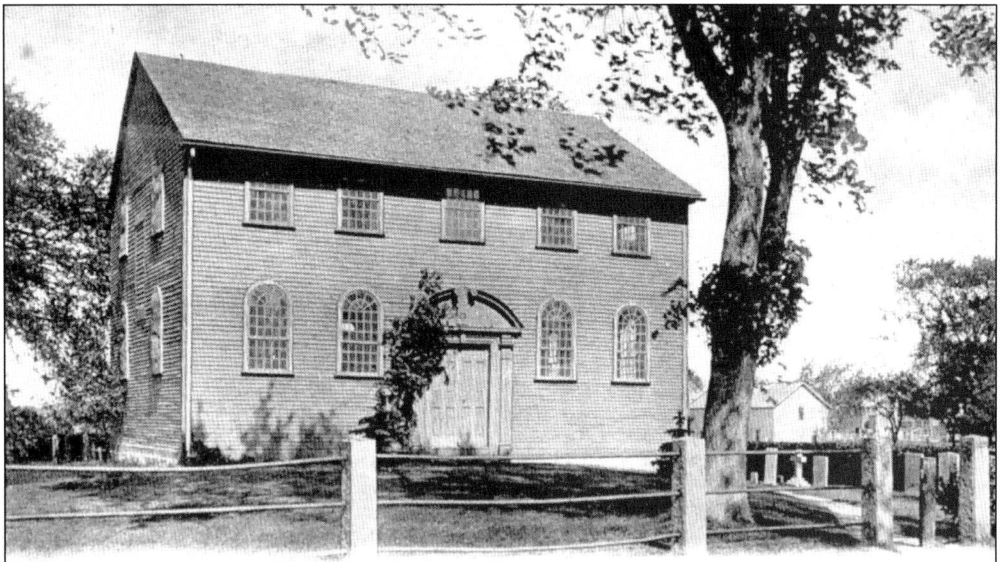

Old Church, erected 1707. Wickford, R. I.

Postcard views of the exterior and interior of the Old Narragansett Church show a building unchanged through the centuries. The church had been utilized almost continuously for 200 years when these photographs were taken. The only time it was not used as a church was during and just after the Revolutionary War, when anti-British sentiments caused the Anglican Church to fall out of favor. Instead it was used as a barracks to house local Revolutionary War soldiers.

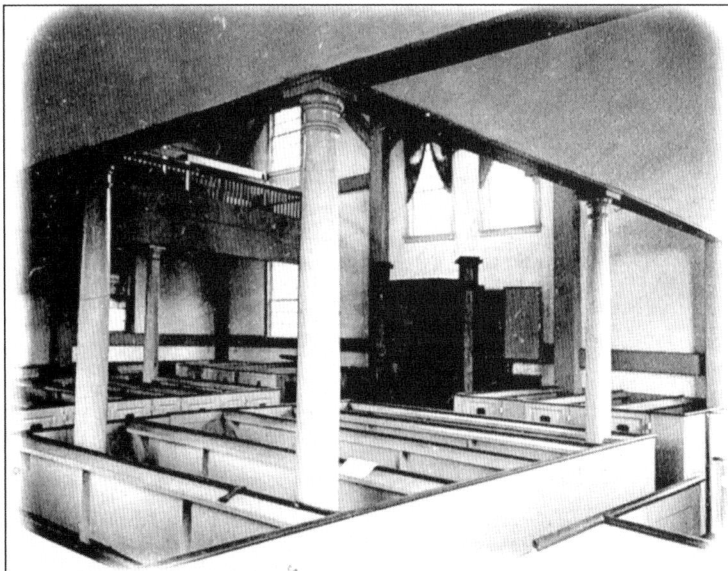

Interior of Old Church, erected 1707. Wickford, R. I.

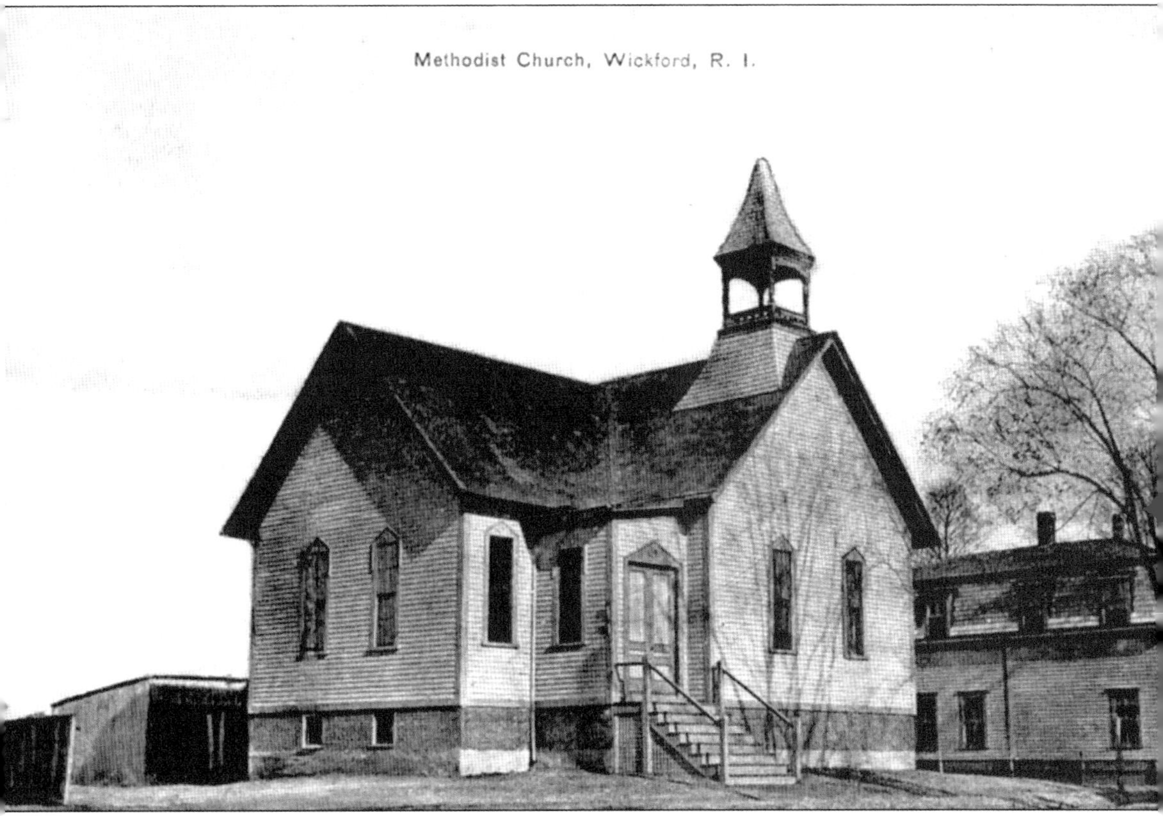

This postcard shows the Wickford Methodist Episcopal Church in its prime. After the congregation dwindled and the church closed, it was subsequently utilized as an ambulance barn and later a commercial building. The Merithew house, which has now also been converted for commercial use, can be seen on the far right.

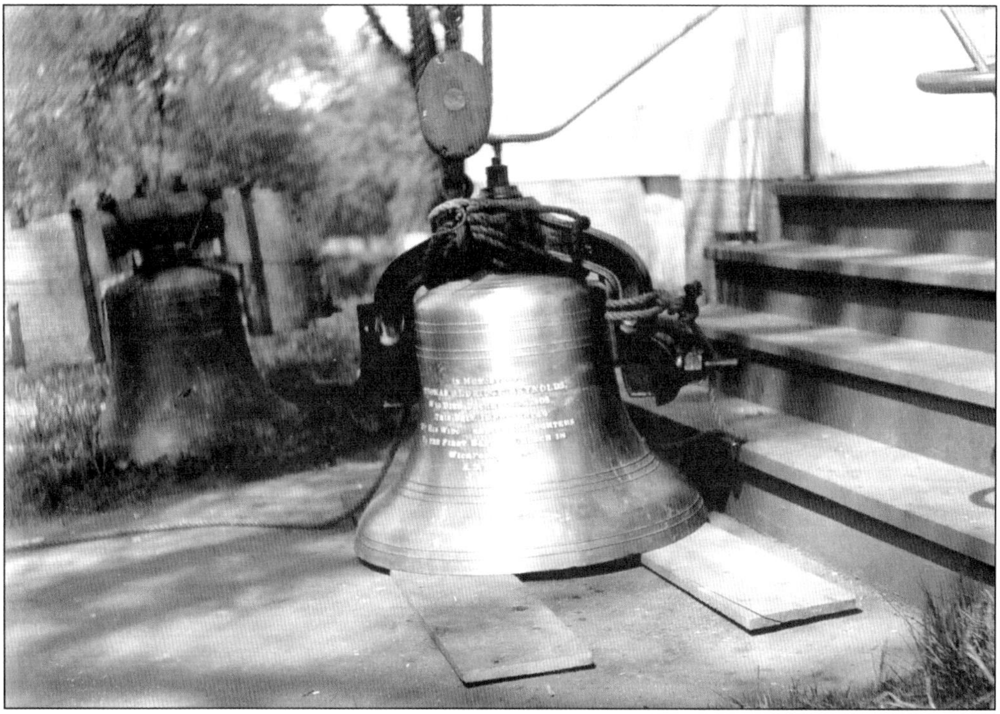

These photographs chronicle the installment of a new memorial bell in the tower of the Wickford Baptist Church. The bell was donated in memory of Thomas A. Reynolds by his family. The old bell can be seen in the background of the photograph above. Doc Young took these pictures in 1908, and nearly 100 years later the bell still rings clear and true.

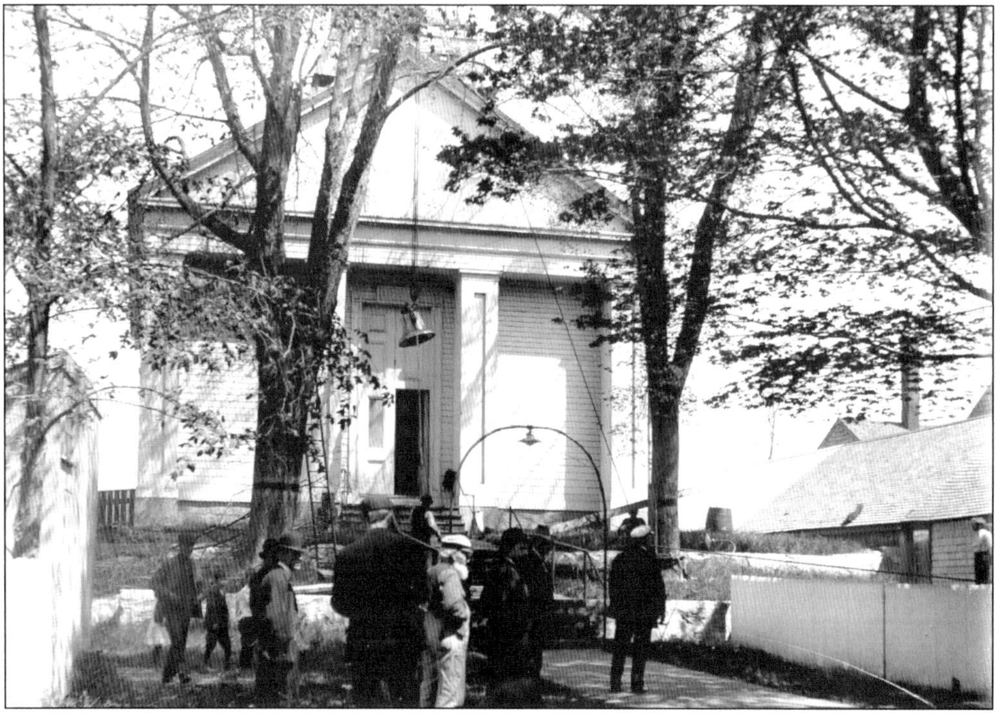

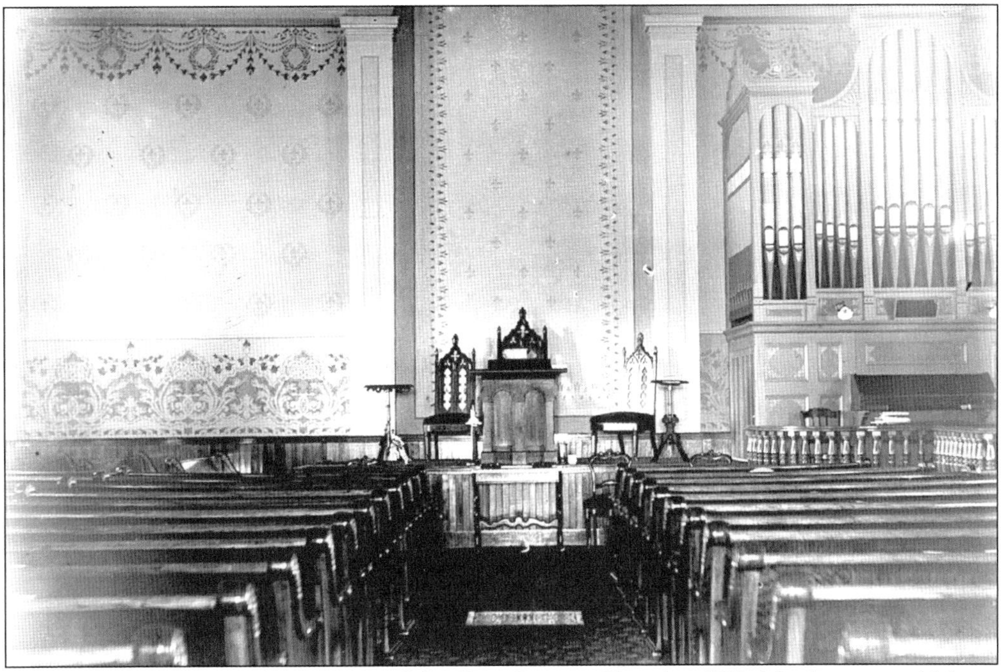

These two views show the interior of the First Baptist Church of Wickford as it would have appeared more than 100 years ago. The photograph above showcases the wonderful hand-stenciled embellishments on the walls, and the photograph below shows the meeting house decked out for the holiday season.

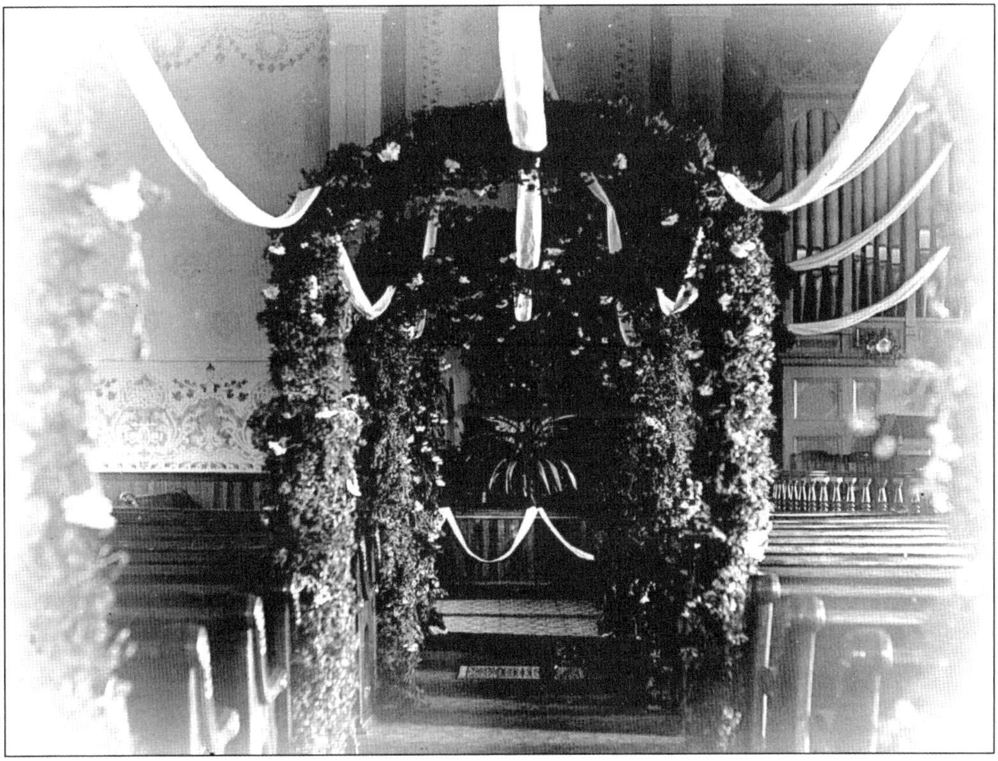

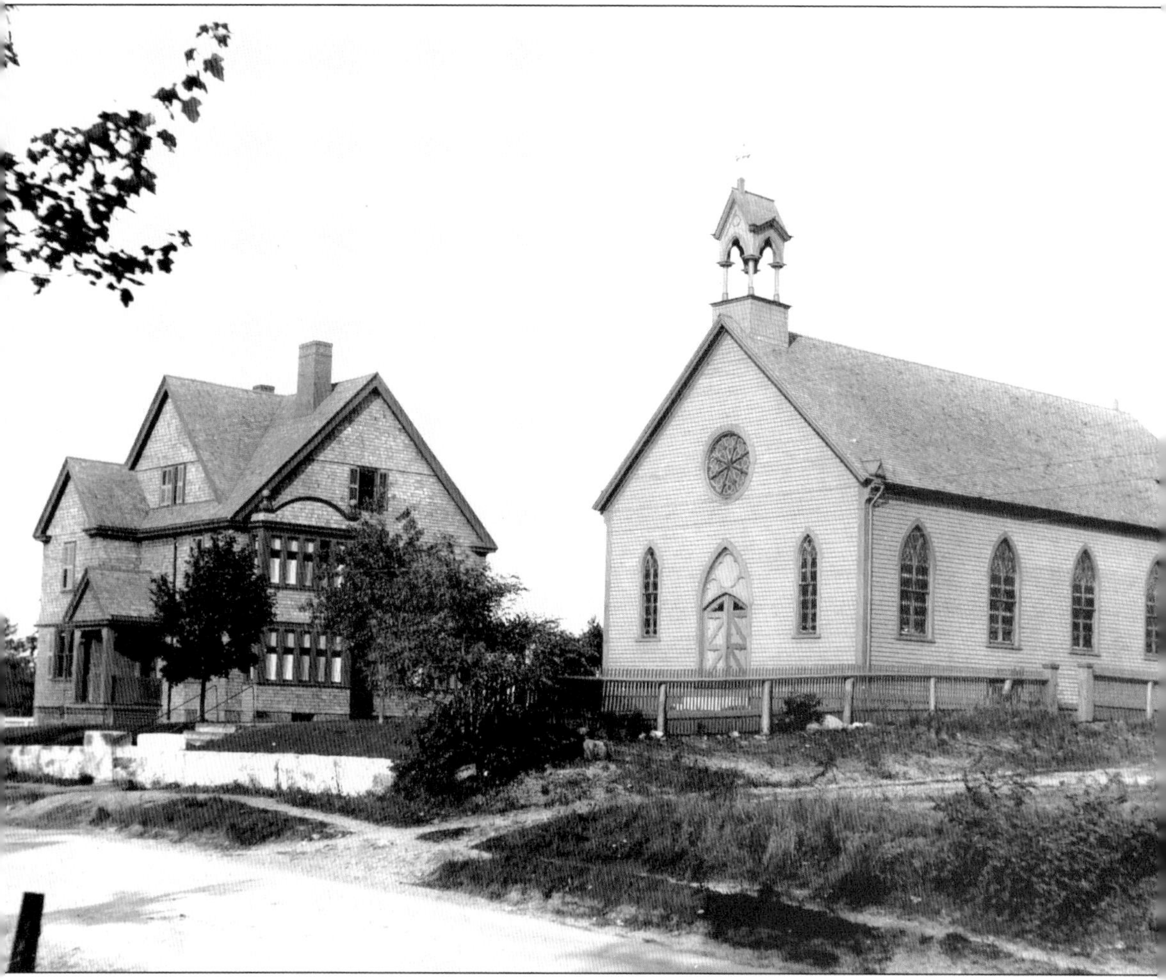

St. Bernard's Catholic Church was located on what was then called Boston Post Road (now Tower Hill Road) between Wickford and Belleville. The location was no coincidence, as it was chosen due to its proximity to the Belleville Station on the Newport and Wickford line and to the textile mills of Belleville, Shady Lea, Silver Spring, Annaquatucket, and Hamilton. The church was originally served by a priest from East Greenwich who would take the train down for services. The St. Bernard's mission was opened specifically to serve the needs of the many Irish and French-Canadian immigrants who had come to North Kingstown to work in its many fabric mills.

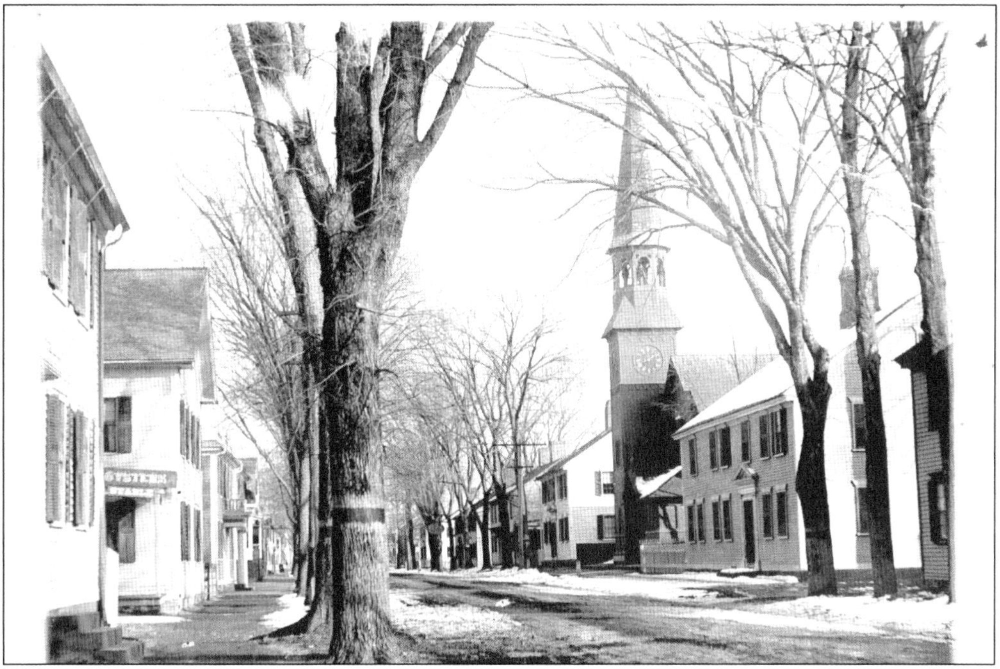

These Doc Young photographs showcase the main church of St. Paul's Episcopal Church on Main Street in Wickford. Built on two small house lots, the church building, with its clock tower and bell steeple, was the centerpiece of the village and a welcome sight for countless mariners as they approached the safety of the harbor. The photograph below showcases the interior of the church, which is little changed today.

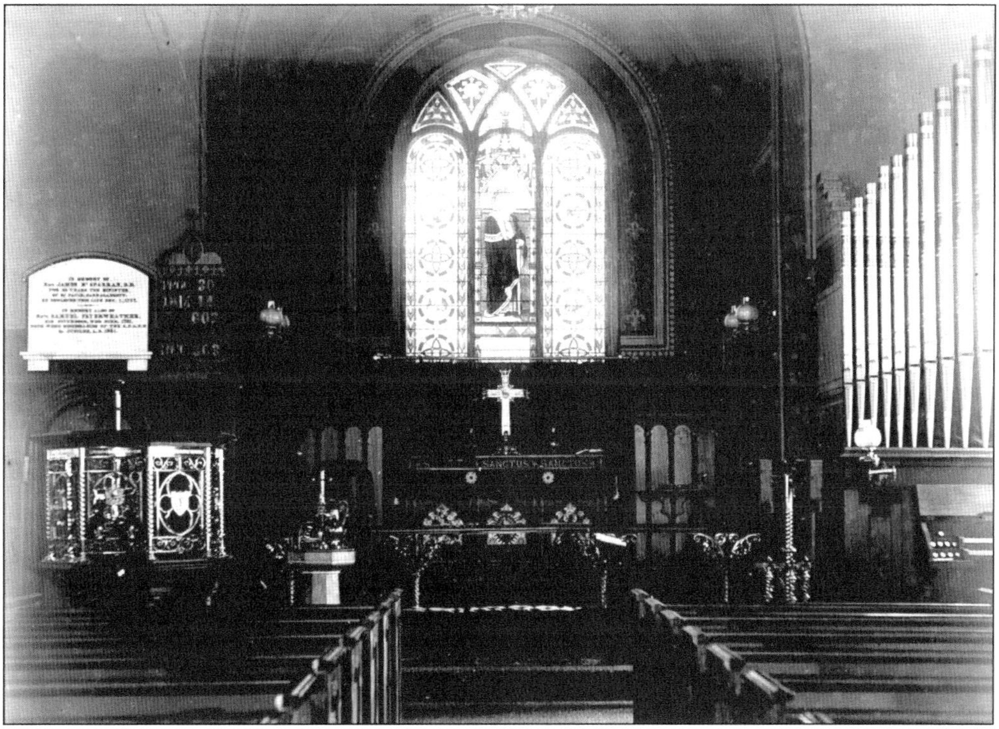

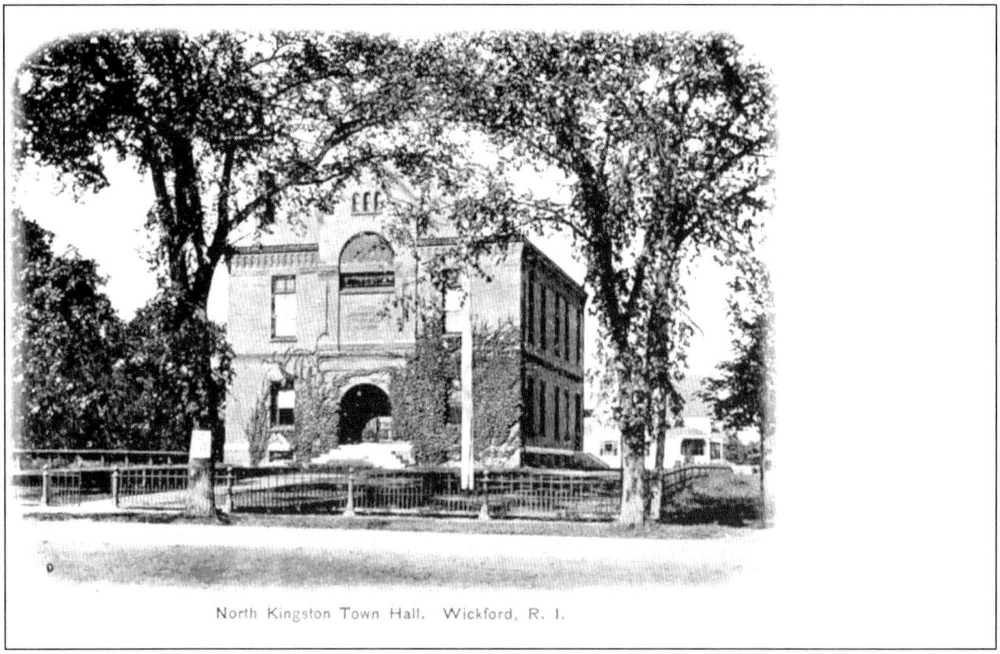

The stately North Kingstown Town Hall is shown in this Sealey's drugstore postcard. Built in 1888 by a committee headed by future governor William Gregory, the lower level held the offices of the town government, and the upper floor housed a large meeting room for town council meetings. The ornate iron fence circling the building was donated to the scrap metal drives of World War II as a show of patriotism.

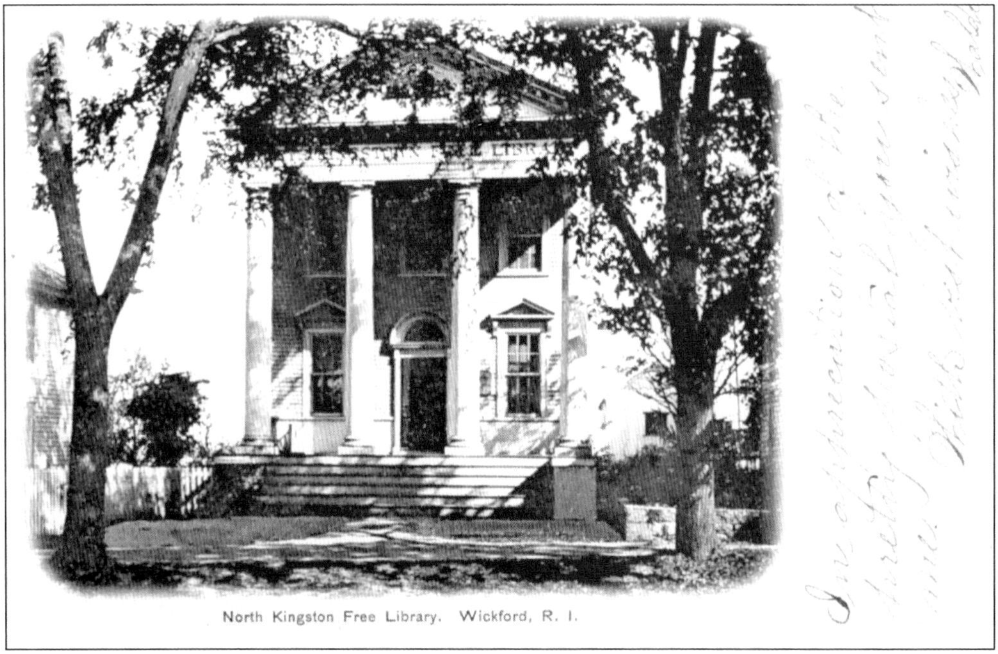

The North Kingstown Free Library was built on land donated by C. Allen Chadsey with money left specifically for that purpose from his estate. The building is still utilized by the town of North Kingstown and serves as a town hall annex building.

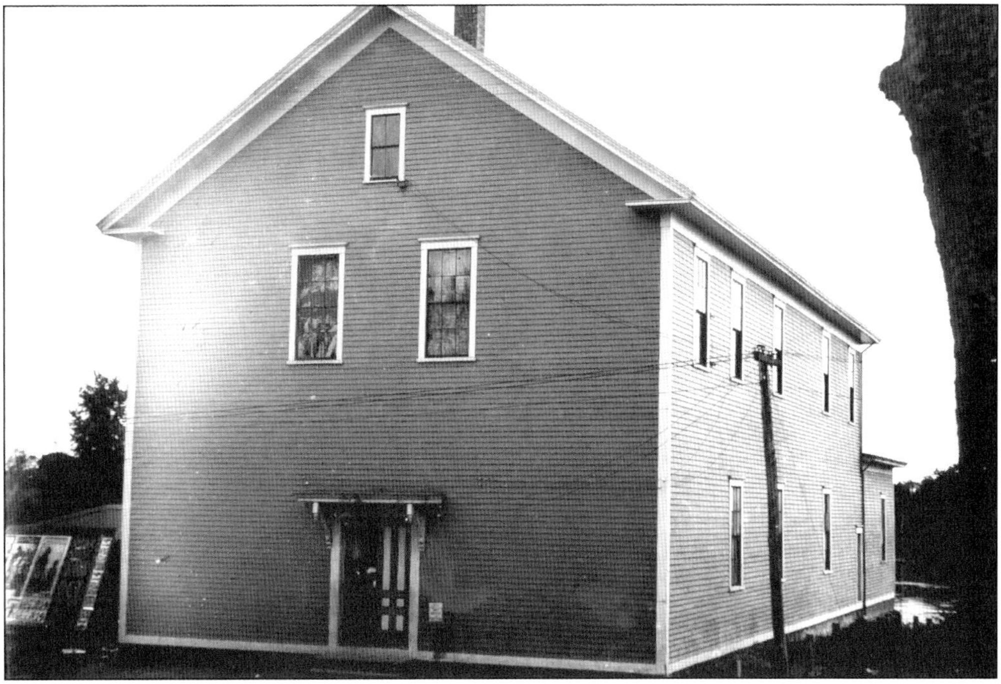

These two photographs showcase the same building some 105 years apart. The Odd Fellows Hall was constructed by a consortium of civic groups, including the Odd Fellows, the Masons, the Redmen, and the Tall Cedars in 1884. They all used the hall for their meetings, dances, teas, and other social functions. By 1895, it was used solely by the Odd Fellows, who rented it out to the school department for assemblies, graduations, and, eventually, basketball games. After the dissolution of the local Odd Fellows chapter, the building was used as a movie theater, an auction hall, and an antique store.

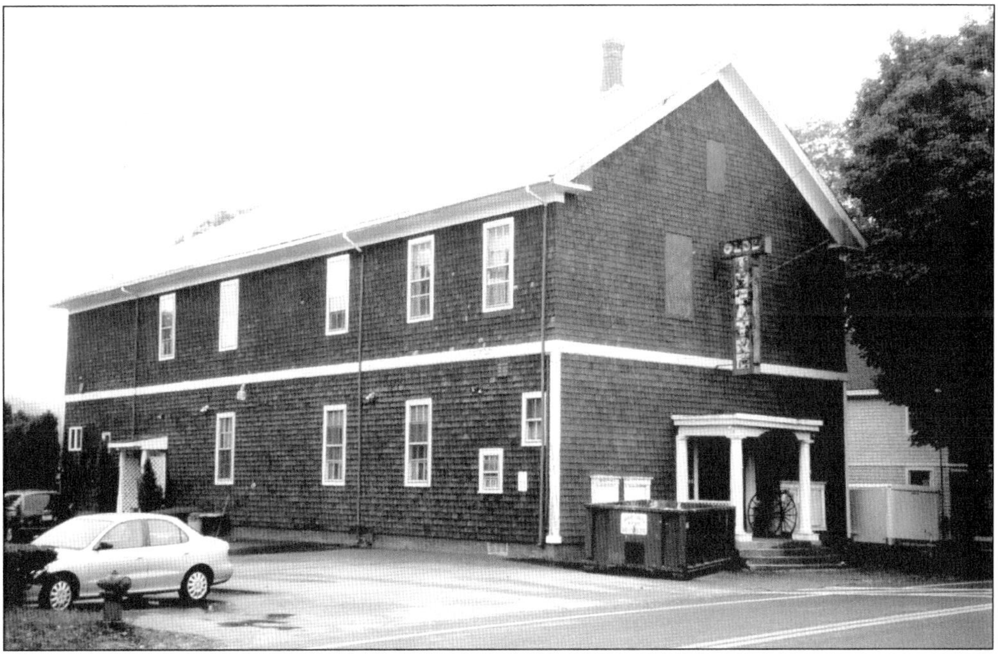

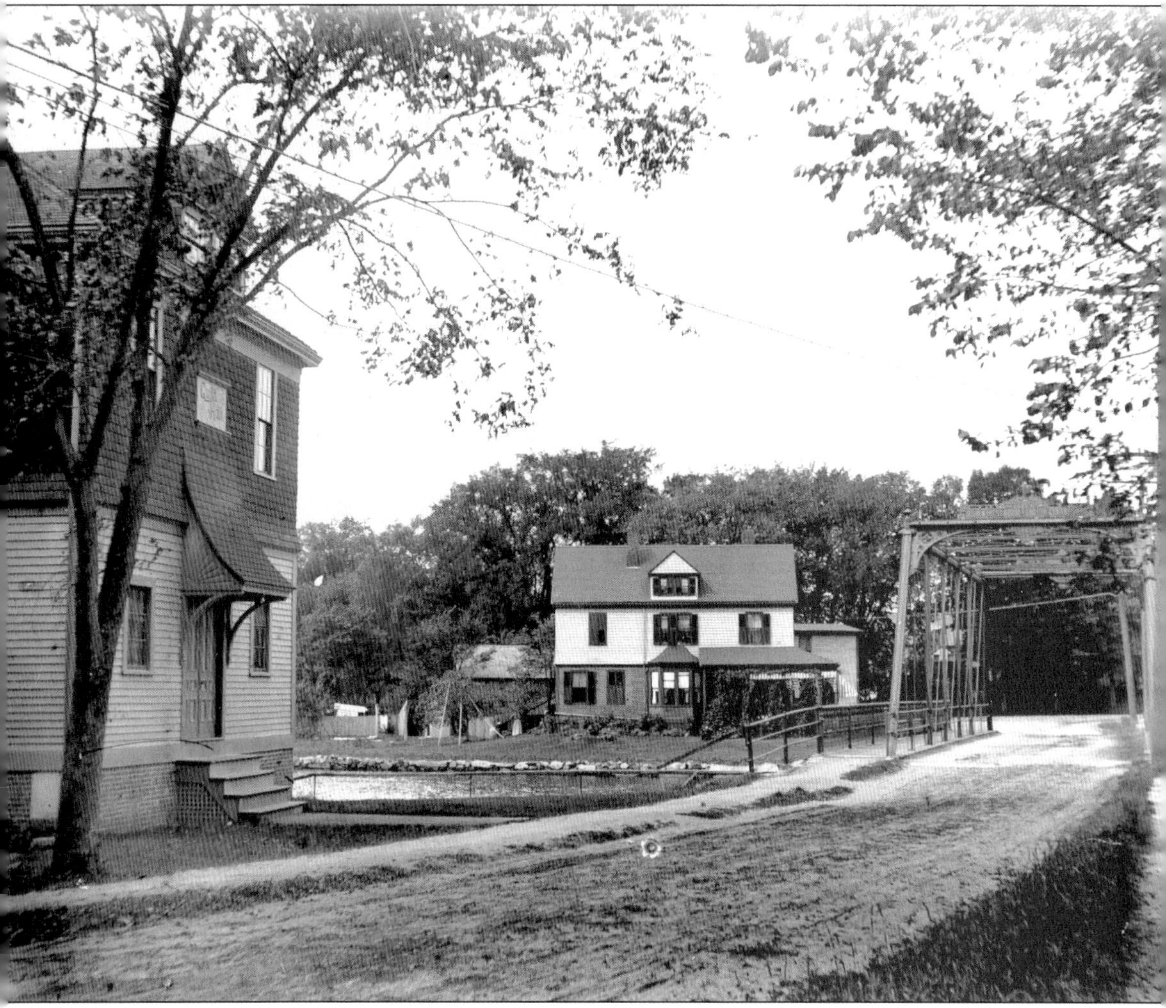

This Doc Young photograph features the St. Paul's Guild Hall, located just across the bridge from Wickford on the road to Hamilton. The guildhall was the site of many community functions in addition to being the meeting place of all the organizations associated with the church. The town library was located in this building prior to the construction of the library building in the village.

Eight

The Character of the Community

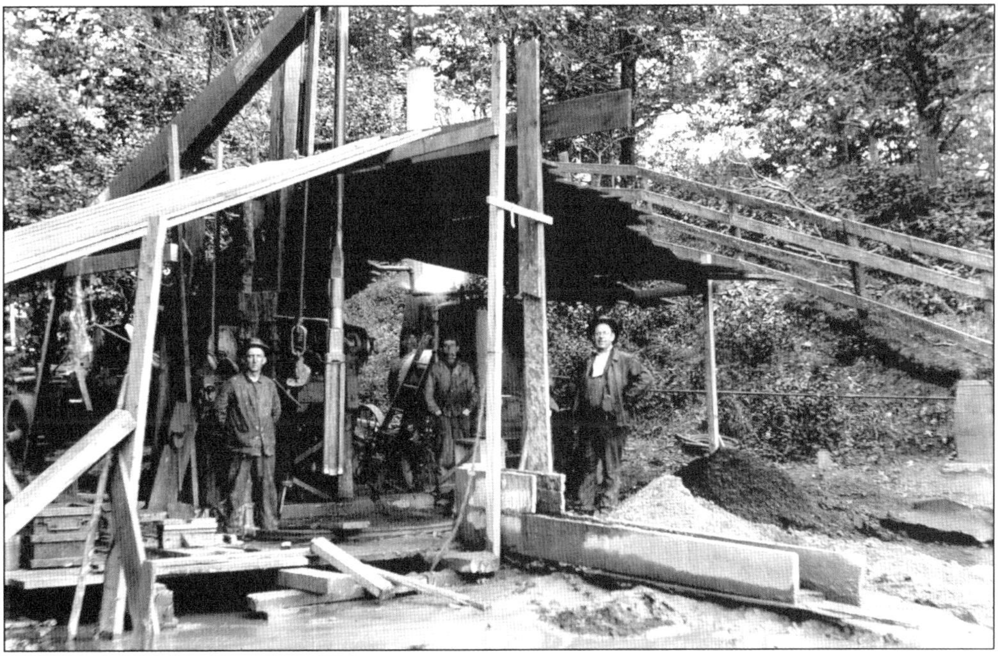

These gentlemen are busy drilling the first community well in the town of North Kingstown. This well was a private affair and serviced the summer homes of a number of the wealthy visitors who stayed there each season. The well was located on the west side of Boston Neck Road and was powered by a large windmill that was visible to sailors on the bay.

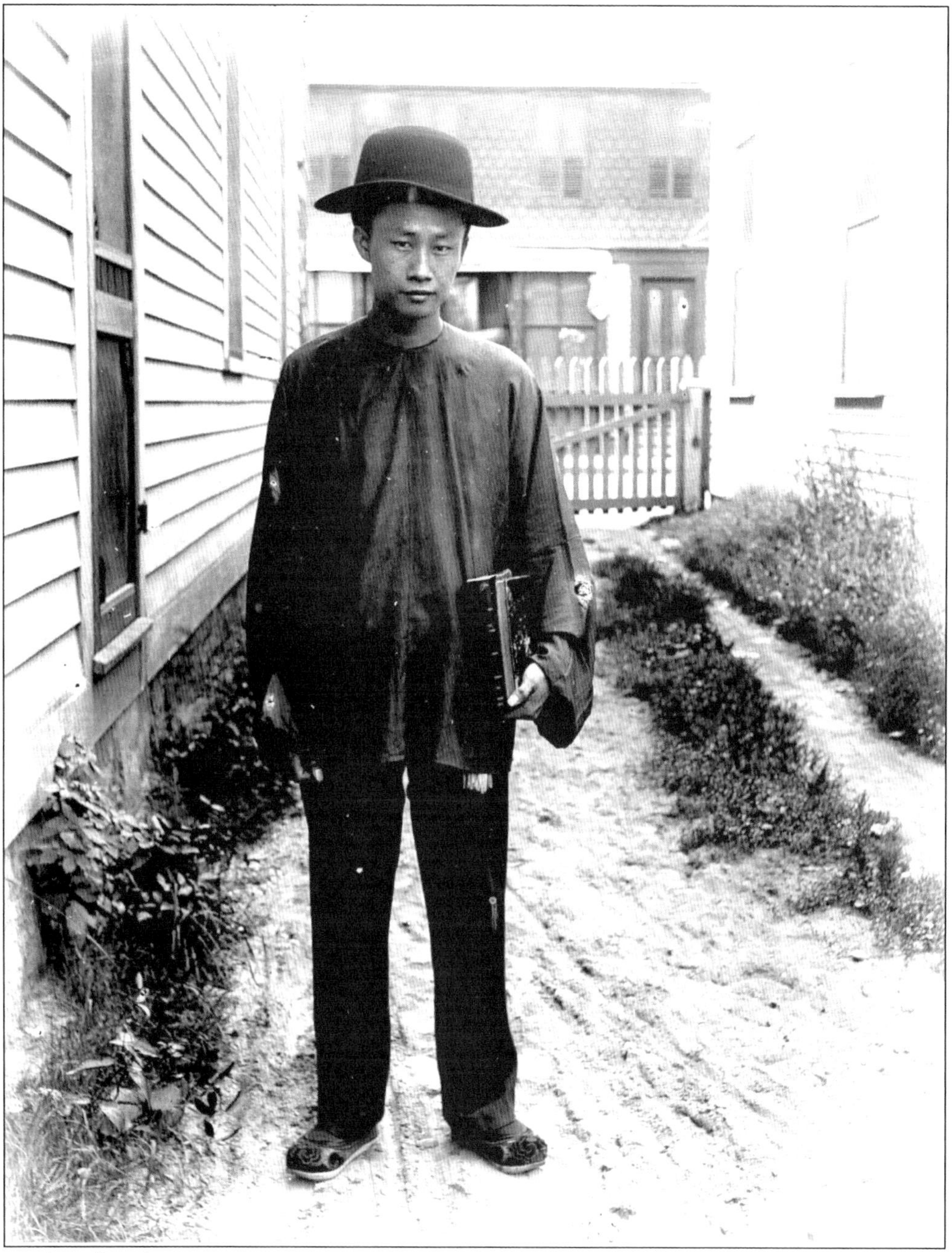

As the village became more prosperous in the first quarter of the 20th century, it attracted many different types of businesses, including a Chinese laundry housed in the building once used by Hainsworth Plumbing. The son of the laundry owner is seen here with his schoolbooks. The awning of Ryan's Market can be made out in the background.

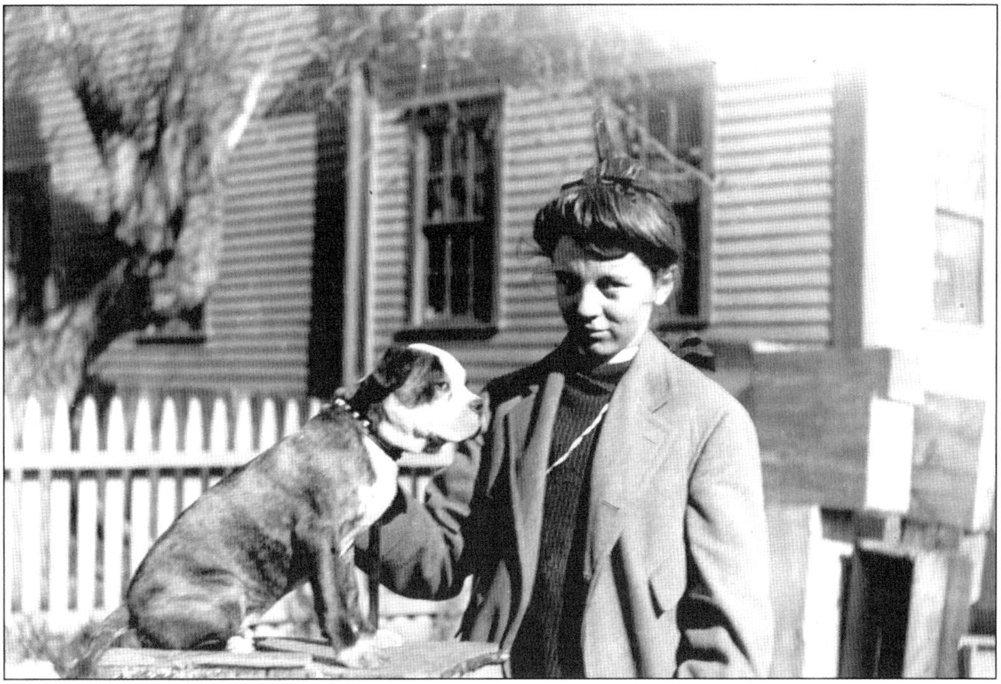

Townsfolk appear with their pets in these two photographs taken by Doc Young. The photograph below shows the effects of the breakdown of the image on its glass-plate negative. A number of the plates in the Young collection were completely ruined in this fashion.

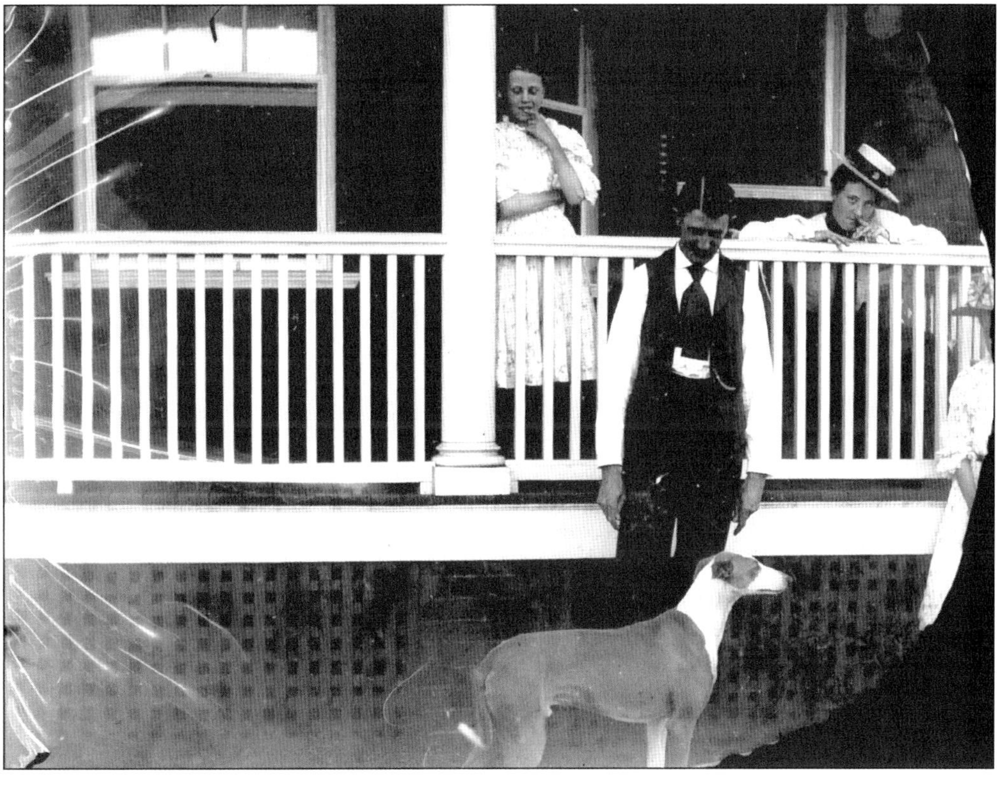

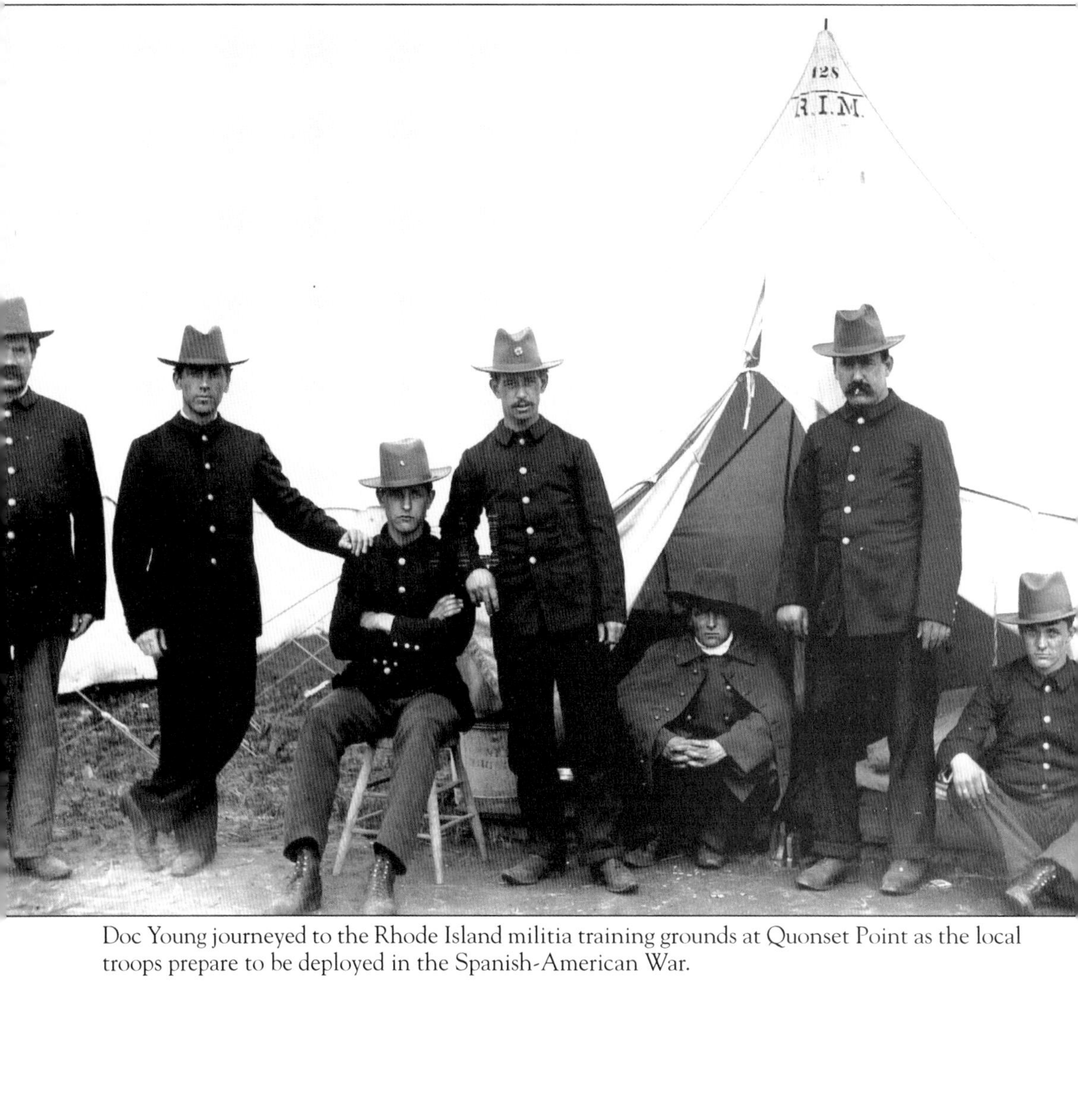

Doc Young journeyed to the Rhode Island militia training grounds at Quonset Point as the local troops prepare to be deployed in the Spanish-American War.

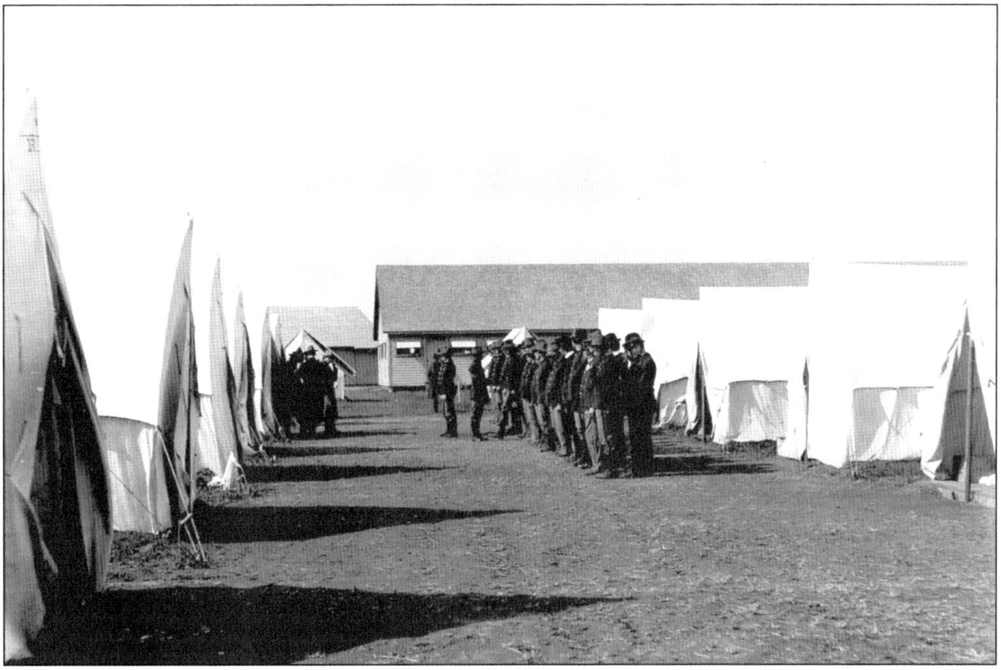

Here are more photographs taken at the Quonset Training Camp at the end of Camp Avenue in North Kingstown. The Fairman designation on the caps of the three gentleman in the photograph below indicates that they are members of the all-volunteer Fairman Marching Band, which accompanied the Rhode Island troops into battle.

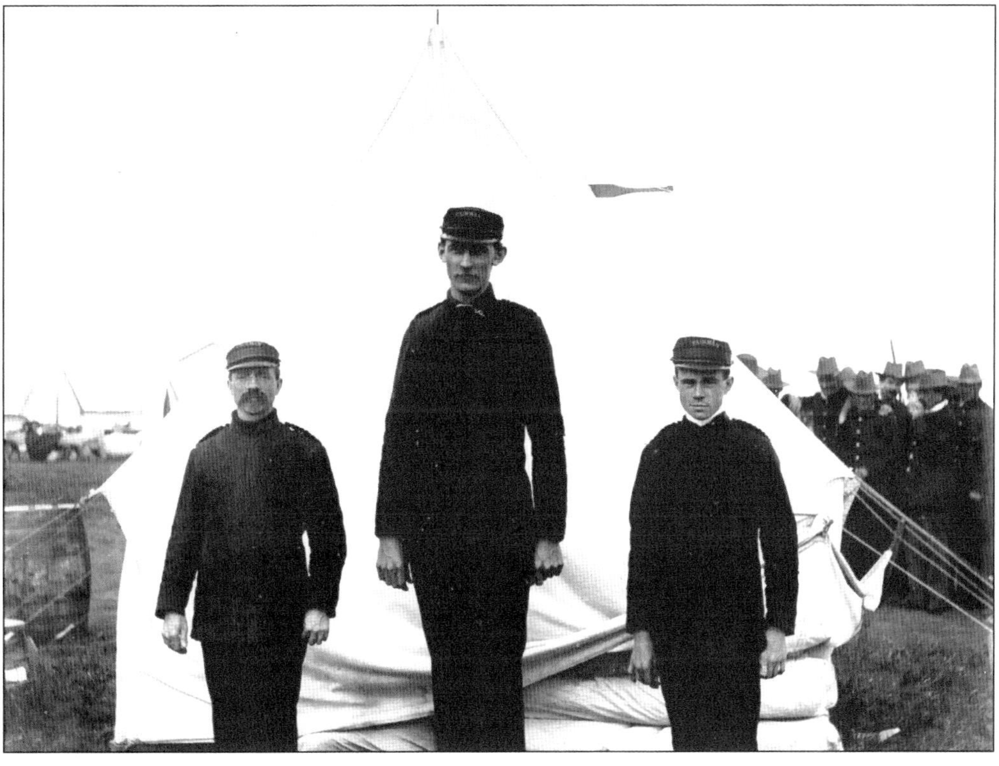

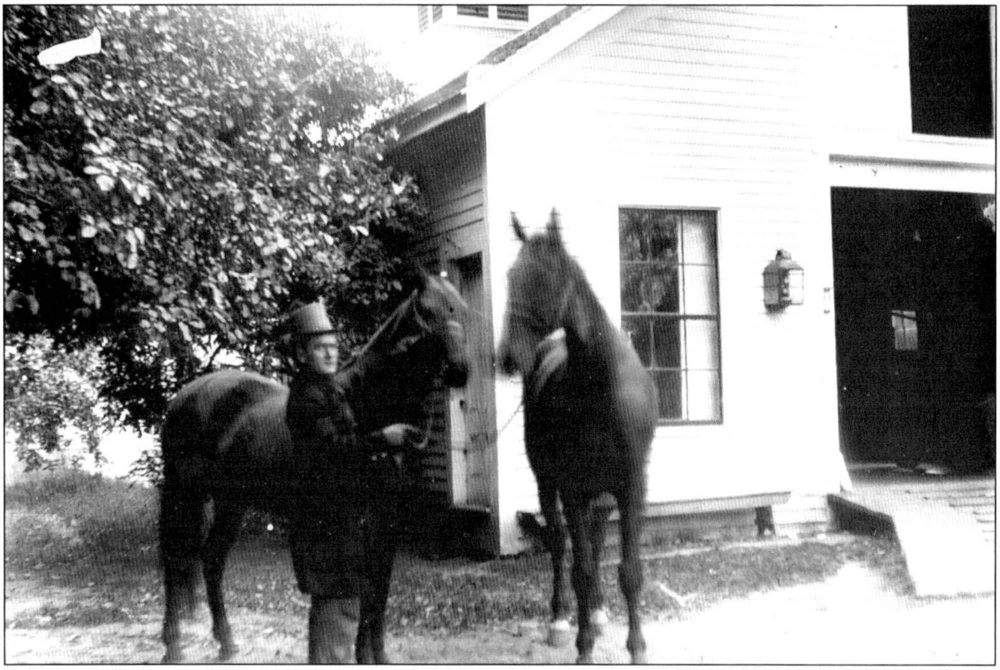

A groomsman handles a pair of horses. This gentleman was probably a local who worked for a wealthy summer resident.

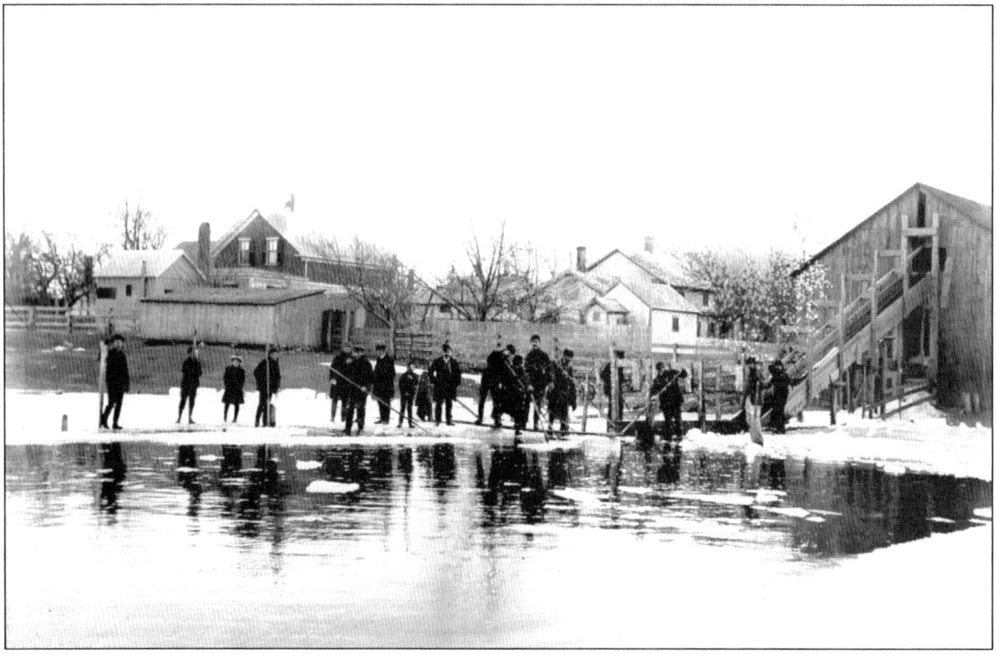

Men are busy cutting ice on Bush Hill Pond off of Fowler Street in Wickford and storing it for later use in the adjacent icehouse. Tightly packed in sawdust, the ice would last well into the summer. With North Kingstown's many millponds, the ice business was big business, and there were as many as a dozen icehouses across the community.

This portrait of a child wearing her father's hat is one of Doc Young's most affecting photographs. The identity of the child is unknown.

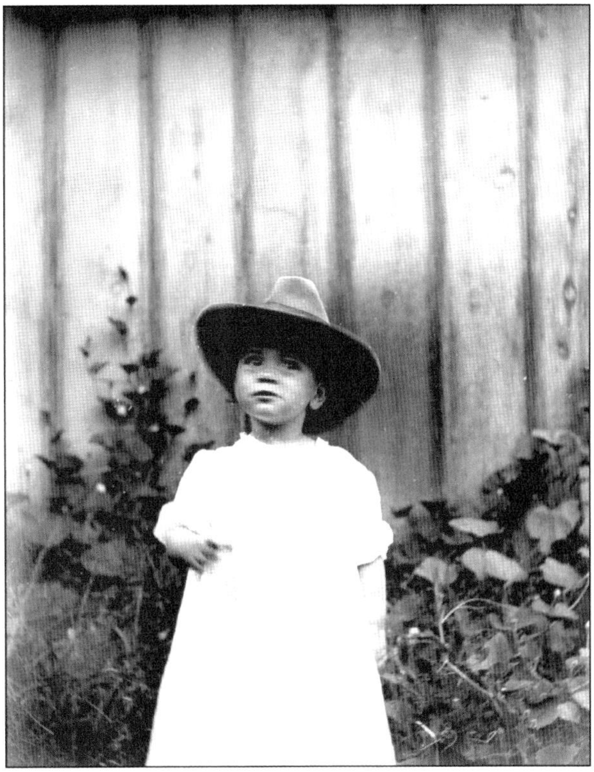

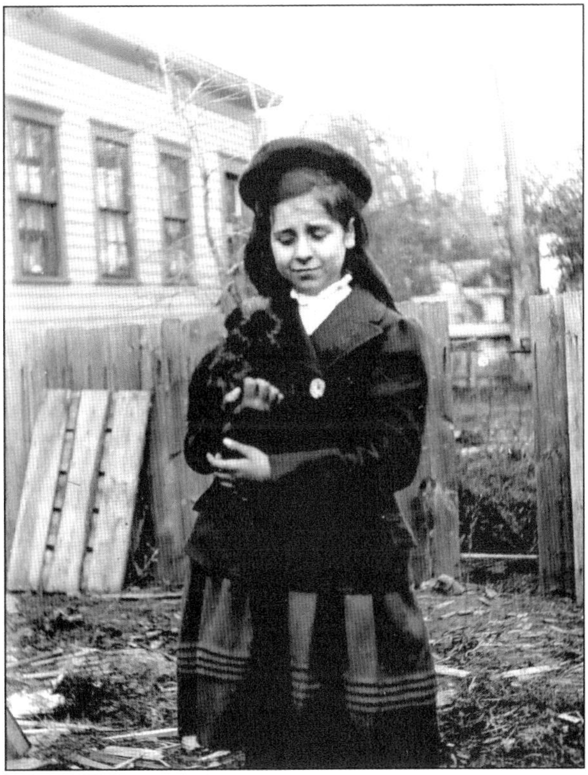

Young Ethel Hainsworth holds her new puppy. The steeple of St. Paul's Episcopal Church can be seen in the background.

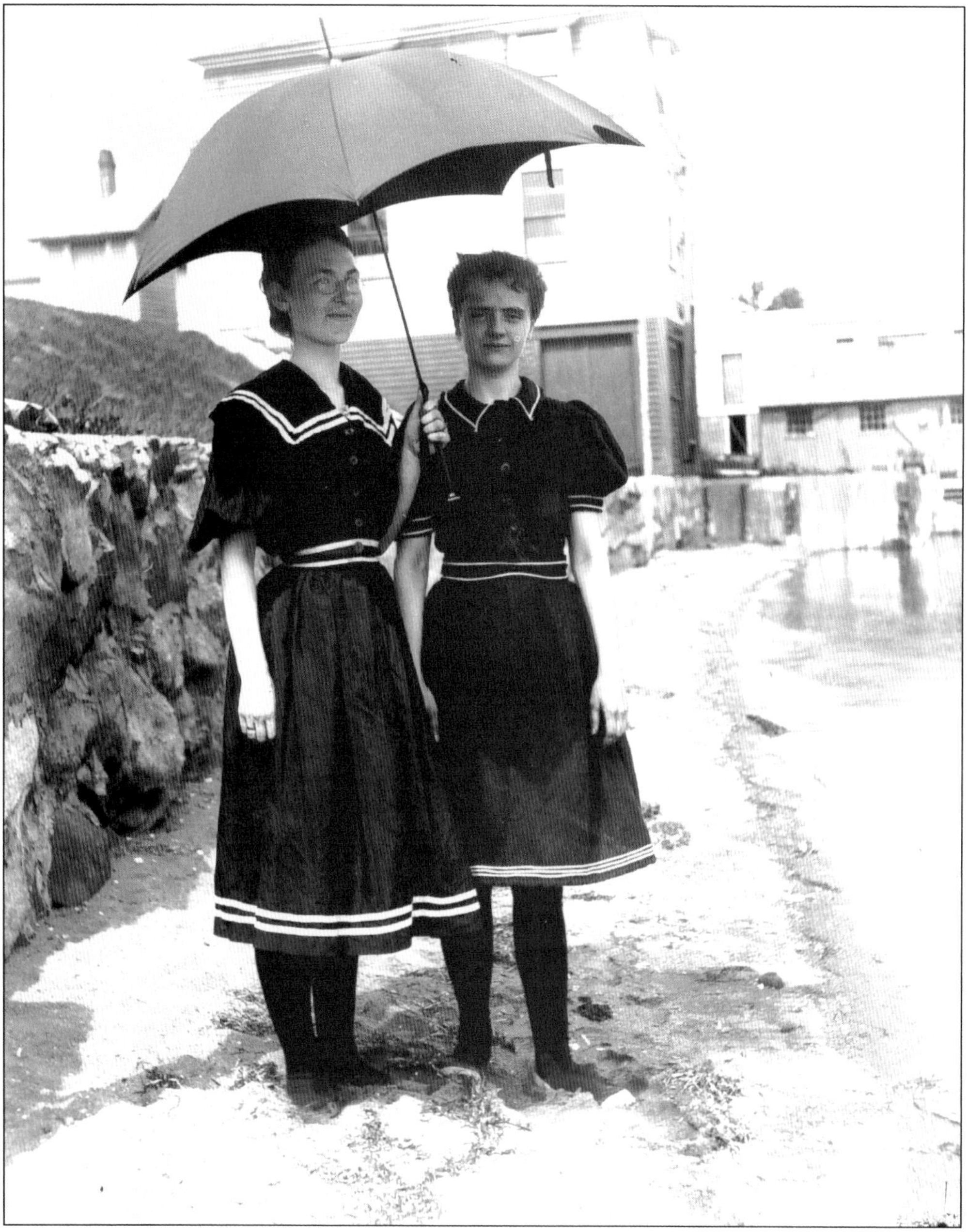

Two Wickford bathing beauties prepare for a day at the beach. Modesty in dress was still very prevalent in the 1880s as these swimsuits attest.

An unidentified, dapper gentleman mugs for Doc Young's camera.

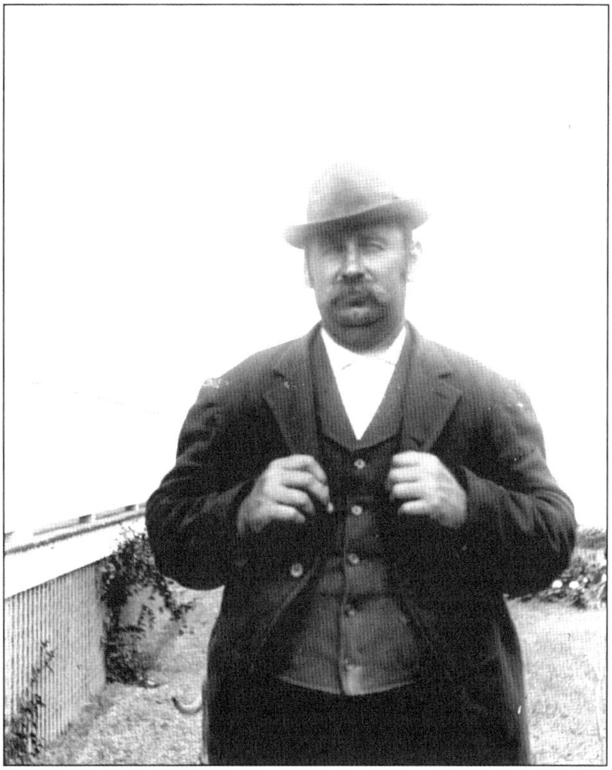

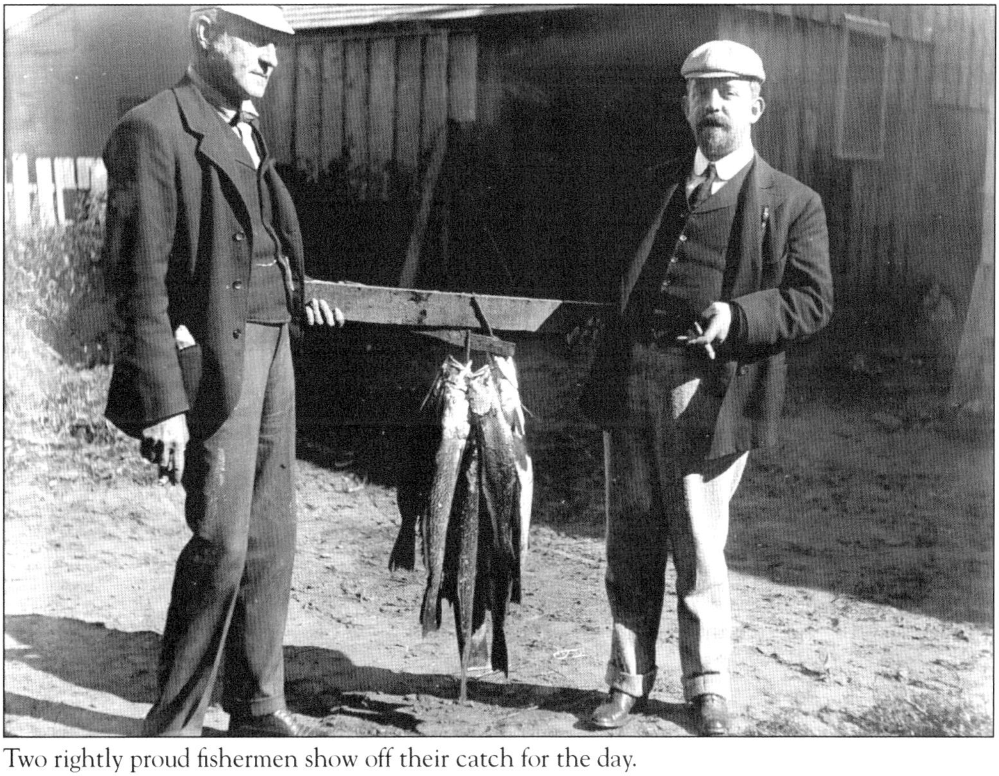

Two rightly proud fishermen show off their catch for the day.

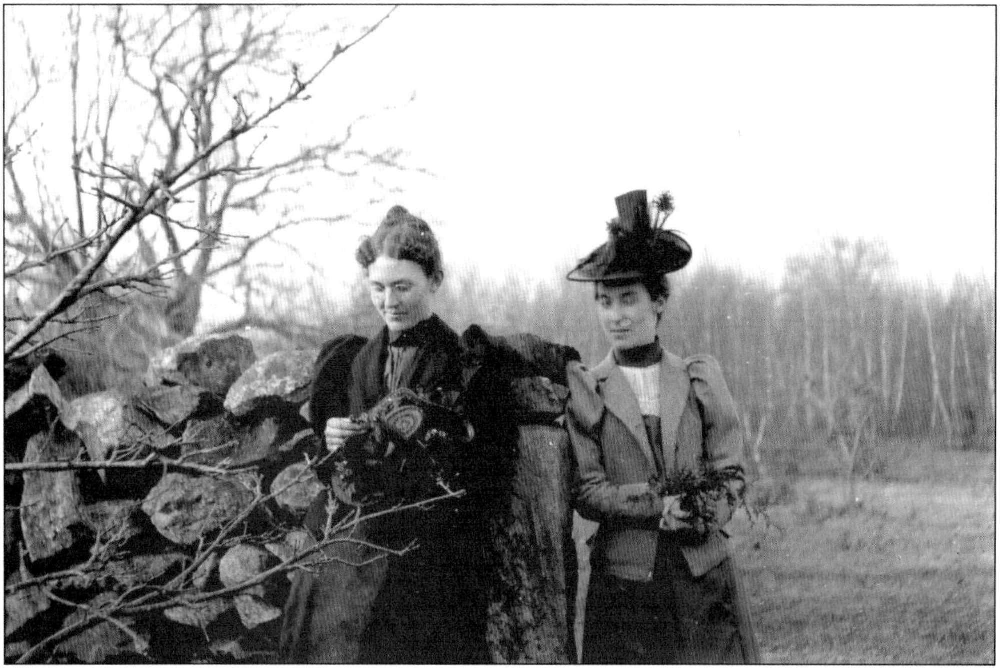

Another earmark of the 1890s was elaborate ladies' hats. In this photograph, two women of North Kingstown show off their stylish bonnets.

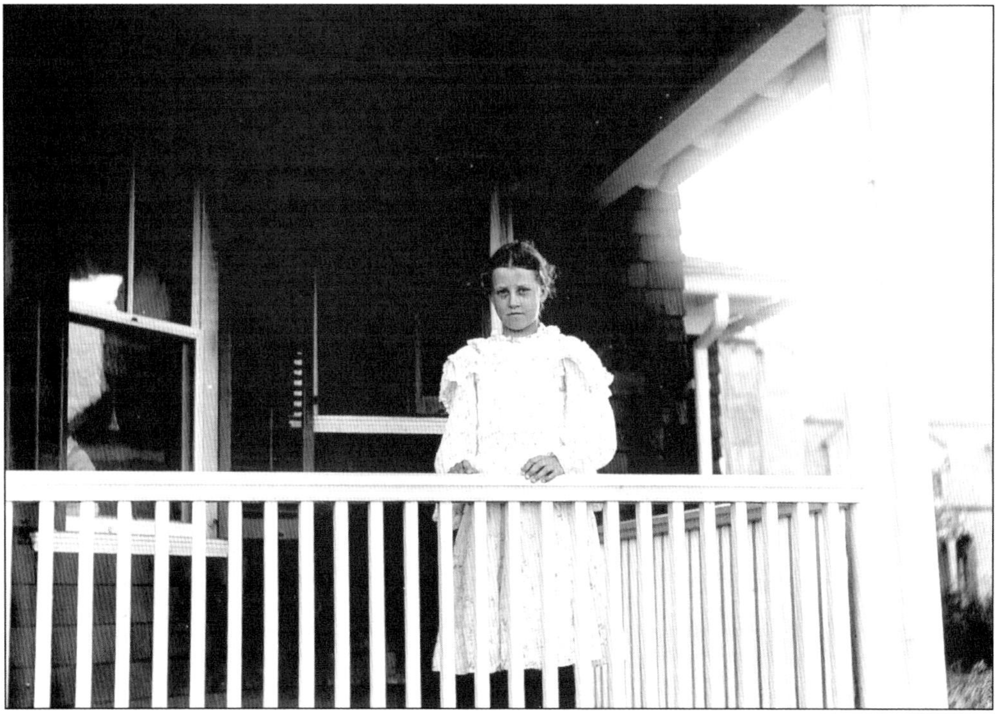

This young girl stands on the back porch of Doc and Mamie Young's home in her Sunday best. She may have been a relation to the Youngs.

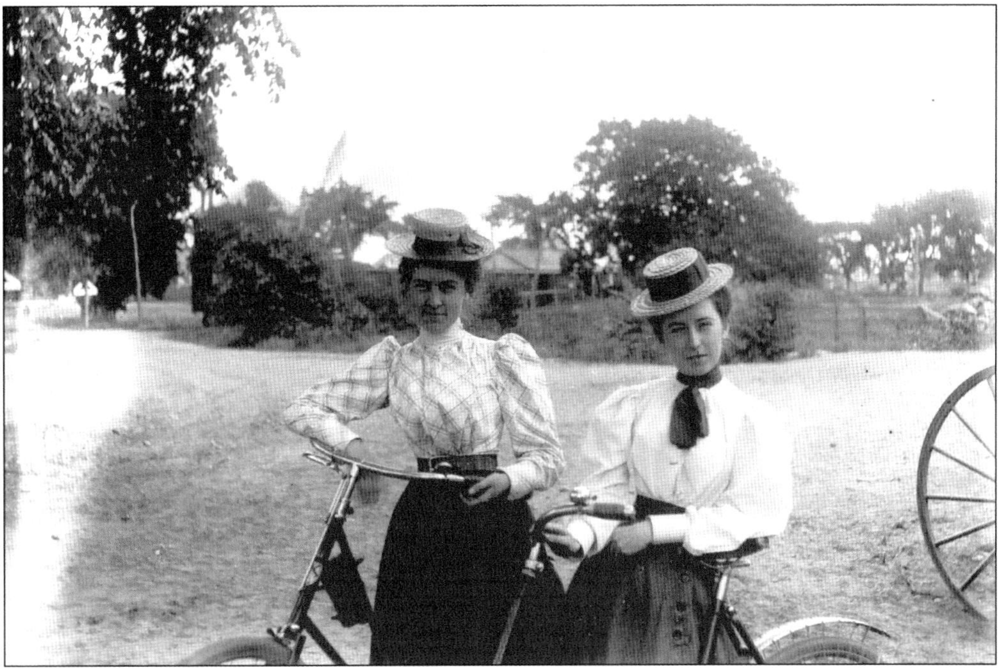

Bicycling on a summer's day was a popular pastime during the last quarter of the 19th century. Here two women show off their riding outfits.

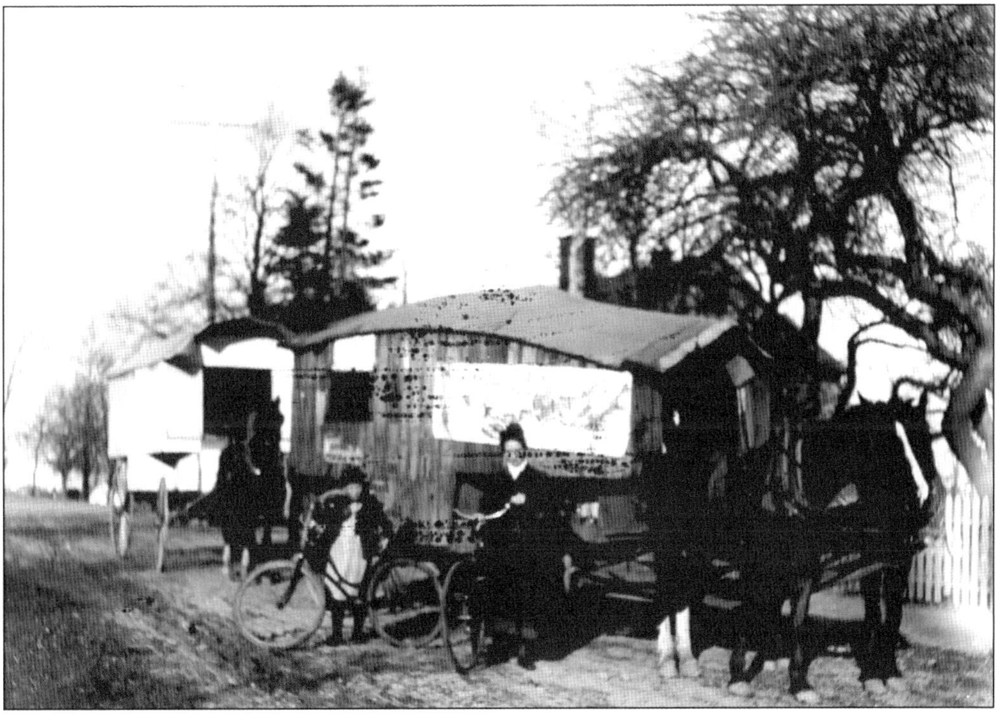

Two locals on bicycles survey the wagons of a group of Gypsies traveling through town in this photograph taken at the top of Phillips Street in an area known as Collation Corner.

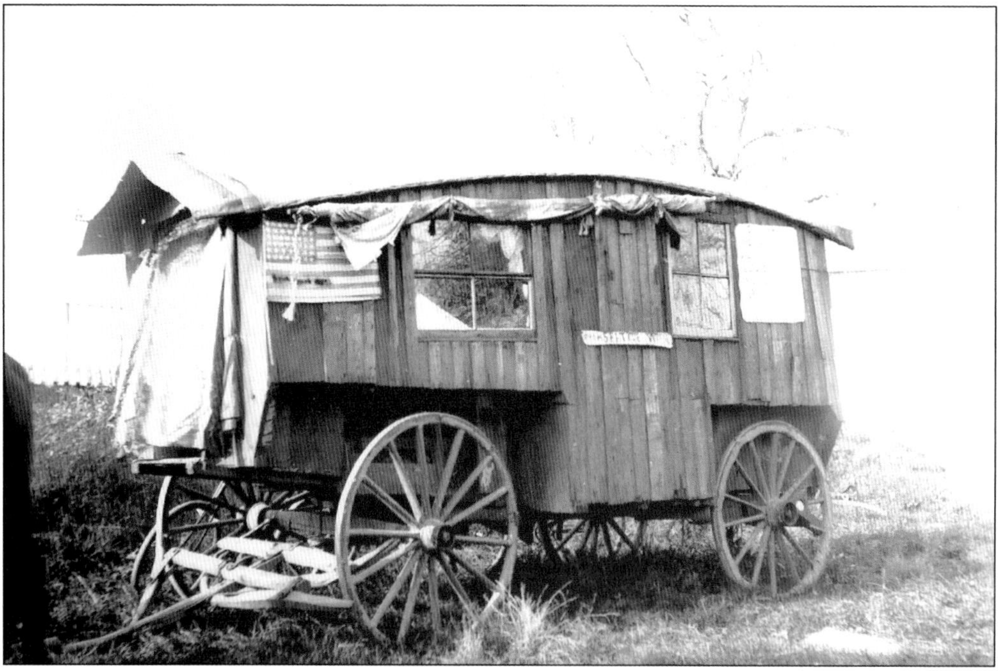

Two more views of the Gypsy wagons are featured in these photographs. The sign on the top wagon tells of a book they are selling that details the escapades of their purported journey across the country from Seattle, Washington.

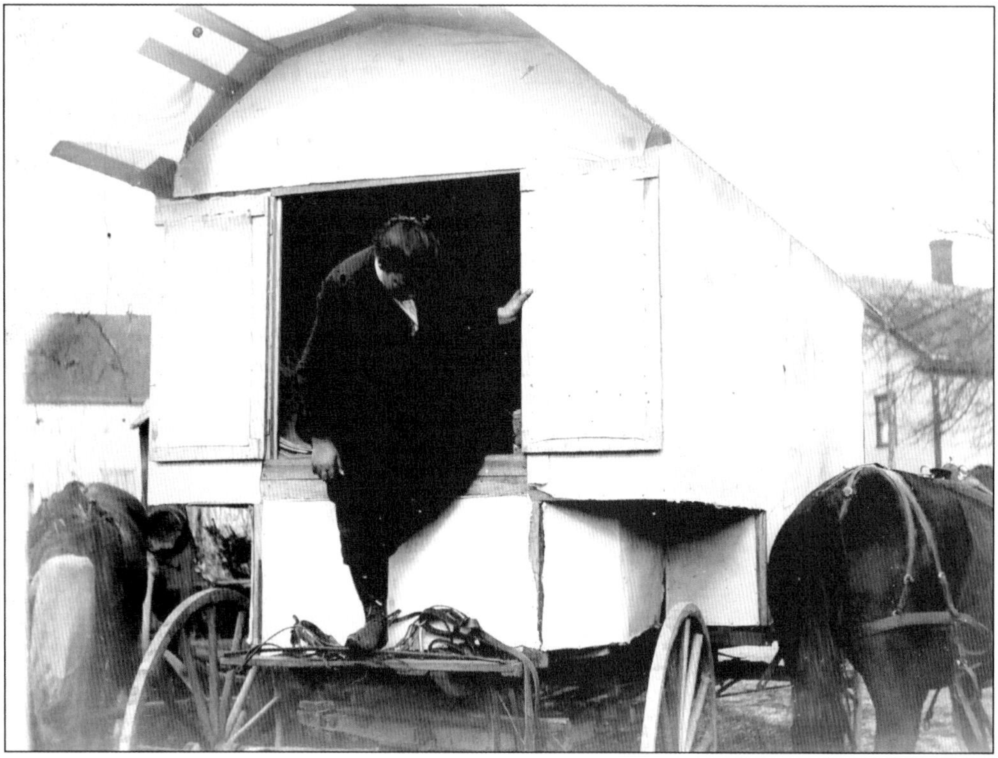

Nine

North Kingstown Homes

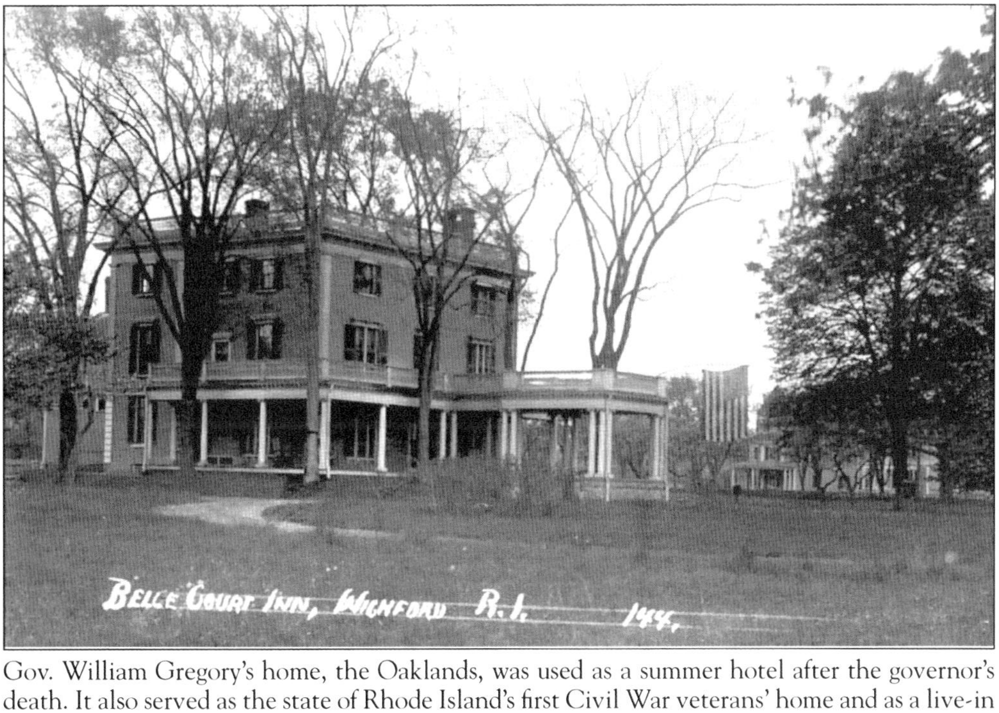

Gov. William Gregory's home, the Oaklands, was used as a summer hotel after the governor's death. It also served as the state of Rhode Island's first Civil War veterans' home and as a live-in school for the deaf. It was nearly destroyed in a fire that occurred while it served as a school and was later rebuilt without the third floor.

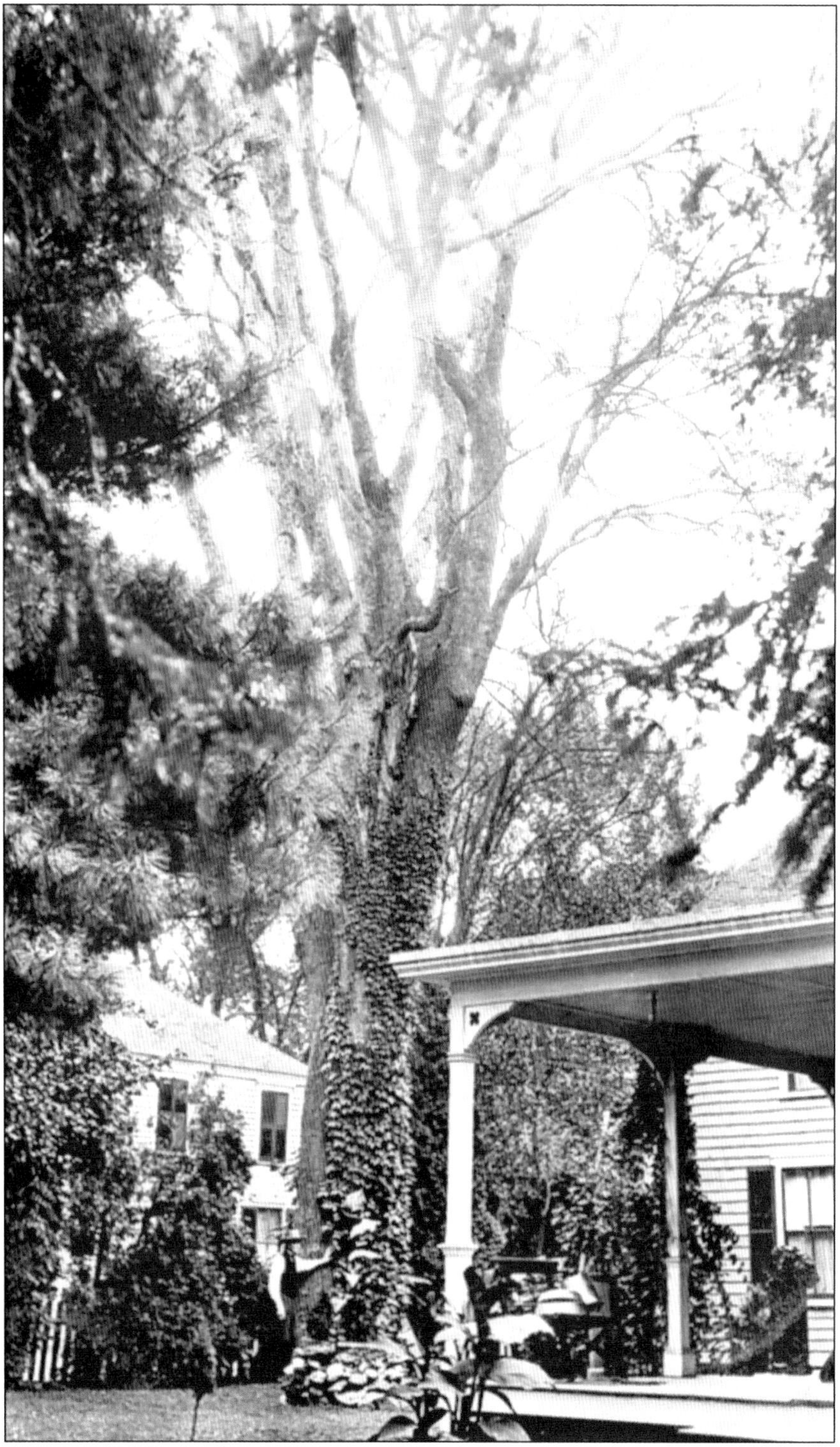

Christopher Wightman stands proudly next to one of the village's famous giant elms in the backyard of the Wightman homestead house that once stood on the corner of Main and Fowler Streets.

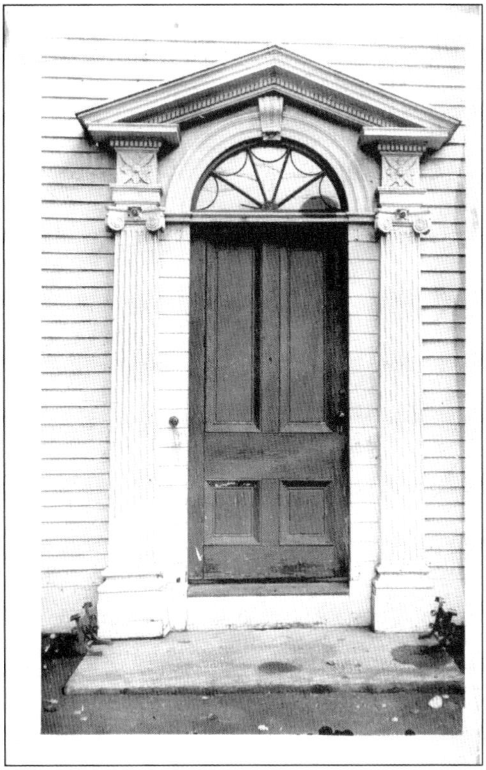

An entire series of postcards was made in the 1920s that showcased Wickford's many magnificent colonial doorways. Two of them are shown here.

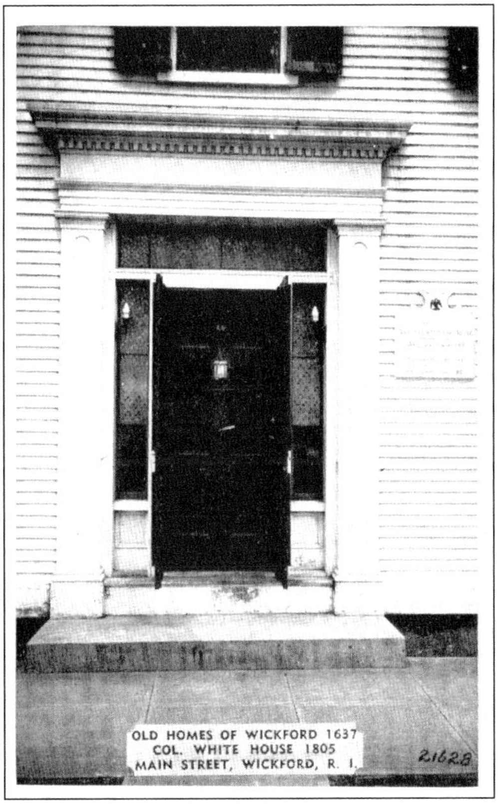

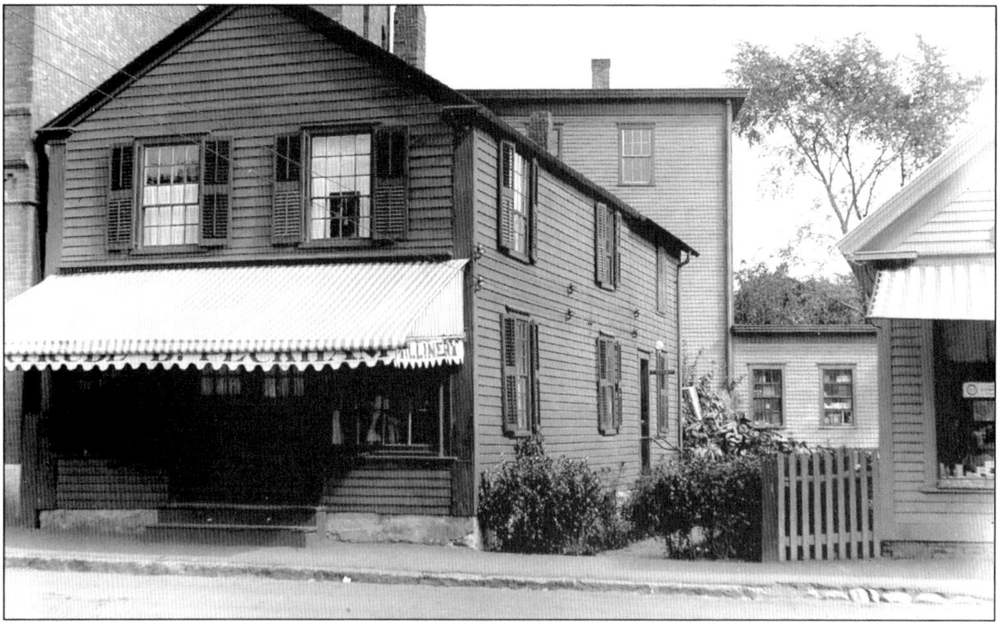

This shop, near the corner of Brown and Main Streets, houses Gertrude Peckham's Millinery Shop, where dresses were made-to-order for her discerning patrons. Upstairs is the Wickford Club, a private gentleman's club that still exists today in the same location. Jacob Turck and his family originally owned the building. Turck was a German immigrant shoemaker who settled here and became an integral part of the community.

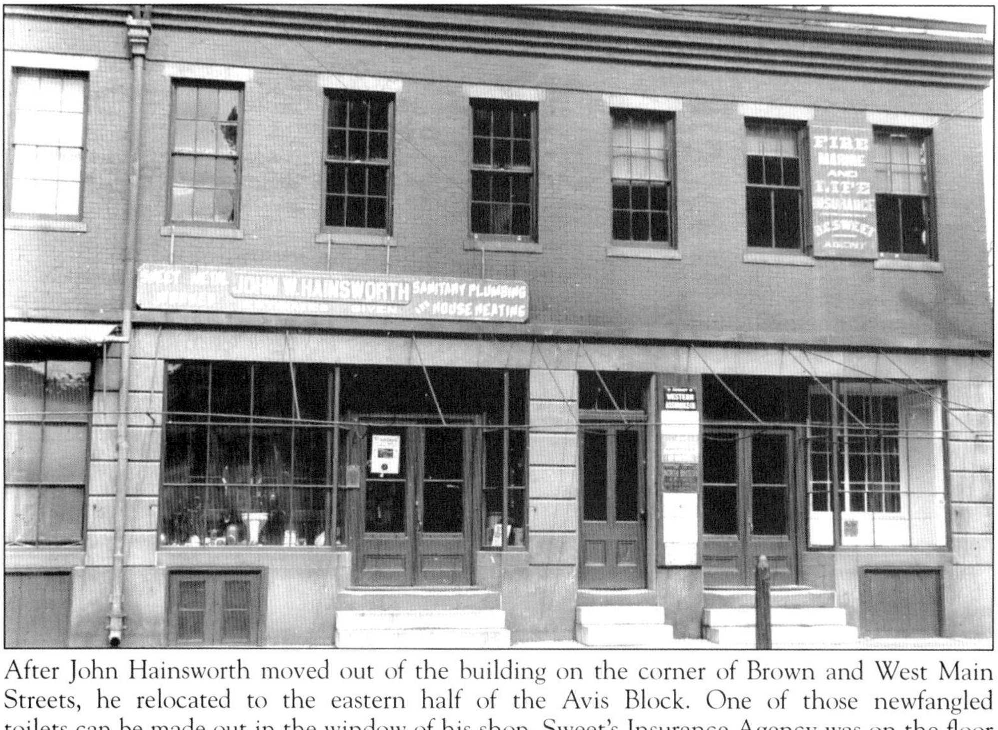

After John Hainsworth moved out of the building on the corner of Brown and West Main Streets, he relocated to the eastern half of the Avis Block. One of those newfangled toilets can be made out in the window of his shop. Sweet's Insurance Agency was on the floor above Hainsworth.

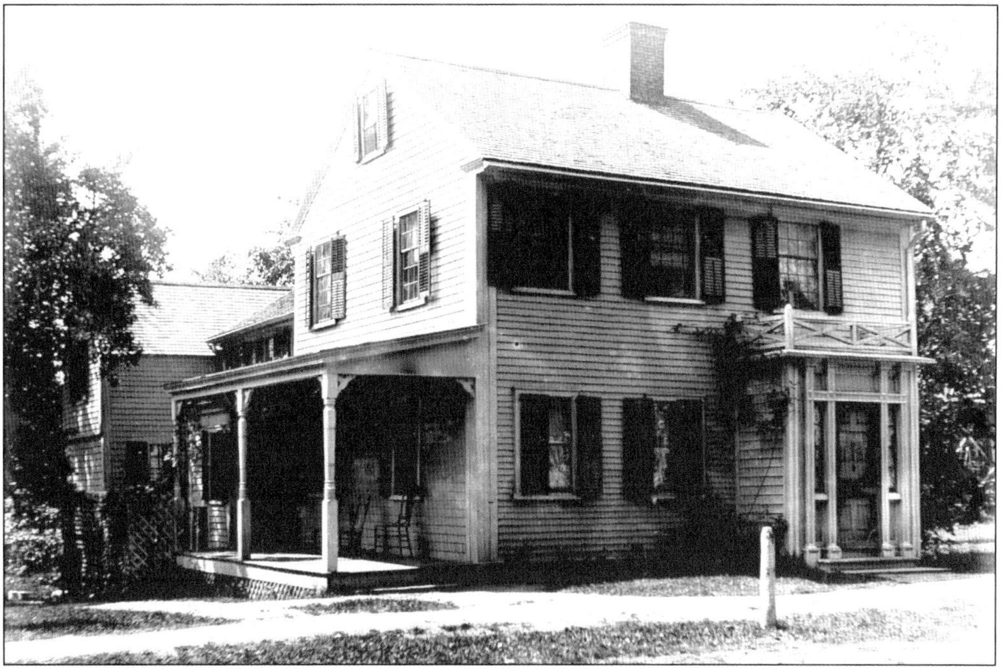

The oldest home in the Quality Hill section of the village, this house was originally built by the Spink family. During its early years, a hatmaker's shop was located here.

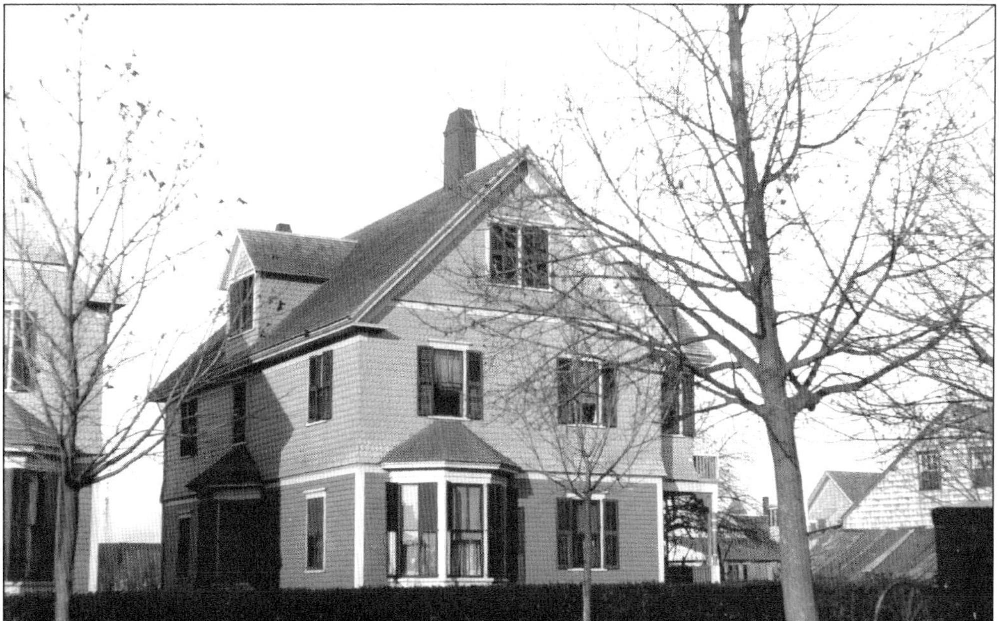

In this photograph, one of the Lewis brothers's houses on Bay Street can be seen. Just visible to the left is another Lewis brother house that is the mirror image of this one. Frugal Yankees to the core, the two fisherman brothers split the price of one set of plans. When asked why they were built with exactly the opposite configuration, the reply was, "Well I certainly don't want my brother to always know who I've got visiting me."

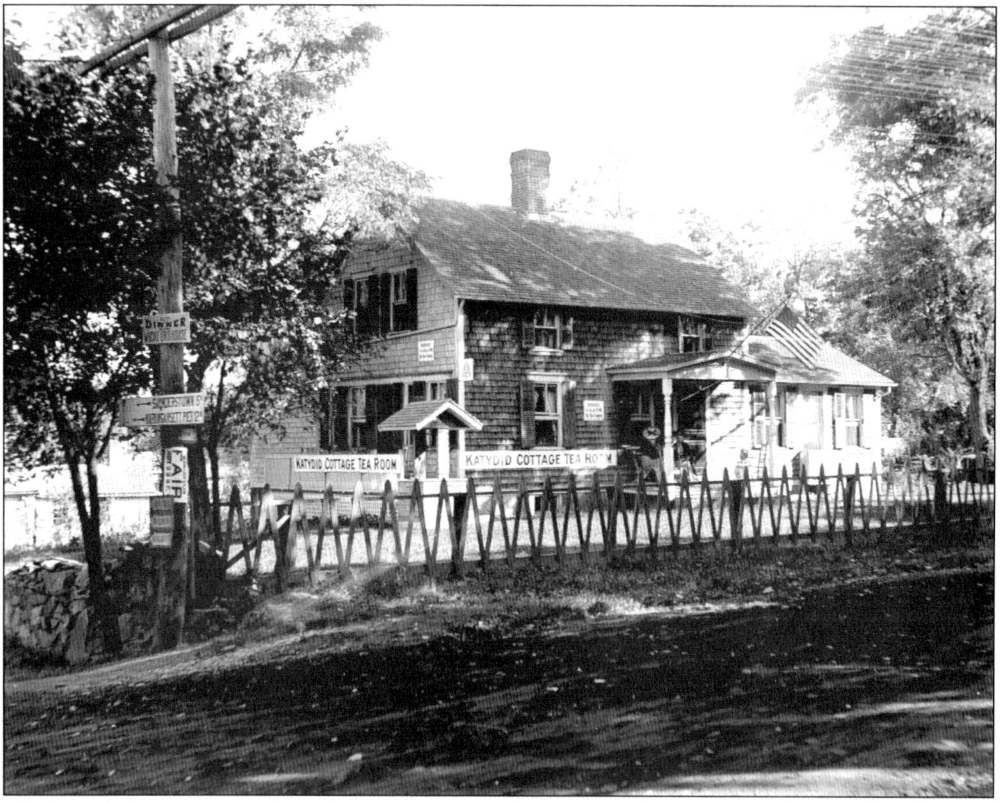

The Katydid Cottage Tea Room was run for years by Lucille Luth. One hundred years later, it is little changed in appearance but has been broken up into apartments, one of which was rented by a young Ross Perot while he served in the navy at Quonset Point.

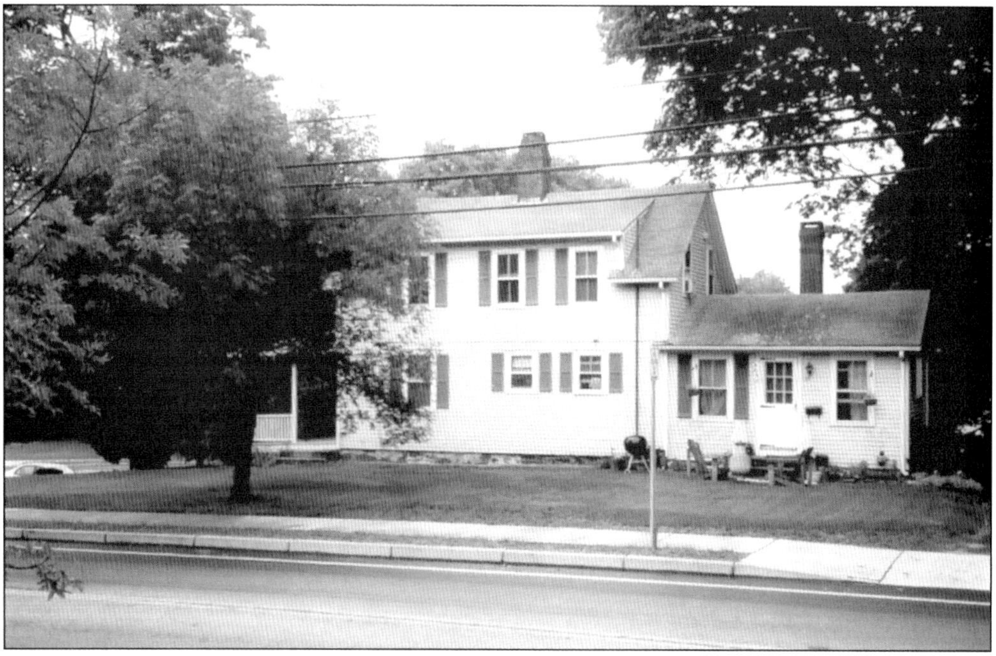

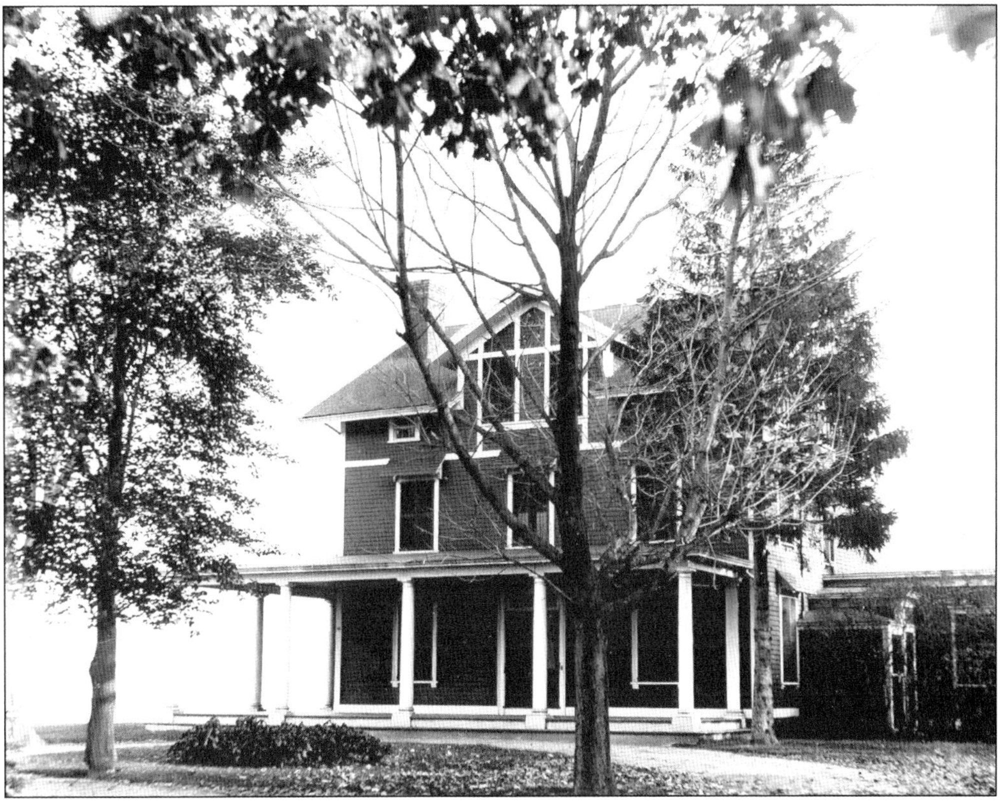

Here is an early photograph of the Gov. Elisha Dyer summer home, the Beachwoods. As mentioned previously, it served as a summer hotel for many years. It is now remarkably similar and is used as the North Kingstown Senior Center. Note the beech tree in both photographs.

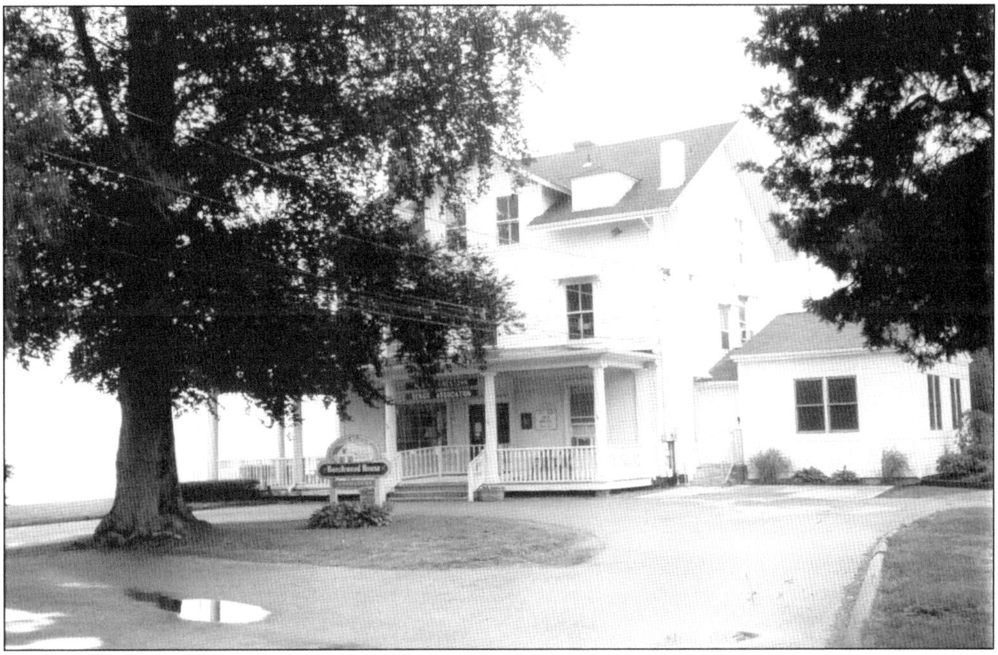

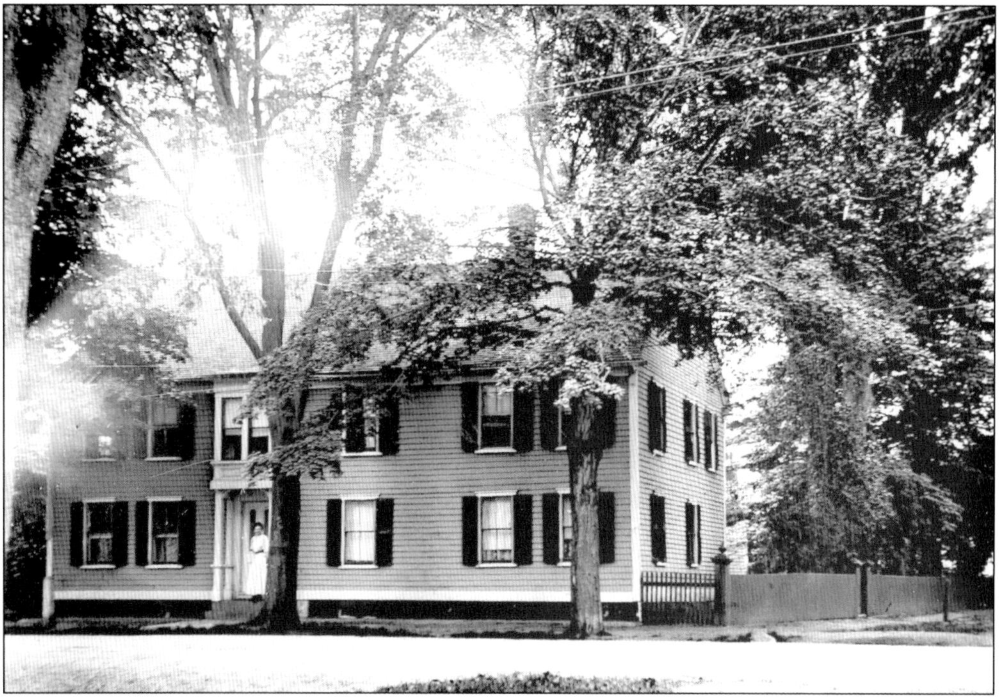

This is the Wightman homestead house on the corner of Main and Fowler Streets. The stately colonial home was so damaged by the 1938 hurricane that it was later demolished.

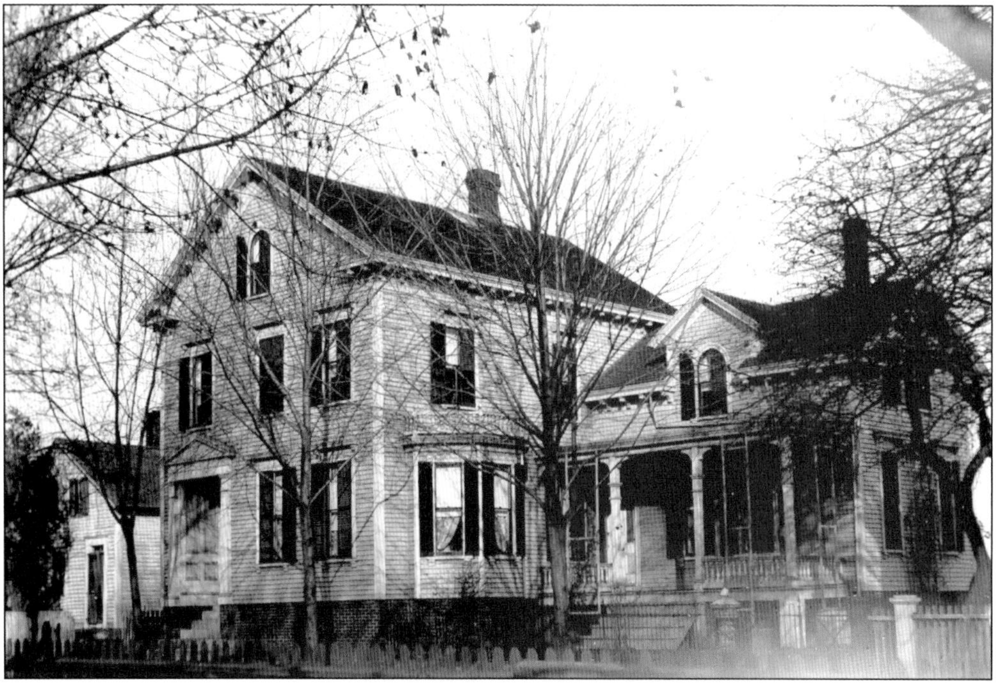

Another fine home, this is the Melissa Babcock House on Pleasant Street. It, too, was divided into apartments during the early 1940s to take advantage of the shortage of housing for the onrush of military personnel assigned to Quonset and Davisville.

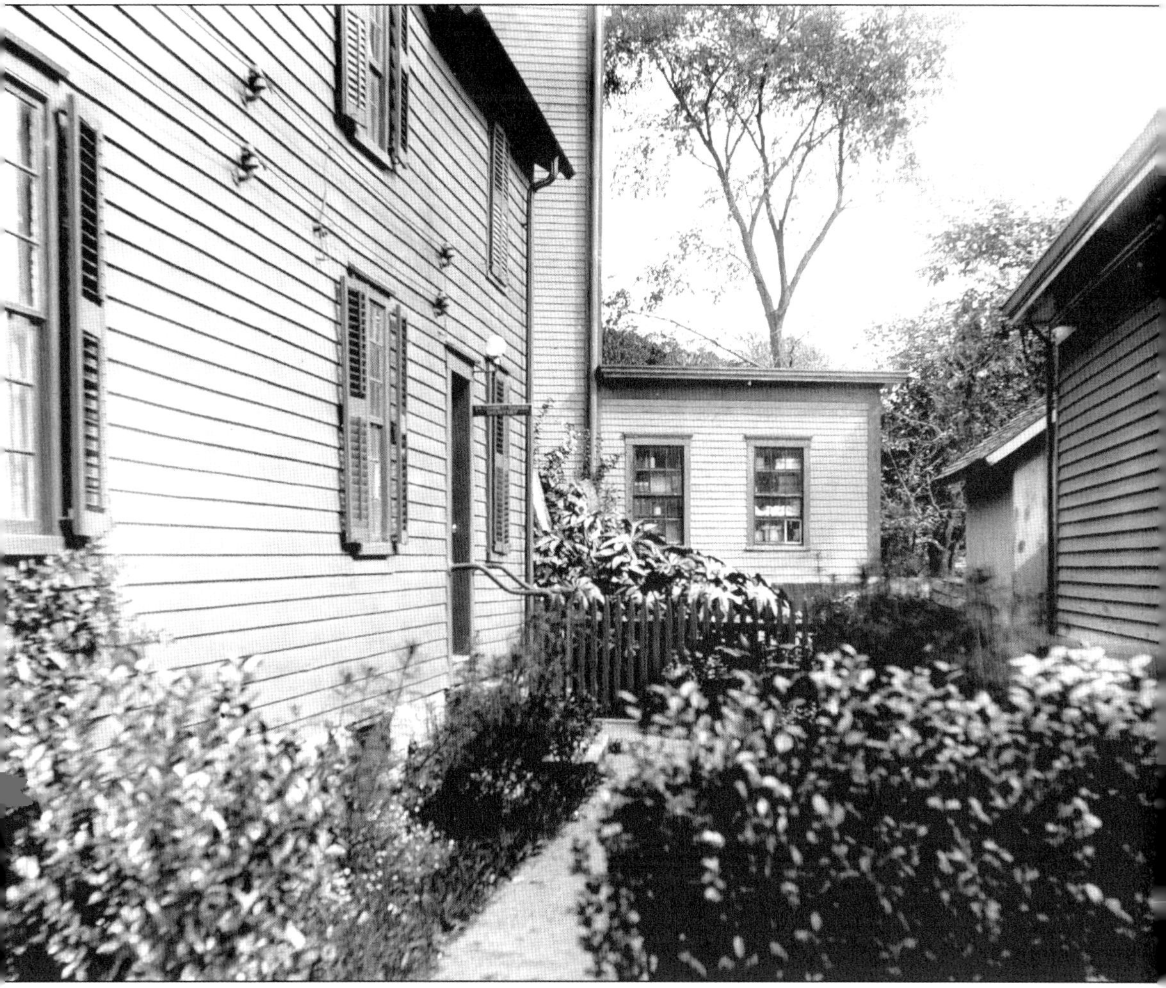

This photograph features the entrance and nearby gardens at the local dentist's shop of Garrett Rogers. It was located on Brown Street in the village of Wickford.

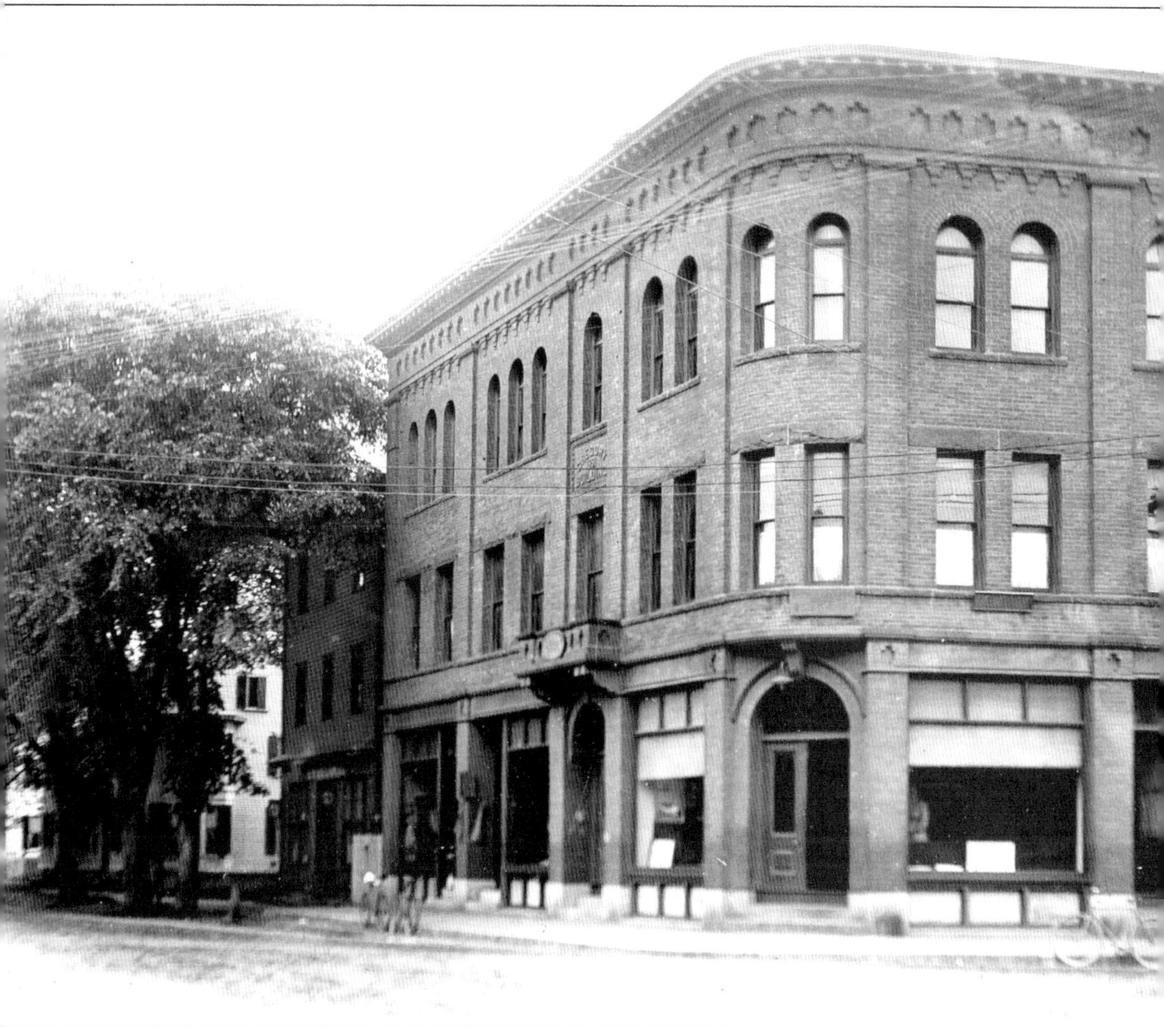

William Gregory, a prominent citizen and mill owner who eventually rose to be the governor of Rhode Island, had big dreams for the downtown section of Wickford. This business block was to be the first of three that he envisioned for the village. His unexpected death at an early age waylaid his grand plans. The Gregory Building eventually housed the town's post office. At the beginning of the 20th century, it was the location for many of the earliest classes of North Kingstown's fledgling high school.

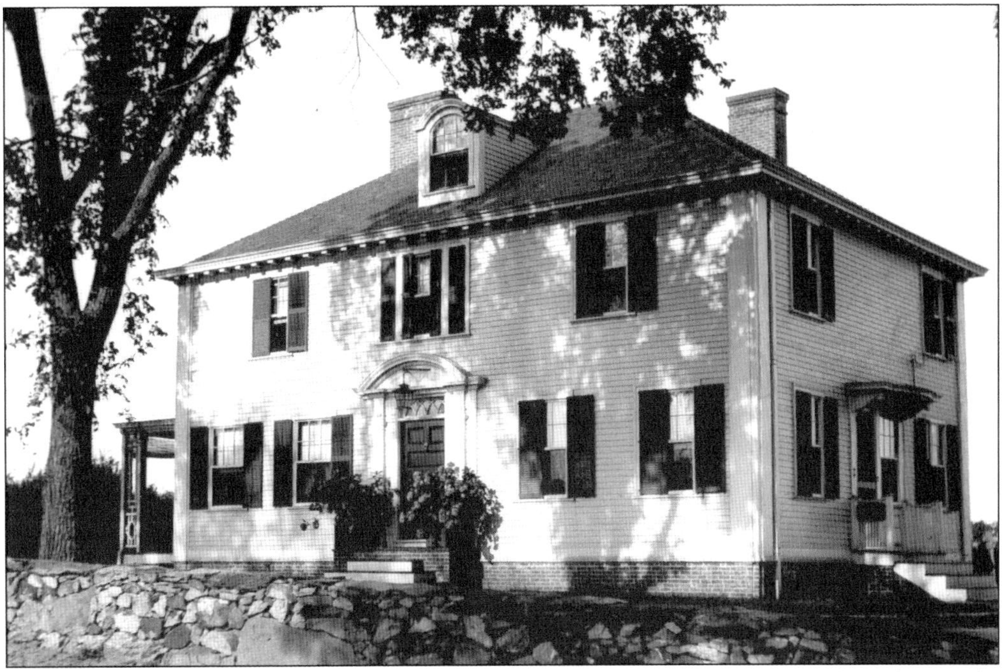

This was the home of the village's real doctor, Doc Metcalf. The entrance to the right was for his family, the entrance on the left was for his patients, and the front door was for show. Doc Metcalf purchased one of the first automobiles in the village to use while making house calls. Very early on, he crashed it into the back wall of his barn. When asked about it, he replied, "Well, the horse always seemed to know when to stop."

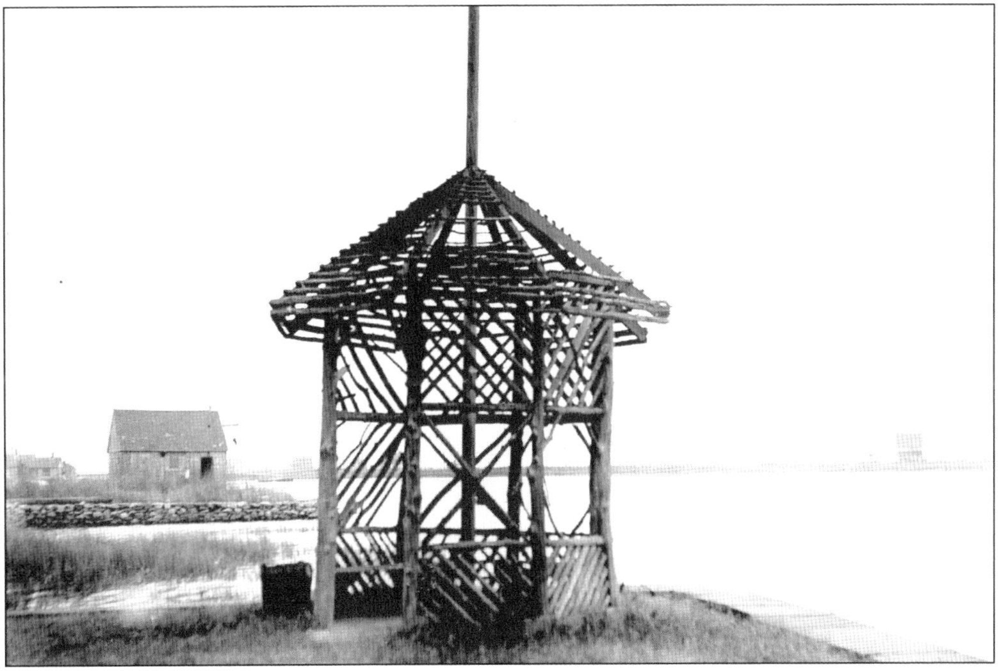

This rustic gazebo was found near the end of Main Street and shows up on the wonderful print "A Bird's Eye View Of Wickford—1888."

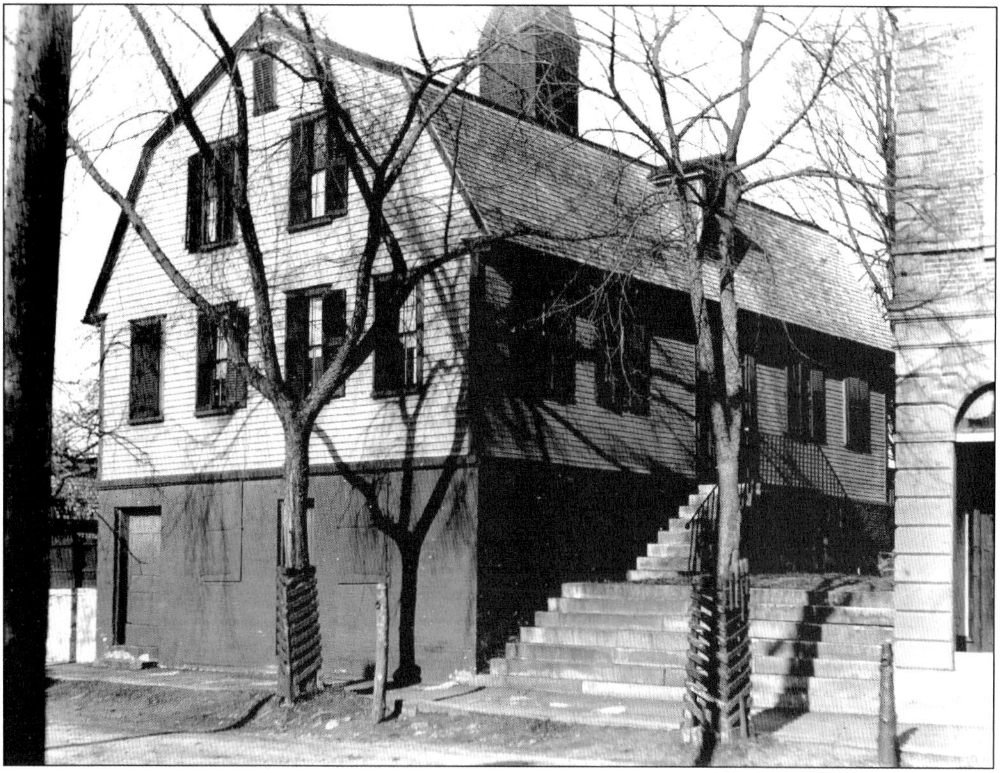

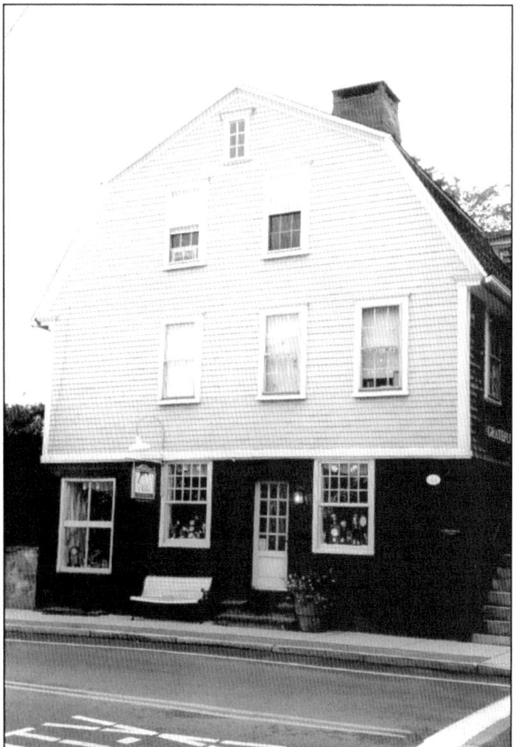

These two photographs are taken of the Samuel Brenton House about 100 years apart. The house, constructed during the time of the Revolution, has been home to everything from taverns to a hippie-era gift shop. It is said that two young lovers in the late 18th century scratched their names into an upstairs window and the markings are still there today.

Ten

The Textile Mill Villages

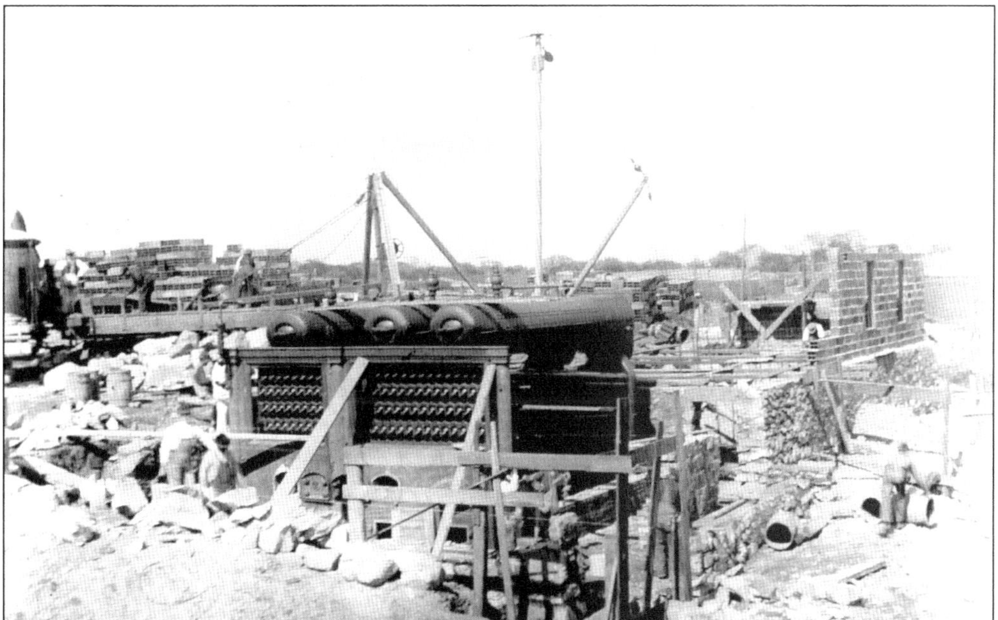

Doc Young was interested in all things and recorded as much as possible with his camera. This photograph shows a mill building under construction, most probably in the Hamilton Web mill complex.

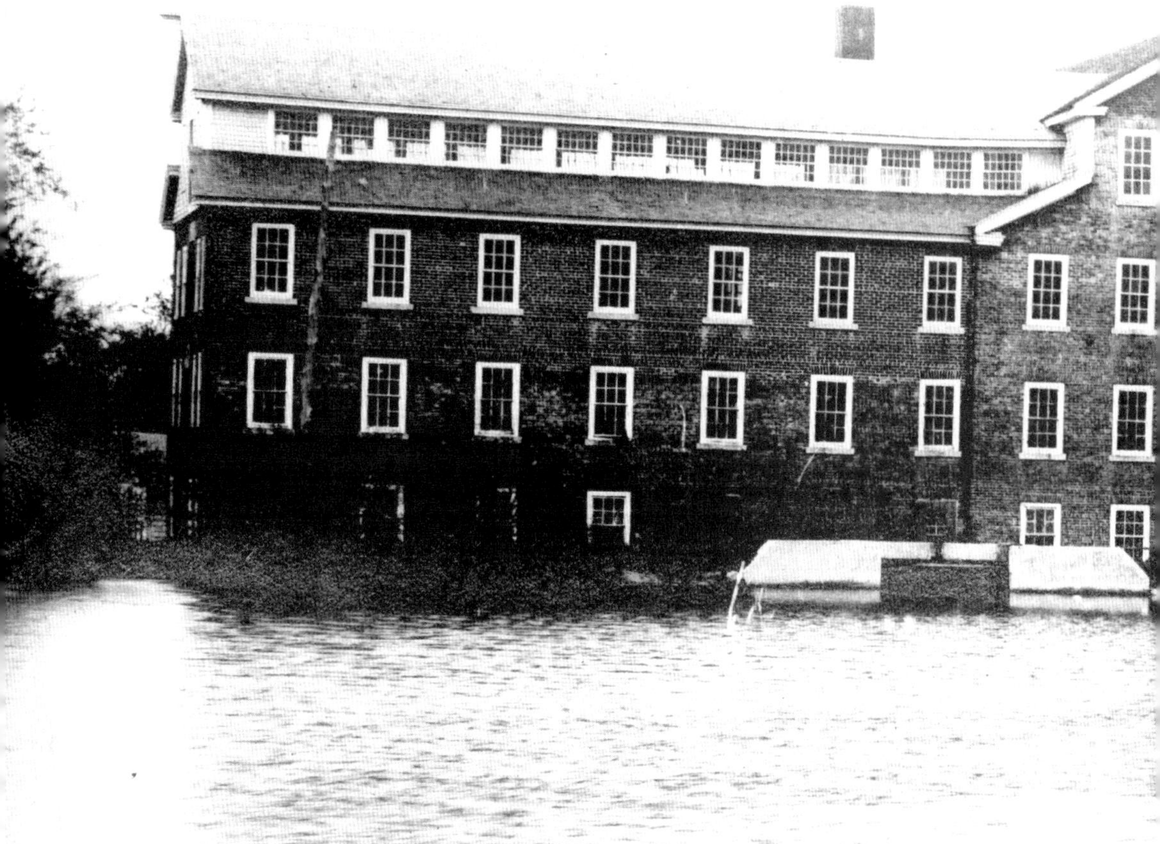

The big mill at Belleville must have been an imposing sight to the countless Irish and French-Canadian immigrants who worked there. This photograph was taken from across the millpond.

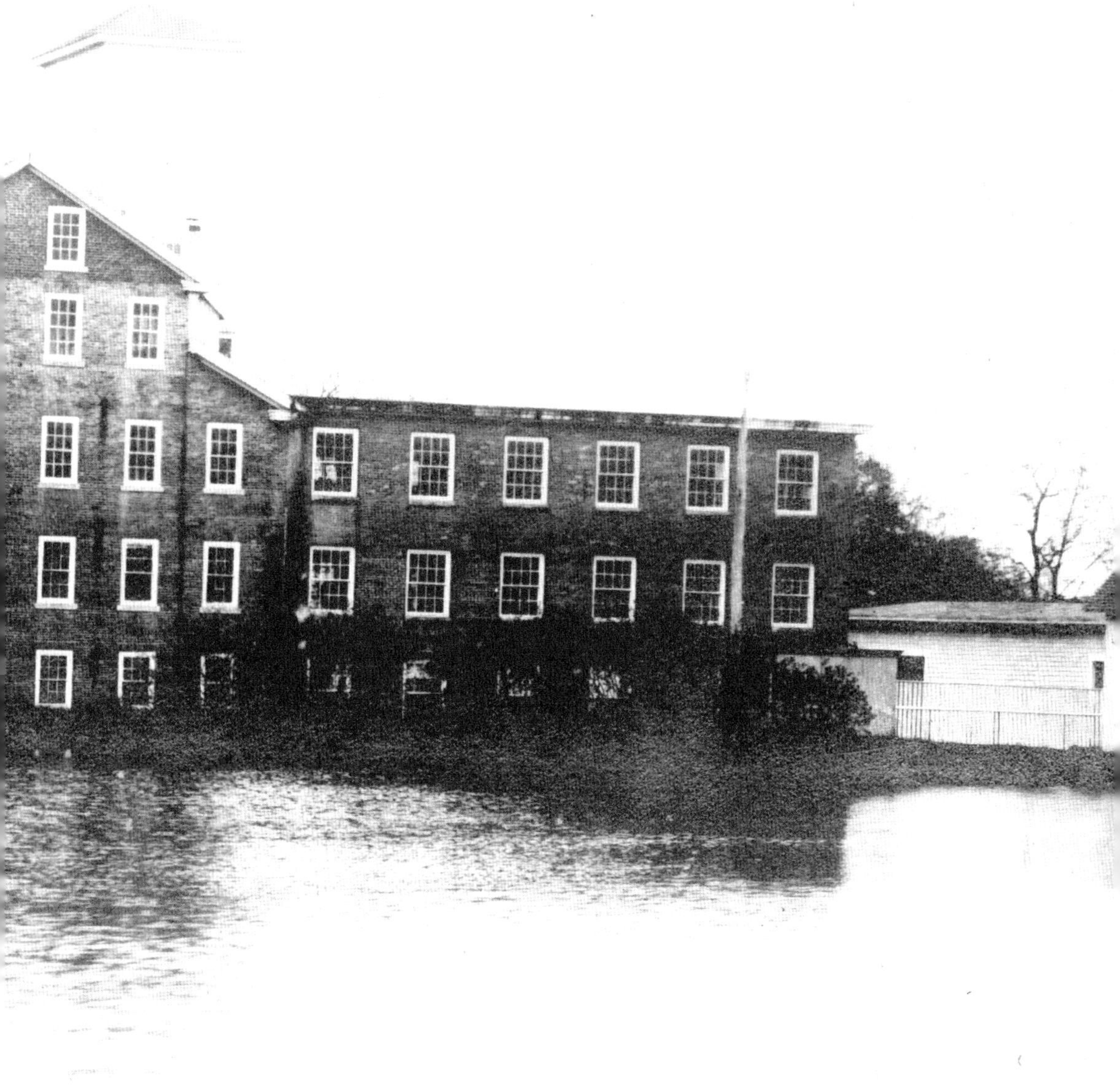

The mill burned to the ground in a spectacular blaze in the early 1960s. Some of the mill's brick walls fell into the millpond during the fire and are there to this day.

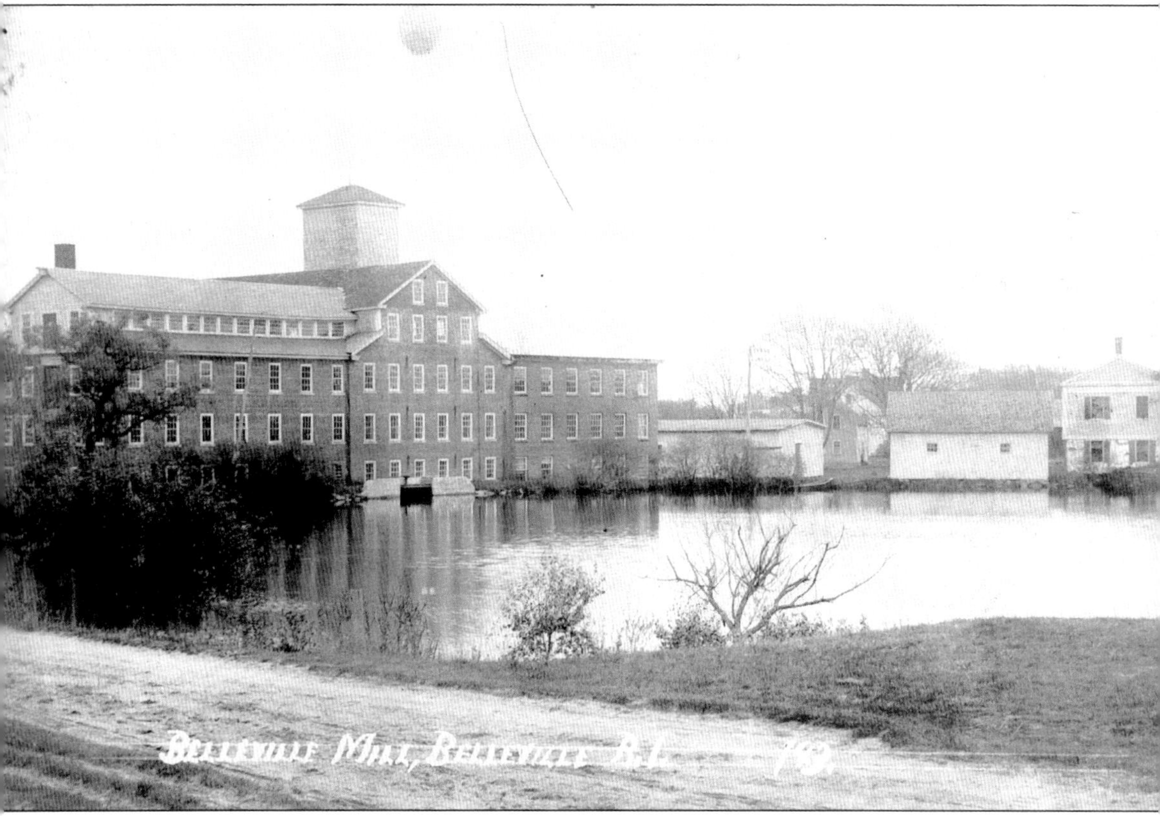

This photograph postcard of the Belleville mill complex was taken from a different angle. The two buildings to the far right and those seen off in the distance survived the blaze and are still extant today.

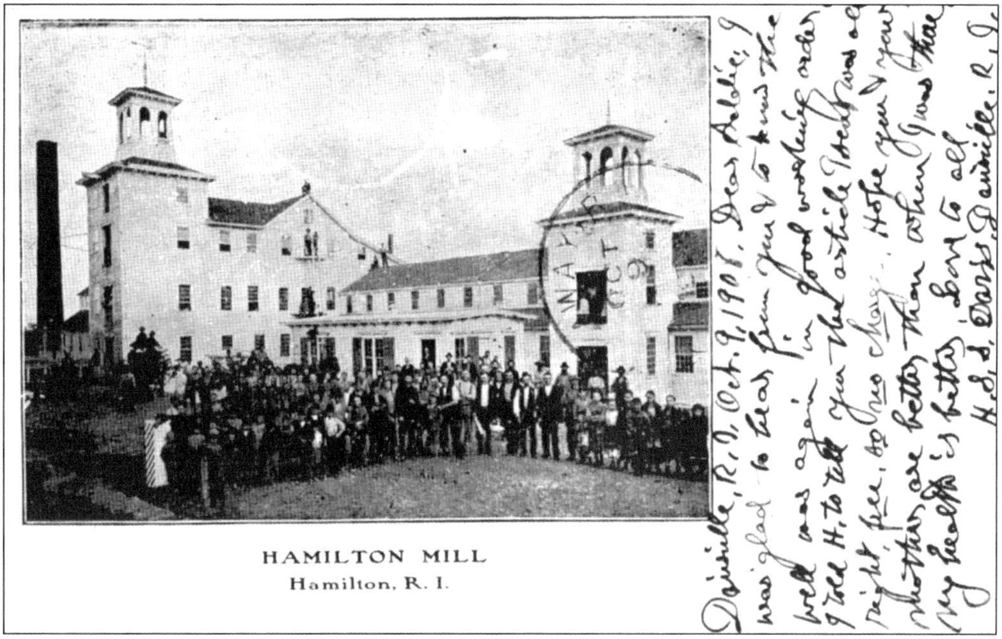

Here are two different photograph postcards of the Hamilton Web mill complex in the village of Hamilton. The employees, many of whom were children, are shown in the photograph above. The Hamilton Web Mill survived into the early 1970s due to the fact that they were manufacturing a very specialized narrow fabric used for everything from boot pulls to belts and guitar straps.

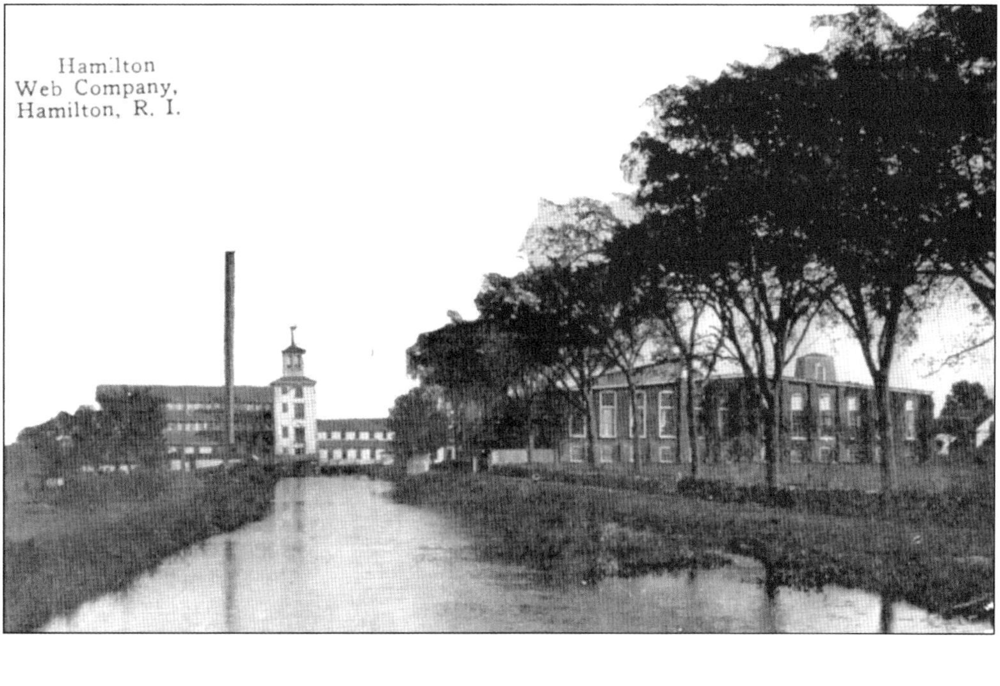

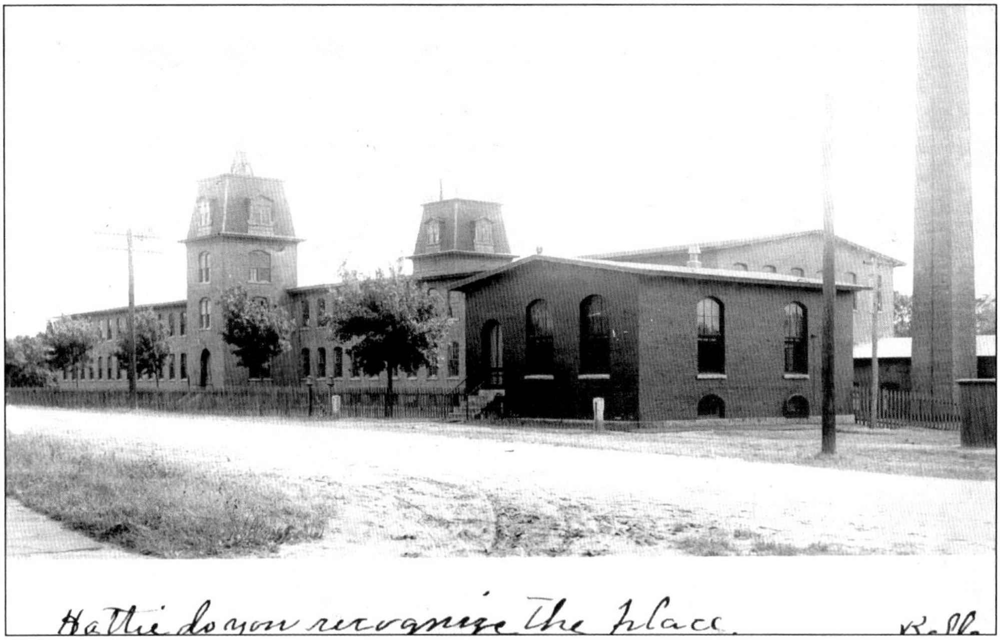

This c. 1890 photograph postcard shows the Lafayette mill of Robert Rodman, the area's largest employer. Generation upon generation of people worked at this Ten Rod Road mill. The building in the foreground was Rodman's office, from which he and his sons ran their textile empire.

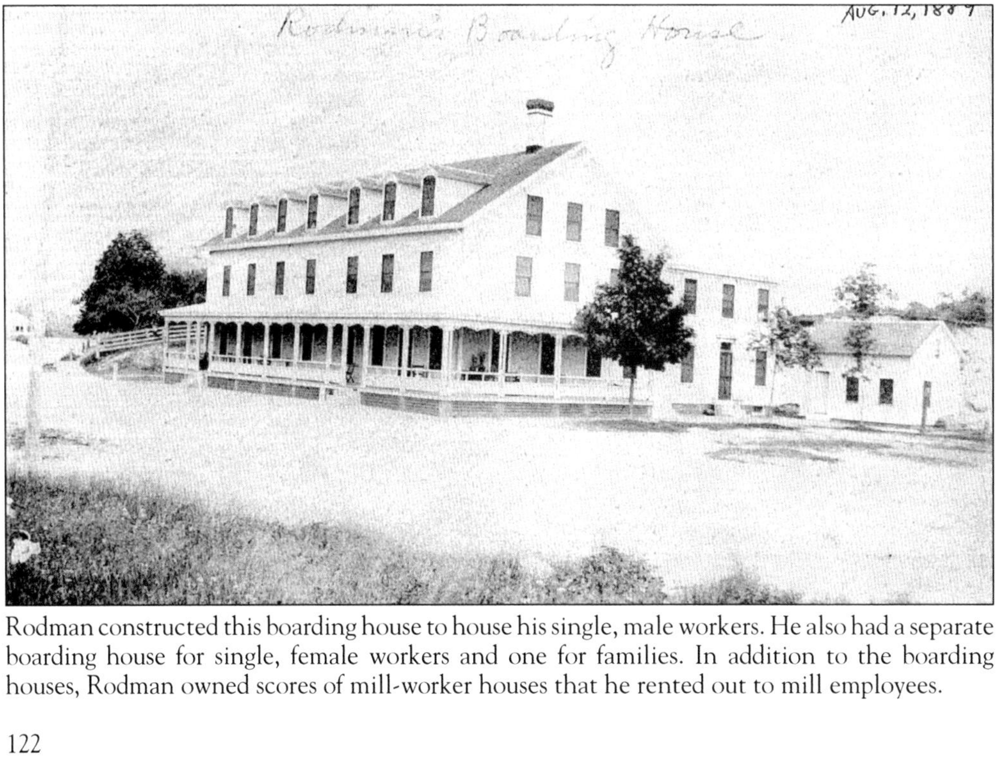

Rodman constructed this boarding house to house his single, male workers. He also had a separate boarding house for single, female workers and one for families. In addition to the boarding houses, Rodman owned scores of mill-worker houses that he rented out to mill employees.

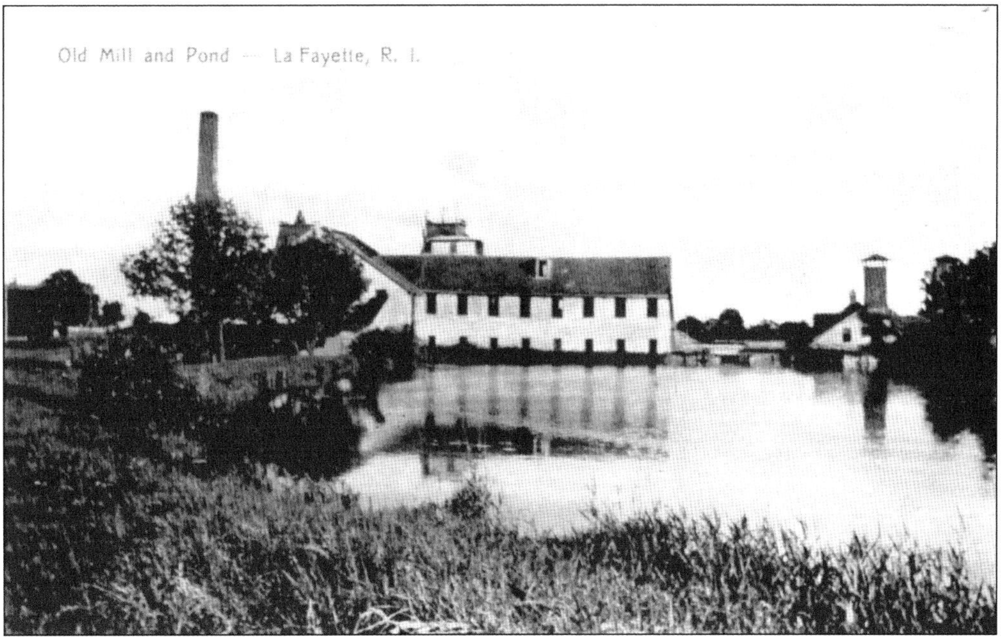

These postcard views of the Lafayette mill village were created specifically for sale in the company store.

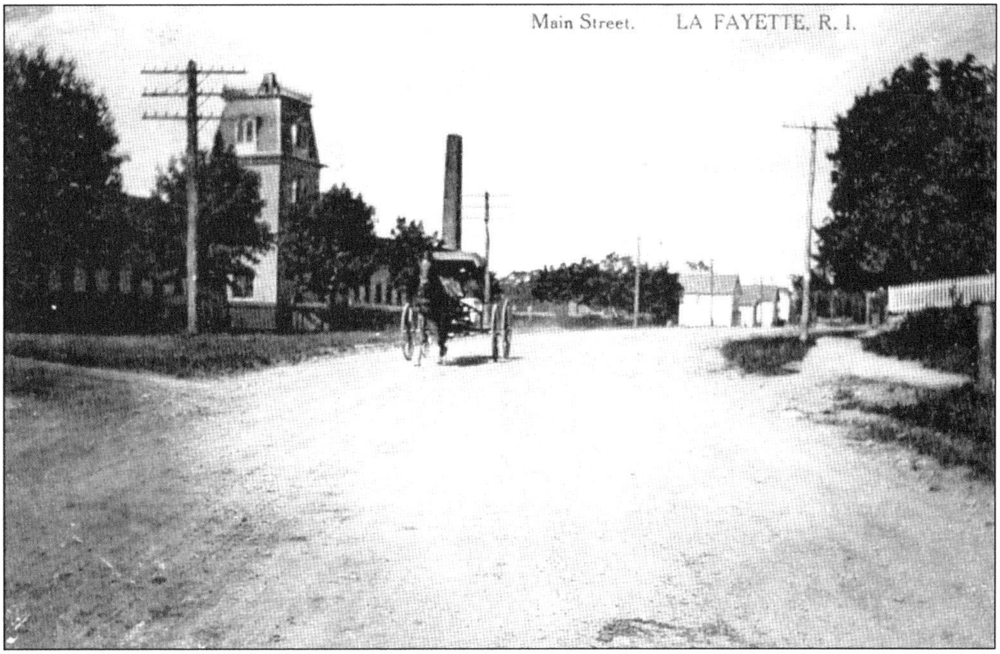

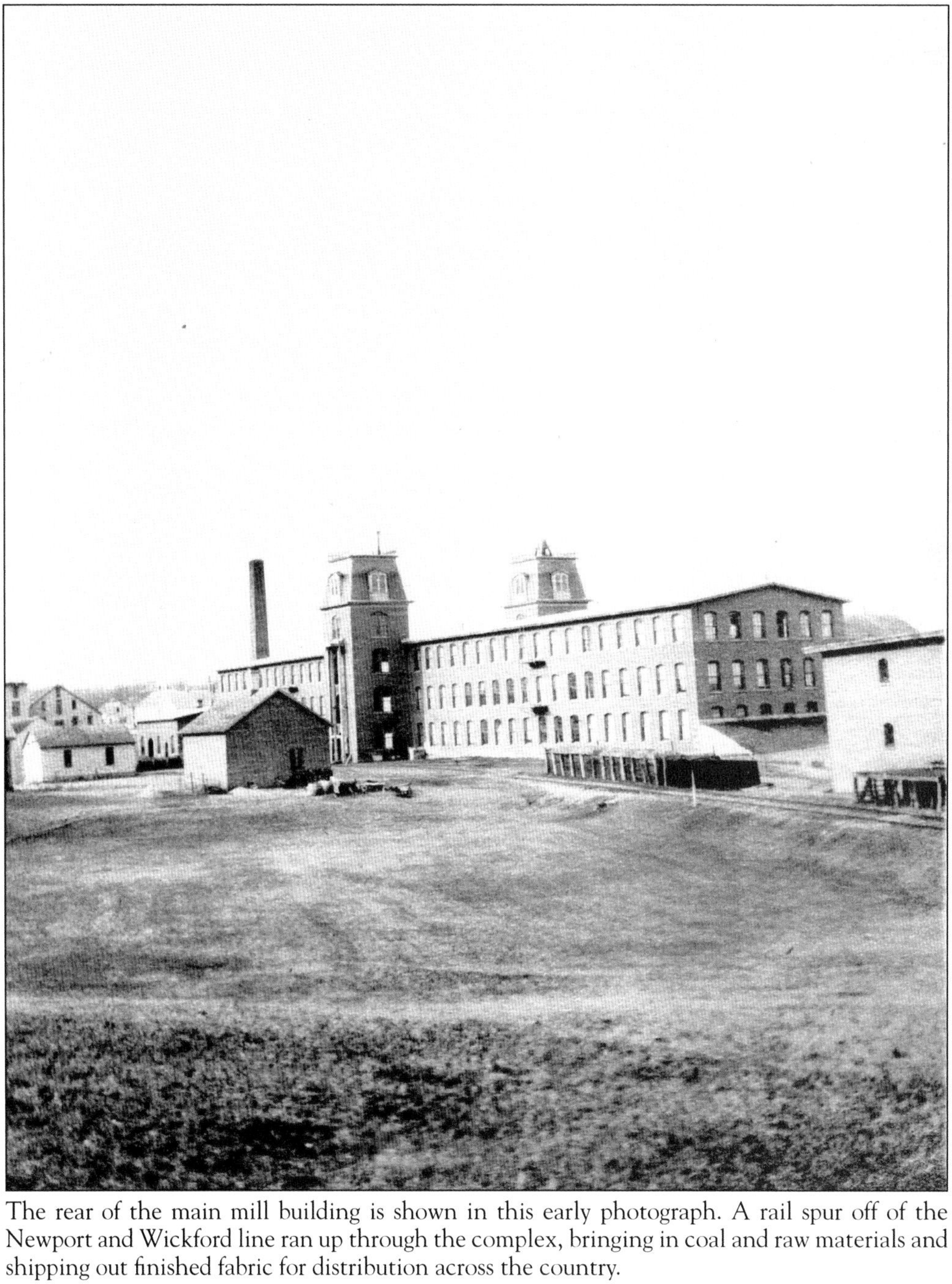

The rear of the main mill building is shown in this early photograph. A rail spur off of the Newport and Wickford line ran up through the complex, bringing in coal and raw materials and shipping out finished fabric for distribution across the country.

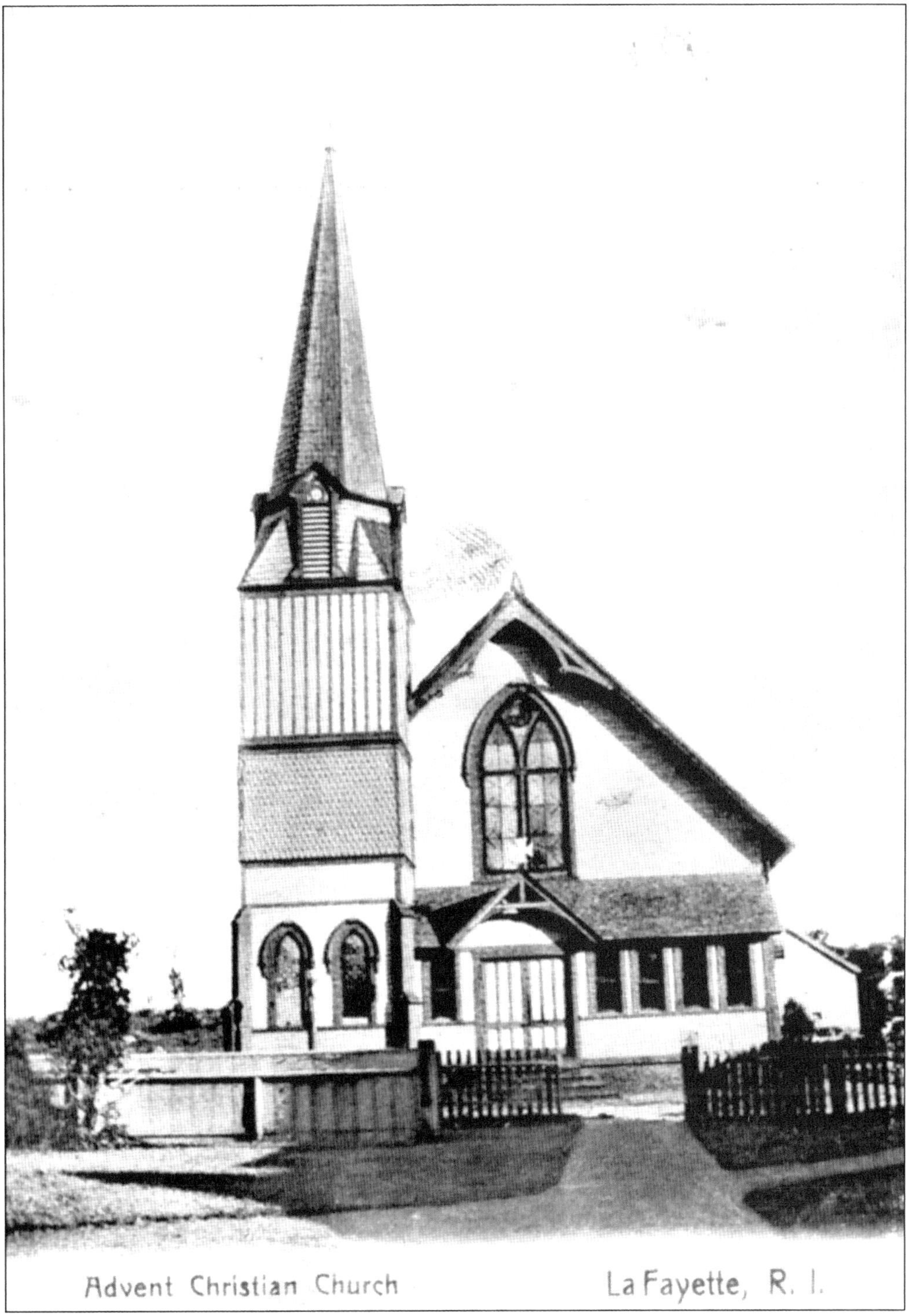

The Advent Christian Church was constructed largely with funds donated by the Rodman family. This postcard, too, was made for sale in the company store. The church is still standing today and is used as a warehouse for a local furniture retailer.

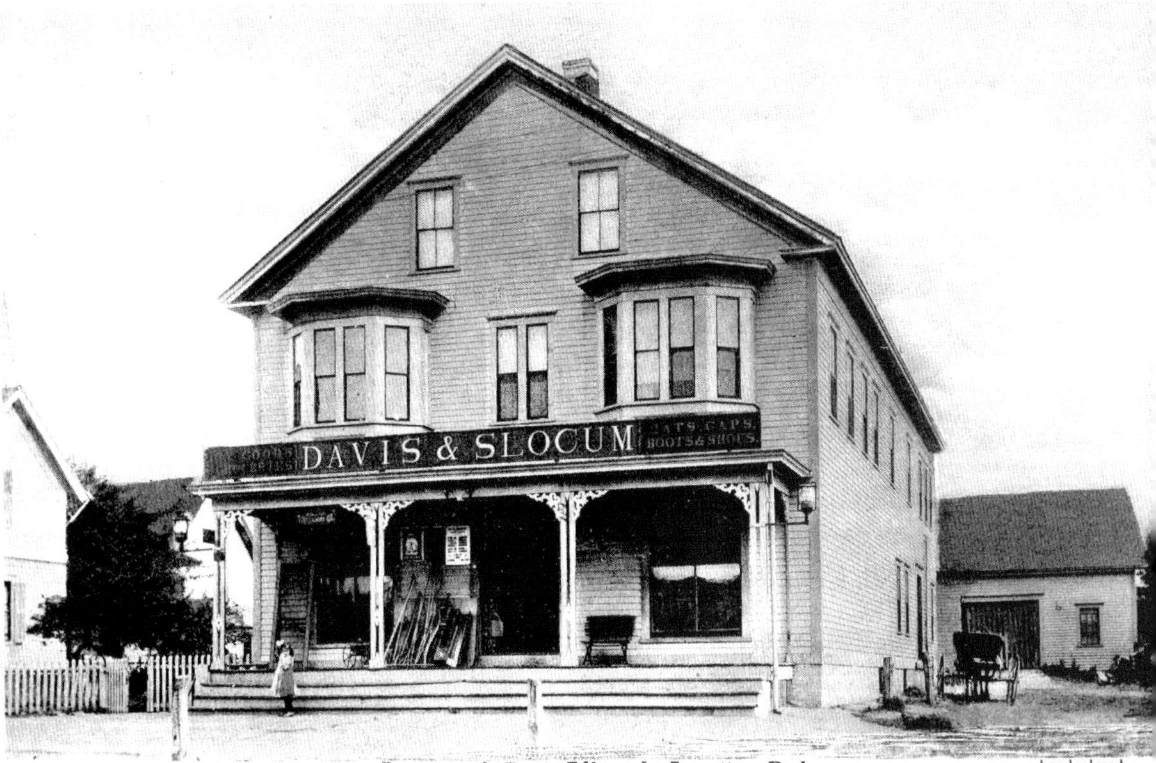

Store and Post Office LaFayette, R. I. handcolored

The Rodman company store, seen here, also served as the village post office. The building has now been broken up into apartments.

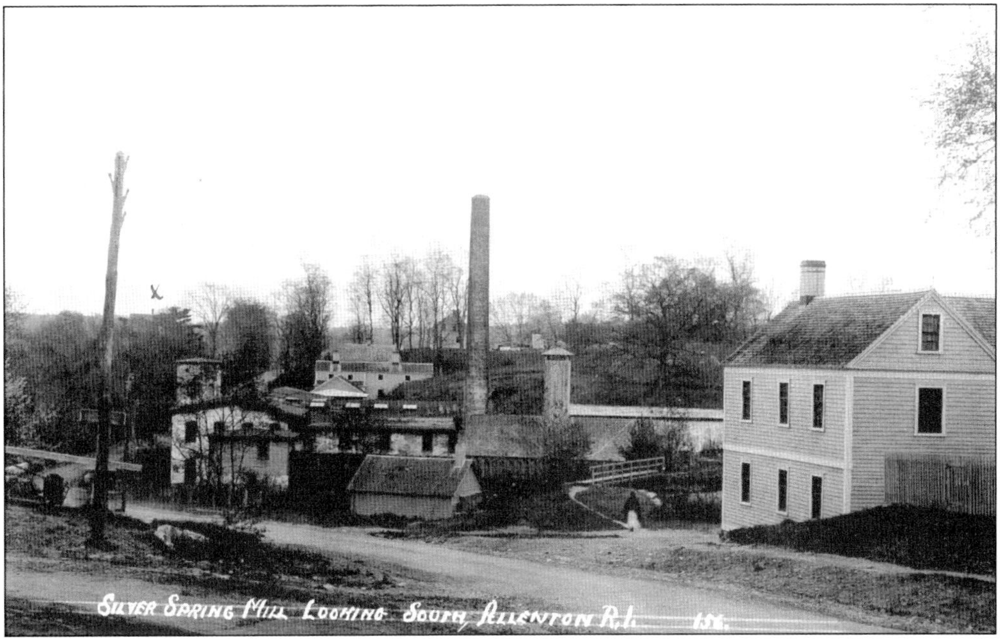

Robert Rodman also owned this mill located in the village of Silver Spring and operated it in conjunction with his Lafayette complex. The millpond and the village take their names from the original dammed spring that used to spit up flecks of shiny mica.

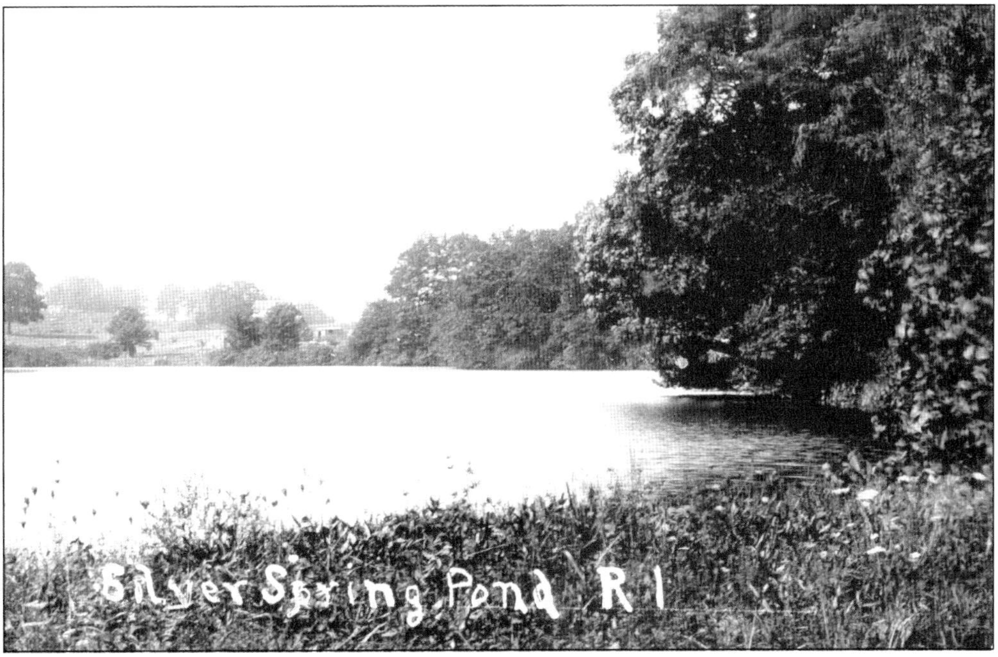

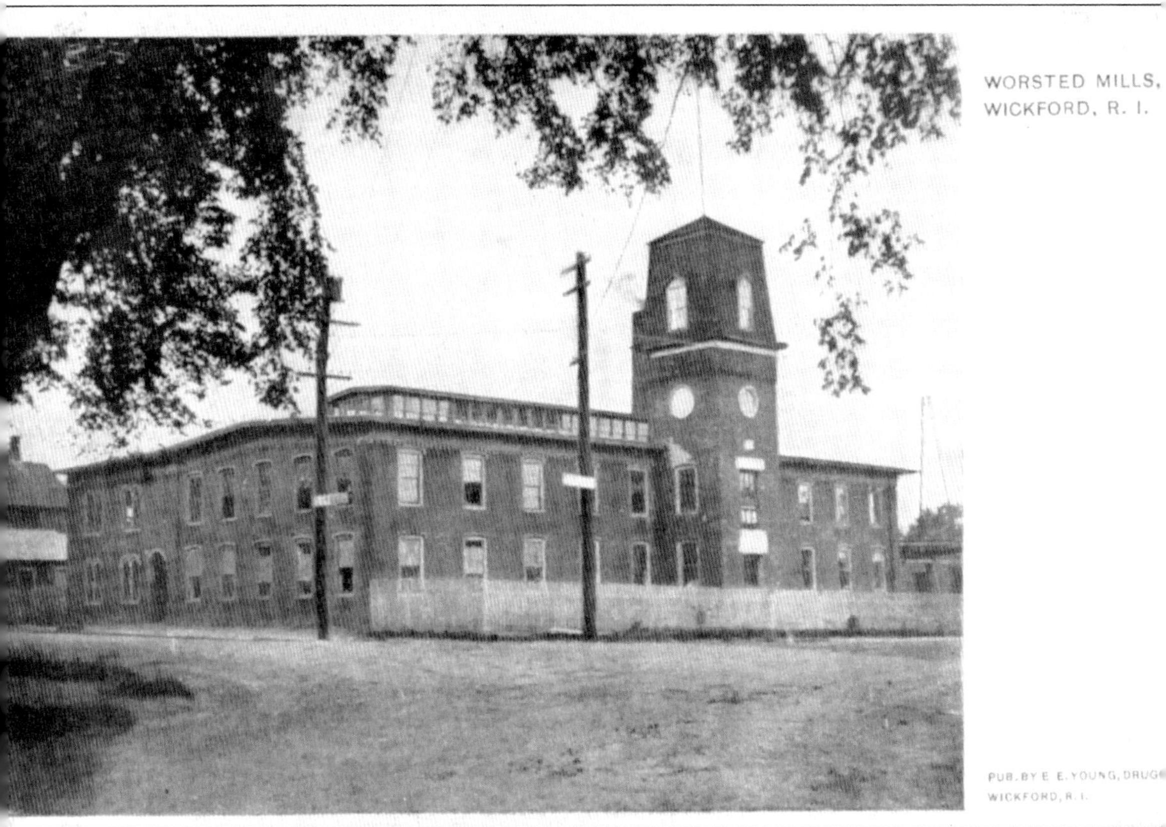

Located in the village of Wickford, Gov. William Gregory's worsted fabric mill is seen in this Doc Young postcard photograph. The mill was constructed on the site of a colonial shipyard. The building still exists today and has been sub-divided into a multi-use site.